The *Best* of COUNTRY COOKING
2001

Editor: Jean Steiner
Art Director: Bonnie Ziolecki
Food Editor: Janaan Cunningham
Associate Editors: Heidi Reuter Lloyd, Susan Uphill, Julie Schnittka
Food Photography Artists: Stephanie Marchese, Vicky Marie Moseley
Food Photography: Dan Roberts, Rob Hagen
Photo Studio Manager: Anne Schimmel
Production: Ellen Lloyd, Catherine Fletcher
Publisher: Roy Reiman

For additional copies of this book or information on other books, write *Taste of Home* Books, P.O. Box 908, Greendale WI 53129, call toll-free 1-800/344-2560 to order with a credit card or visit our Web site at **www.reimanpub.com**.

PICTURED ON COVER. From the top: Fried Chicken Coating Mix (p. 41), Crunchy Dilled Slaw (p. 56) and Summer Berry Cheese Pie (p. 124).

PICTURED ABOVE. Clockwise from top left: Mustard-Glazed Ham, Potato Rolls, Spring Fruit Salad and Creamy Asparagus Casserole (all recipes on p. 146).

Cooks Across the Country Share Tried-and-True Recipes

ARE YOU READY to take another tour into the recipe files of the best at-home cooks in North America? With 370 recipes in *The Best of Country Cooking 2001*—the fourth in our cookbook series of family-pleasing recipes—you can sample a deliciously different dish every day.

This giant collection includes the very best recipes from recent issues of *Country Woman, Country, Country EXTRA, Reminisce* and *Reminisce EXTRA* magazines. All are hearty, wholesome and proven favorites of a family just like yours.

You see, these recipes weren't developed in some high-tech industrial "kitchen". Instead, they're from the personal recipe files of hundreds of everyday cooks across the country. Each and every dish has been sampled and approved by the toughest critic around—a hungry family!

What's more, every recipe in this book was tested—many of them twice—by us as well. So you can be doubly confident each and every dish is a "keeper" that doesn't require a tryout first.

Looking to liven up your weekday dinners? You have 77 Main Dishes to choose from, including Zippy Swiss Steak (Henderson, Nevada cook Janice Dyer's irresistible family recipe), Raspberry Chicken (an easy-to-make dish with a touch of elegance from Carol Cottrill, Rumford, Maine) and Honey-Baked Ribs (a finger-lickin'-good favorite in Marge Tubbs' Raleigh, North Carolina kitchen).

Take your pick of this beautiful book's 39 satisfying Soups & Salads like Creamy Potato Soup, a surefire way for Michelle Wollenburg to chase away chills in Beatrice, Nebraska. Plus, you can fill your bread basket with fresh-baked Breads & Rolls such as Bacon Cheddar Round from Dorothy Collins, Winnsboro, Texas.

With 84 cakes, cookies, pies and desserts, everyone will save room for dessert. Chocolate Chocolate Chip Cake (from Spanish Fork, Utah cook Roni Goodell) is a chocolate lover's dream. For a tempting taste variation, Virginia Kraus of Pocahontas, Illinois makes mouth-watering Apple Meringue Pie.

In addition, this tried-and-true treasury contains a savory selection of salads, side dishes and snacks. You'll also enjoy some extra-special features most other cookbooks overlook:

Thirty-Minute Meals—Six complete meals (18 recipes in all) that are ready to eat in *less than half an hour*.

Memorable Meals—Six complete meals featuring favorite recipes from home cooks.

Cooking for Two—A separate chapter with 48 recipes all properly proportioned to serve two people.

Want more? *The Best of Country Cooking 2001* offers individual sections on cooking quick-and-easy fare that you can whip up for your hungry family with little effort.

As you page through *The Best of Country Cooking 2001*, watch for the special symbol at right. It signifies a "best of the best" recipe—a winner of a coast-to-coast cooking contest one of our magazines sponsored.

Finally, throughout this colorful collection are lots of helpful kitchen tips from everyday cooks plus dozens of "restricted diet" recipes marked with this check ✓ that use less fat, sugar or salt.

Now you and your family can *taste* why we call this book "The Best"!

CONTENTS

Snacks & Beverages...4

Main Dishes...12

Soups & Salads...46

Side Dishes &
Condiments...62

Breads & Rolls...76

Cakes, Cookies
& Candies...90

Pies & Desserts...110

Meals in Minutes...128

Our Most
Memorable Meals...140

Cooking for Two...152

Index begins on page 176

FOR A SUPER START to a supper, or a treat any time of day, turn to these satisfying appetizers, beverages and snacks.

GRAB SOME GOODIES. From top: Starry Fruit Punch (p. 6), Festive Veggie Pizza (p. 5), Sweet-Hot Sausage Meatballs (p. 5) and Taco Tater Skins (p. 6).

SWEET-HOT SAUSAGE MEATBALLS

Claire Stryker, Delta, Utah

(Pictured at left)

These great-tasting sausage meatballs seem to disappear before anything else on the table or buffet. They have a delightful tang with a bit of crunch from the water chestnuts. I've used the recipe when entertaining for over 20 years because it's so easy to do and comes out perfect every time.

   2 cans (8 ounces *each*) water chestnuts,
     drained
   1 pound bulk pork sausage
   1 pound bulk hot pork sausage
1/4 cup cornstarch
   1 cup maple syrup
2/3 cup cider *or* red wine vinegar
1/4 cup soy sauce

In a blender or food processor, process water chestnuts until minced. Transfer to a bowl; add sausage. Mix well. Shape into 1-in. balls. Place in ungreased 15-in. x 10-in. x 1-in. baking pans. Bake, uncovered, at 350° for 20-25 minutes or until meat is no longer pink. Meanwhile, in a saucepan, combine cornstarch, syrup, vinegar and soy sauce; stir until smooth. Bring to a boil; cook and stir for 2 minutes or until thickened and bubbly. Drain meatballs; add to sauce and heat through. **Yield:** 12-14 servings.

FESTIVE VEGGIE PIZZA

Carol Severson, Shelton, Washington

(Pictured at left)

The popularity of this dish starts with its appearance. You can sprinkle the pizza with plenty of colorful toppings. Guests will be attracted right away. Then, when they have a taste, one slice just won't be enough! It's also a good way to get kids to eat veggies.

Pastry for single-crust pie
   2 packages (3 ounces *each*) cream cheese,
     softened
1/4 cup crumbled blue cheese, optional
1/4 cup mayonnaise
1/4 teaspoon onion salt
1/4 teaspoon garlic salt
   1 cup quartered cherry tomatoes
1/2 cup chopped broccoli
1/2 cup sliced fresh mushrooms
1/3 cup sliced ripe olives
1/4 cup chopped radishes
   1 tablespoon minced fresh parsley, optional

On an ungreased baking sheet, roll out pastry into an 11-in. circle; prick several times with a fork. Bake at 425° for 8 minutes or until lightly browned. Cool completely on a wire rack. Meanwhile, in a small mixing bowl, beat cream cheese, blue cheese if desired, mayonnaise, onion salt and garlic salt. Place crust on a large serving plate. Spread cream cheese mixture to within 1 in. of edge. Cover and chill for at least 4 hours. Top with tomatoes, broccoli, mushrooms, olives, radishes and parsley if desired. Cut into serving-size pieces. **Yield:** 10-12 servings.

TREE AND STAR CRAB SANDWICHES

Karen Gardiner, Eutaw, Alabama

This fun-to-eat finger food starts with a flavorful crab filling. I regularly serve the spread at Christmas get-togethers, and it's a hit every time. Folks always fall for the festive bread tree and star shapes I cut out with cookie cutters.

3/4 cup mayonnaise
3/4 cup shredded sharp cheddar cheese
   1 can (6 ounces) crabmeat, drained, flaked
     and cartilage removed
   2 tablespoons French salad dressing
1/2 teaspoon prepared horseradish
Dash hot pepper sauce
  48 bread slices
Fresh dill sprigs

In a bowl, combine the first six ingredients; set aside. Using 2-1/2-in. cookie cutters, cut stars and Christmas trees out of bread (two stars or trees from each slice). Spread half of the cutouts with crab mixture; top with remaining cutouts. Garnish with dill. **Yield:** 4 dozen.

STARRY FRUIT PUNCH

Betty Romine, Lake Jackson, Texas

(Pictured on page 4)

Besides quenching thirst, this fruity beverage saves time in the kitchen, too. For the star-shaped molds, you just mix and freeze three basic ingredients.

> 2 cups sugar
> 2 packages (.23 ounce *each*) unsweetened
>   lime soft drink mix
> 6 cups water

PUNCH:

> 1-1/2 cups sugar
> 1 package (6 ounces) raspberry gelatin
> 2 cups boiling water
> 6-1/2 cups cold water
> 6 ounces limeade concentrate
> 6 ounces lemonade concentrate
> 1 can (46 ounces) pineapple juice, chilled
> 2 liters ginger ale, chilled

In a bowl, dissolve sugar and drink mix in water. Pour into twelve 1/2-cup star-shaped molds or one 6-cup mold. Freeze overnight. In a large bowl, dissolve sugar and gelatin in boiling water. Stir in cold water and concentrates. Chill. Transfer to a punch bowl just before serving; stir in pineapple juice and ginger ale. Add three small ice molds or one large mold. Replenish small ice molds as needed. **Yield:** 4 quarts.

TACO TATER SKINS

Phyllis Douglas, Fairview, Michigan

(Pictured on page 4)

My husband, kids and I make a meal out of these skins. But they're also great for parties as appetizers. I did some experimenting to come up with the recipe.

> 6 large russet potatoes
> 1/2 cup butter *or* margarine, melted
> 2 tablespoons taco seasoning
> 1 cup (4 ounces) shredded cheddar cheese
> 15 bacon strips, cooked and crumbled
> 3 green onions, chopped

Salsa *and/or* sour cream, optional

Bake potatoes at 375° for 1 hour or until tender. Remove from oven. Reduce heat to 350°. When cool enough to handle, cut the potatoes lengthwise into quarters. Scoop out pulp, leaving a 1/4-in. shell (save pulp for another use). Combine the butter and taco seasoning; brush over both sides of potato skins. Place skin side down on a greased baking sheet. Sprinkle with cheese, bacon and onions. Bake for 5-10 minutes or until the cheese is melted. Serve with salsa and/or sour cream if desired. **Yield:** 2 dozen.

CHEESY HERBED SNACK SQUARES

Peggy Kleis, Climax Springs, Missouri

(Pictured at left)

We have six children, and they all enjoy these snack squares. I've given the recipe to a number of people, and they like to add their own twists to it.

> 1 loaf (1 pound) frozen bread dough
> 1 tablespoon butter *or* margarine, melted
> 1 teaspoon instant beef bouillon granules
> 2 teaspoons *each* caraway seeds, poppy
>   seeds, sesame seeds and celery seed
> 1 teaspoon dill weed
> 1/4 teaspoon garlic powder
> 2 cups (8 ounces) shredded cheddar
>   cheese

Thaw bread and let rise according to package directions. Pat into a greased 15-in. x 10-in. x 1-in. baking pan. Brush with butter; sprinkle with seasonings and cheese. Bake at 425° for 12-15 minutes or until golden brown. Cut into squares; serve warm. **Yield:** 12-15 servings.

MUSHROOM PARTY PUFFS

Patricia Kile, Greentown, Pennsylvania

If you like mushrooms, you'll love this appetizer! As soon as I tasted it for the first time at a friend's house, I had to get the recipe. Not on the rich side—but full of cheese and seasonings—the puffs are satisfying by themselves or as accompaniments to other dishes.

36 medium fresh mushrooms
3 tablespoons butter *or* margarine
1 cup mayonnaise*
1 cup (4 ounces) finely shredded Swiss
  cheese
1/4 cup Dijon mustard
1/4 cup minced fresh parsley
1/2 teaspoon onion powder
2 egg whites

Remove and discard mushroom stems. In a skillet, saute mushroom caps in butter. In a bowl, combine mayonnaise, cheese, mustard, parsley and onion powder. Beat egg whites until stiff; fold into mayonnaise mixture. Spoon into mushroom caps. Place in an ungreased 15-in. x 10-in. x 1-in. baking pan. Bake at 450° for 8-10 minutes or until golden brown. **Yield:** 12-15 servings. ***Editor's Note:** Light or fat-free mayonnaise may not be substituted for regular mayonnaise.

ORANGE-PECAN HOT WINGS

June Jones, Hudson, Florida

(Pictured above right)

We like to use oranges and orange juice in lots of different ways—we even have an orange tree in our backyard. These chicken wings are a fun appetizer that our friends are very fond of. They like the tasty combination of sweet and spicy flavors.

3 pounds whole chicken wings*
3 eggs
1 can (6 ounces) frozen orange juice
  concentrate, thawed
2 tablespoons water
1 cup all-purpose flour
1/2 cup finely chopped pecans
1/2 cup butter *or* margarine, melted

RED HOT SAUCE:
2 cups ketchup
3/4 cup packed brown sugar
2 to 3 tablespoons hot pepper sauce

Cut chicken wings into three pieces; discard wing tips. In a bowl, whisk eggs, orange juice concentrate and water. In another bowl or a resealable plastic bag, combine flour and pecans. Dip wings

in egg mixture, then roll or toss in flour mixture. Pour butter into a 15-in. x 10-in. x 1-in. baking pan. Arrange wings in a single layer in pan. Bake, uncovered, at 375° for 25 minutes. Meanwhile, combine sauce ingredients. Spoon half over the wings; turn. Top with remaining sauce. Bake 30 minutes longer or until meat juices run clear. **Yield:** 8-10 servings. ***Editor's Note:** 3 pounds of uncooked chicken wing sections can be substituted for the whole chicken wings. Omit the first step of the recipe.

TANGY TURKEY MEATBALLS

Carol Brewer, Los Alamitos, California

These tangy meatballs are perfect for taking to potlucks. They take little time to prepare, and they disappear in no time. The turkey is a nice change of pace from ground beef.

2 cups soft bread crumbs
1/2 cup finely chopped onion
2 pounds ground turkey
1 jar (12 ounces) currant jelly
1 bottle (12 ounces) chili sauce

In a bowl, combine crumbs, onion and turkey; mix well. Shape into 1-in. balls. Place in a lightly greased 13-in. x 9-in. x 2-in. baking dish. Combine jelly and chili sauce; pour over meatballs. Cover and bake at 350° for 40 minutes. Uncover; bake 10 minutes longer or until meat is no longer pink. **Yield:** about 5 dozen.

Spiced Up Seeds Are a Savory Snack

TACO PUMPKIN SEEDS

Here is a hot idea from our test kitchen—toast seeds from a freshly cut pumpkin in taco seasoning and a bit of garlic salt. The combination packs a tasty punch!

- 1 cup seeds from freshly cut pumpkin, washed and dried
- 2 tablespoons vegetable oil
- 1 to 2 tablespoons taco seasoning
- 1/4 to 1/2 teaspoon garlic salt

In a skillet, saute pumpkin seeds in oil for 5 minutes or until lightly browned. Using a slotted spoon, transfer seeds to an ungreased 15-in. x 10-in. x 1-in. baking pan. Sprinkle with taco seasoning and garlic salt; stir to coat. Spread into a single layer. Bake at 325° for 15-20 minutes or until crisp. Remove to paper towels to cool completely. Store in an airtight container for up to 3 weeks. **Yield:** 1 cup.

SWEET 'N' SOY SNACK MEATBALLS

Jodi Klassen, Coaldale, Alberta

My mom gave me this recipe when I got married over 10 years ago. They're great for any occasion because they're easy to make and get eaten quickly.

- 1 egg
- 1/4 cup finely chopped onion
- 1 tablespoon ketchup
- 1-1/2 teaspoons salt
- 1/2 teaspoon pepper
- 1/2 teaspoon seasoned salt
- 1/2 teaspoon Worcestershire sauce
- 2 pounds ground beef
- 3/4 cup dry bread crumbs

SAUCE:
- 2 tablespoons plus 1-1/2 teaspoons cornstarch
- 1 cup orange marmalade
- 3 to 4 tablespoons soy sauce
- 2 tablespoons lemon juice
- 2 garlic cloves, minced

In a bowl, combine the first seven ingredients. Crumble meat over mixture. Sprinkle with crumbs; mix gently. Shape into 1-in. balls. Place 1 in. apart in an ungreased 15-in. x 10-in. x 1-in. baking pan. Bake, uncovered, at 350° for 20-25 minutes or until meat is no longer pink. Meanwhile, combine sauce ingredients in a saucepan.

Bring to a boil; cook and stir for 2 minutes or until thickened. Remove meatballs to a serving dish; top with sauce. **Yield:** 5 dozen.

SAUSAGE CHEESE SQUARES

Helen McFadden, Sierra Vista, Arizona

My grandsons tried these savory morsels for the first time as youngsters and loved them. Though they're all grown up now, the boys still request the squares—and I'm happy to comply!

- 1 tube (8 ounces) refrigerated crescent rolls
- 1 package (8 ounces) brown-and-serve sausage links, thawed and sliced 1/2 inch thick
- 2 cups (8 ounces) shredded Monterey Jack cheese
- 4 eggs
- 3/4 cup milk
- 2 tablespoons chopped green pepper
- 1/2 teaspoon salt
- 1/4 teaspoon pepper

Unroll crescent dough; place in an ungreased 13-in. x 9-in. x 2-in. baking dish. Press onto bottom and 1/2 in. up sides to form a crust. Top with sausage and cheese. Beat eggs in a bowl; add the milk, green pepper, salt and pepper. Carefully pour over cheese. Bake, uncovered, at 425° for 20-25 minutes or until a knife inserted near the center comes out clean. Cut into small squares. **Yield:** 12-16 servings.

PINK RHUBARB PUNCH

Rebecca Mininger, Orrville, Ohio

Rhubarb is the featured ingredient in this blush-colored punch. A friend passed the recipe on to me. We enjoy it so much for family parties and potluck dinners that I thought others might, too.

8 cups chopped fresh *or* frozen rhubarb
8 cups water
2-1/2 cups sugar
2 tablespoons strawberry gelatin
2 cups boiling water
2 cups pineapple juice
1/4 cup lemon juice
6 cups ginger ale, chilled

In a large saucepan, bring rhubarb and water to a boil. Reduce heat; simmer for 10 minutes. Drain, reserving liquid (save rhubarb for another use). In a large bowl, combine sugar, gelatin and boiling water until dissolved. Add pineapple and lemon juices; mix well. Stir in rhubarb liquid; refrigerate. Just before serving, pour into a punch bowl and add ginger ale. **Yield:** about 5 quarts.

BACON-BROCCOLI CHEESE BALL

Tamara Rickard, Bartlett, Tennessee

(Pictured at right)

Needing to put together a quick appetizer one night when unexpected company dropped in, I created this easy-to-make cheese ball. For variety, you can shape it into a log instead of a ball, or substitute favorite herbs for the pepper.

1 package (8 ounces) cream cheese, softened
1 cup (4 ounces) finely shredded cheddar cheese
1/2 teaspoon pepper
1 cup finely chopped broccoli florets
6 bacon strips, cooked and crumbled
Assorted crackers

In a mixing bowl, beat cream cheese, cheddar cheese and pepper until blended. Stir in broccoli. Shape into a ball and roll in bacon. Cover and refrigerate. Remove from the refrigerator 15 minutes before serving. Serve with crackers. **Yield:** 2-1/2 cups.

CREAMY GUACAMOLE

Phyllis Allan, Vero Beach, Florida

As a transplanted New Englander, I was anxious to use some of Florida's fresh fruits in new recipes. I came across this one and it quickly became a favorite.

1 medium ripe avocado, halved, seeded and peeled
2 teaspoons lime juice
2 packages (3 ounces *each*) cream cheese, softened
1/2 teaspoon Worcestershire sauce
1/4 teaspoon salt
1/4 teaspoon hot pepper sauce
Tortilla chips

In a small mixing bowl, beat avocado with lime juice. Add the cream cheese, Worcestershire sauce, salt and hot pepper sauce; beat until smooth. Serve with tortilla chips. Store in the refrigerator. **Yield:** 1-1/3 cups.

▰▰▰▰▰▰▰▰▰▰▰
FLAVORFUL SAUSAGE BALLS

Olive Lamb, Cushing, Oklahoma

(Pictured above)

I whip up a batch of these meatballs in a matter of minutes. They're great for busy days when you need something fast that's full of flavor. But we like them so much, I make them even on days I have time to spare.

> 1 pound bulk pork sausage
> 1 egg, beaten
> 1/2 cup dry bread crumbs
> 3/4 cup ketchup
> 1/4 cup packed brown sugar
> 2 tablespoons vinegar
> 2 tablespoons soy sauce

In a bowl, combine sausage and egg. Sprinkle with bread crumbs; mix well. Shape into 1-in. balls. In a skillet, brown meatballs; drain. Combine remaining ingredients; pour over meatballs. Simmer for 10 minutes or until meat is no longer pink. **Yield:** 2-1/2 dozen.

▰▰▰▰▰▰▰▰▰▰▰
SUGAR 'N' SPICE NUTS

Lori Brouwer, Cumberland, British Columbia

It just isn't Christmas at my house until these crunchy munchers are in the oven. The wonderful aroma of ginger, cinnamon and nuts fills the kitchen with festivity when I bake this snack.

> 3 egg whites
> 2 tablespoons water
> 3 cups walnut halves

> 2 cups pecan halves
> 1 cup whole unblanched almonds
> 2 cups sugar
> 2 tablespoons ground cinnamon
> 2 teaspoons ground ginger
> 2 teaspoons grated orange peel
> 1 teaspoon salt
> 1 teaspoon ground nutmeg
> 1 teaspoon ground allspice
> 1/2 teaspoon ground cloves

In a mixing bowl, beat egg whites and water until frothy. Add nuts; stir gently to coat. Combine the remaining ingredients. Add to nut mixture and stir gently to coat. Spread into two greased 15-in. x 10-in. x 1-in. baking pans. Bake, uncovered, at 300° for 20-25 minutes or until lightly browned, stirring every 10 minutes. Cool. Store in an airtight container. **Yield:** 8 cups.

▰▰▰▰▰▰▰▰▰▰▰
FOUR-FRUIT SMOOTHIE

Kathleen Tribble, Santa Ynez, California

Kids will be glad to sip this cool and tangy treat, and you'll be glad to know it's full of good-for-you fruit! Besides the beverage's smooth taste, adults are sure to love its short preparation time. After cutting up the banana, processing the ingredients in a blender is all it takes.

> 1 cup orange juice
> 1 package (10 ounces) frozen sweetened raspberries, partially thawed
> 1 cup frozen unsweetened strawberries
> 1 medium ripe banana, cut into chunks
> 6 ice cubes
> 1 to 2 tablespoons sugar

In a blender, combine the first six ingredients. Cover and process until smooth. Pour into chilled glasses. **Yield:** 4 cups.

▰▰▰▰▰▰▰▰▰▰▰
HAM PECAN PINWHEELS

Dorothy Anderson, Ottawa, Kansas

Your party will be on a roll when you serve these appetizers. The addition of garlic and crunchy pecans really dresses up ordinary ham roll-ups for the holidays.

> 1 package (8 ounces) cream cheese, softened
> 1/4 cup mayonnaise
> 1 garlic clove, minced
> 1 cup chopped pecans
> 8 to 10 slices deli ham

In a mixing bowl, beat the cream cheese, mayonnaise and garlic until smooth. Stir in pecans.

Spread about 3 tablespoonfuls mixture on each ham slice. Roll up tightly; cover and refrigerate for at least 2 hours. Cut into bite-size pieces. **Yield:** 4 dozen.

BACON CHEESEBURGER BALLS

Cathy Lendvoy, Boharm, Saskatchewan

When I serve these, my husband and sons are often fooled into thinking we're having plain meatballs until they cut into the flavorful filling inside.

1 egg
1 envelope onion soup mix
1 pound ground beef
2 tablespoons all-purpose flour
2 tablespoons milk
1 cup (4 ounces) finely shredded cheddar cheese
4 bacon strips, cooked and crumbled
COATING:
2 eggs
1 cup crushed saltines (about 30 crackers)
5 tablespoons vegetable oil

In a bowl, combine egg and soup mix. Crumble beef over mixture and mix well. Divide into 36 portions; set aside. In a bowl, combine the flour and milk until smooth. Add cheese and bacon; mix well. Shape cheese mixture into 36 balls. Shape one beef portion around each cheese ball. In a shallow bowl, beat the eggs. Place cracker crumbs in another bowl. Dip meatballs into egg, then coat with crumbs. In a large skillet over medium heat, cook meatballs in oil for 10-12 minutes or until the meat is no longer pink and coating is golden brown. **Yield:** 3 dozen.

SWEET-SOUR CHICKEN DIPPERS

Kari Caven, Post Falls, Idaho

(Pictured at right)

Since you can chop up all the ingredients the night before, this can be ready in about 30 minutes. So it's a great snack or appetizer...similar to chicken nuggets.

1 can (8 ounces) crushed pineapple
1-1/2 cups sugar
1 can (14-1/2 ounces) diced tomatoes, undrained
1/2 cup vinegar
1/2 cup chopped onion
1/2 cup chopped green pepper
1 tablespoon soy sauce
1/4 teaspoon ground ginger
1 tablespoon cornstarch
BATTER:
1 cup all-purpose flour
1 cup cornstarch
2 teaspoons baking powder
2 teaspoons baking soda
2 teaspoons sugar
1-1/3 cups cold water
Oil for deep-fat frying
1-1/2 pounds boneless skinless chicken breasts, cut into chunks

Drain pineapple, reserving juice. In a saucepan, combine sugar, tomatoes, vinegar, onion, green pepper, soy sauce, ginger and pineapple. Simmer for 20 minutes. In a bowl, combine cornstarch and the reserved pineapple juice until smooth; add to tomato mixture. Bring to a boil; boil and stir for 2 minutes or until slightly thickened. Remove from the heat; set aside. In a bowl, combine the flour, cornstarch, baking powder, baking soda, sugar and water until smooth. In a deep-fat fryer, heat oil to 375°. Dip chicken pieces in batter; drop into oil and fry until golden brown and juices run clear, about 5 minutes. Serve immediately with sweet-sour sauce. **Yield:** 4 dozen appetizers.

Main Dishes

GLAZED HAM BALLS

Esther Leitch, Fredericksburg, Virginia

(Pictured at left)

Over the years, I have found this recipe ideal for using leftovers from a baked ham.

   3 eggs
   1 cup milk
1-1/4 cups quick-cooking oats
2-1/2 pounds ground fully cooked ham
SAUCE:
   1 cup plus 2 tablespoons packed brown
     sugar
   3 tablespoons cornstarch
  1/2 teaspoon ground cloves, optional
1-3/4 cups pineapple juice
  1/2 cup light corn syrup
   3 tablespoons cider vinegar
4-1/2 teaspoons Dijon mustard

In a bowl, combine the eggs, milk, oats and ham; mix well. Shape into 1-1/2-in. balls. Place in a greased 15-in. x 10-in. x 1-in. baking pan. In a saucepan, combine the brown sugar, cornstarch and cloves if desired. Stir in pineapple juice, corn syrup, vinegar and mustard until smooth. Bring to a boil over medium heat; cook and stir for 2 minutes. Pour over ham balls. Bake, uncovered, at 350° for 35-40 minutes or until browned. **Yield:** 10 servings.

FIESTA MEATBALLS

Patricia Archie, Glendo, Wyoming

(Pictured at left)

When I serve this flavorful combination, my rancher husband comes back for more.

   1 egg
1-1/2 teaspoons Worcestershire sauce
  1/4 cup finely chopped onion
  1/4 cup finely chopped celery
2-1/2 teaspoons garlic salt, *divided*
  1/4 teaspoon pepper
   1 pound ground beef
   1 cup soft bread crumbs

   1 tablespoon cornstarch
   1 cup beef broth
   1 can (14-1/2 ounces) stewed tomatoes
   2 cups sliced zucchini
   1 teaspoon dried oregano
  1/2 teaspoon sugar
  1/2 teaspoon dried basil

In a large bowl, combine the egg, Worcestershire sauce, onion, celery, 1-1/2 teaspoons garlic salt and pepper. Add beef and mix well. Sprinkle with bread crumbs; mix just until combined. Shape into 2-in. balls. Place in an ungreased 15-in. x 10-in. x 1-in. baking pan. Bake, uncovered, at 375° for 20 minutes or until meat is no longer pink. Meanwhile, in a saucepan, combine cornstarch and broth until smooth. Stir in the stewed tomatoes, zucchini, oregano, sugar, basil and remaining garlic salt. Bring to a boil; cook and stir for 2 minutes or until thickened. Drain meatballs; top with the tomato mixture. Bake 10 minutes longer or until heated through. **Yield:** 4 servings.

BROCCOLI BRUNCH SKILLET

Frances Rowley, Bartlesville, Oklahoma

Whether for brunch, lunch or supper, this recipe always draws rave reviews.

   6 fresh broccoli spears
   6 slices mozzarella cheese
   6 thin slices fully cooked ham
   1 tablespoon butter *or* margarine
   6 eggs
  1/3 cup water

In a saucepan, bring broccoli and a small amount of water to a boil. Reduce heat. Cover and simmer for 5-8 minutes or until broccoli is crisp-tender; drain. Place one cheese slice over one ham slice and wrap around one broccoli spear. Secure with a toothpick. Repeat. Melt the butter in a 9-in. skillet. Arrange ham rolls in a spoke pattern. In a bowl, beat the eggs and water; pour over ham rolls. Cook over medium-low heat for 10 minutes; as eggs set, lift edges, letting uncooked portion flow underneath. Cover and cook 2-3 minutes longer or until the eggs are completely set. Carefully remove toothpicks; cut into wedges. **Yield:** 6 servings.

In a large resealable plastic bag or shallow glass container, combine the first nine ingredients; mix well. Add chicken and turn to coat. Seal or cover and refrigerate for 8 hours or overnight, turning occasionally. Drain and discard marinade. In a shallow dish, combine bread crumbs and sesame seeds. Dredge chicken in the crumb mixture. Place in a greased 13-in. x 9-in. x 2-in. baking dish. Combine butter and shortening; drizzle over chicken. Bake, uncovered, at 350° for 35-40 minutes or until juices run clear. Meanwhile, combine sauce ingredients in a saucepan; heat through. Serve with chicken. **Yield:** 6 servings.

MEATBALL LOVER'S SANDWICH

Kelly Gerhardt, Council Bluffs, Iowa

(Pictured on page 12)

You'll find that these hearty sandwiches will satisfy even the healthiest appetites. My husband and our three children love them! I like the fact that the recipe makes a big batch of meatballs with tangy sauce that's also savory over spaghetti.

    2 eggs
1/3 cup milk
    2 cups soft bread crumbs
1/2 cup finely chopped onion
1-1/2 teaspoons salt
    2 pounds ground beef
    2 garlic cloves, minced
    1 teaspoon butter *or* margarine
    1 cup ketchup
2/3 cup chili sauce
1/4 cup packed brown sugar
    2 tablespoons Worcestershire sauce
    2 tablespoons prepared mustard
    2 teaspoons celery seed
1/2 teaspoon salt
1/4 teaspoon hot pepper sauce
    8 hoagie buns *or* submarine rolls, split
    1 large onion, sliced

In a bowl, beat eggs and milk. Stir in bread crumbs, chopped onion and salt. Add beef; mix well. Shape into 1-in. balls. Place in a lightly greased 15-in. x 10-in. x 1-in. baking pan. Bake, uncovered, at 375° for 15-20 minutes or until meat is no longer pink. In a saucepan, saute garlic in butter. Add ketchup, chili sauce, brown sugar, Worcestershire sauce, mustard, celery seed, salt and hot pepper sauce. Bring to a boil; add meatballs. Reduce heat; cover and simmer for 20 minutes or until heated through, stirring occasionally. Carefully hollow out buns, leaving a 1/2-in. shell. Spoon meatball mixture into buns; top with sliced onion. **Yield:** 8 servings.

SESAME CHICKEN WITH MUSTARD SAUCE

Wanda White, Antioch, Tennessee

(Pictured above)

For variety, you can make a cracker-crumb coating for my chicken...substitute turkey for the chicken...or grill it instead of baking it. Served with the zesty mustard sauce, it's a fun food for dipping.

1-1/2 cups buttermilk
    2 tablespoons lemon juice
    2 teaspoons Worcestershire sauce
    1 teaspoon salt
    1 teaspoon pepper
    1 teaspoon paprika
    1 teaspoon soy sauce
1/2 teaspoon dried oregano
    2 garlic cloves, minced
    6 boneless skinless chicken breast halves
      (about 1-1/2 pounds)
    2 cups dry bread crumbs
1/2 cup sesame seeds
1/4 cup butter *or* margarine, melted
1/4 cup shortening, melted
SAUCE:
1-1/2 cups prepared mustard
1-1/2 cups plum jam
4-1/2 teaspoons prepared horseradish
1-1/2 teaspoons lemon juice

REUBEN MEATBALLS

Irlana Waggoner, Hays, Kansas

(Pictured on page 12)

Those who like the taste of Reuben sandwiches and sauerkraut are sure to savor these distinctive meatballs. The recipe was given to me by a good friend, Helga Stremel, who is from Germany and is a wonderful cook.

    1 egg
    1 small onion, finely chopped
  2/3 cup soft bread crumbs
  1/4 cup minced fresh parsley
  1/2 teaspoon salt
  1/2 teaspoon pepper
    1 cup cooked rice
1-1/2 pounds lean ground beef
    2 cups sauerkraut, rinsed and well drained
    1 to 2 teaspoons caraway seeds
    1 can (10-3/4 ounces) condensed cream of mushroom soup, undiluted
  1/2 cup Thousand Island salad dressing
  1/4 cup shredded Swiss cheese
Rye bread, optional

In a bowl, combine the egg, onion, bread crumbs, parsley, salt and pepper. Stir in rice. Crumble beef over the mixture and mix well. Shape into 15 balls. Place in an ungreased 13-in. x 9-in. x 2-in. baking dish. Bake, uncovered, at 350° for 15-20 minutes or until browned; drain. Arrange sauerkraut over meatballs; sprinkle with caraway seeds. Combine soup and salad dressing; spread over the top. Cover and bake for 35-45 minutes or until meat is no longer pink. Uncover; sprinkle with Swiss cheese. Bake 10 minutes longer or until cheese is melted. Serve with rye bread if desired. **Yield:** 5 servings.

BARLEY WRAPS

The folks at the National Barley Foods Council share this scrumptious sandwich recipe that will soon become a staple at your house.

1-1/2 cups water
  1/2 cup medium pearl barley
  1/4 teaspoon salt
  3/4 pound ground turkey
    1 cup chunky salsa
    1 cup fresh *or* frozen corn
    1 can (4 ounces) chopped green chilies, drained
    1 can (2-1/4 ounces) sliced ripe olives, drained
    1 teaspoon ground cumin
  1/2 teaspoon dried oregano
  1/2 teaspoon garlic powder
    3 cups (12 ounces) shredded cheddar cheese
   12 flour tortillas (6 to 7 inches), warmed

In a saucepan, combine water, barley and salt; bring to a boil. Reduce heat; cover and simmer for 45 minutes or until tender. In a skillet, cook turkey until no longer pink; drain. Add the barley, salsa, corn, chilies, olives and seasonings; cover and simmer for 15 minutes. Stir in the cheese. Spoon into tortillas and roll up. **Yield:** 1 dozen.

TACO MEATBALL RING

Brenda Johnson, Davison, Michigan

(Pictured on page 12)

While it looks complicated, this attractive meatball-filled ring is really very easy to assemble. My family loves tacos, and we find that the crescent roll dough is a nice change from the usual tortilla shells or chips. There are never any leftovers when I serve this at a meal or as a party appetizer!

    2 cups (8 ounces) shredded cheddar cheese, *divided*
    2 tablespoons water
    2 to 4 tablespoons taco seasoning
  1/2 pound ground beef
    2 tubes (8 ounces *each*) refrigerated crescent rolls
  1/2 head iceberg lettuce, shredded
    1 medium tomato, chopped
    4 green onions, sliced
  1/2 cup sliced ripe olives
Sour cream
    2 small jalapeno peppers, seeded and sliced*
Salsa, optional

In a bowl, combine 1 cup cheese, water and taco seasoning. Add beef and mix well. Shape into 16 balls. Place 1 in. apart in an ungreased 15-in. x 10-in. x 1-in. baking pan. Bake, uncovered, at 400° for 12 minutes or until meat is no longer pink. Drain meatballs on paper towels. Reduce heat to 375°. Arrange crescent rolls on a greased 15-in. pizza pan, forming a ring with pointed ends facing the outer edge of the pan and wide ends overlapping. Place a meatball on each roll; fold point over meatball and tuck under wide end of roll (meatballs will be visible). Bake for 15-20 minutes or until rolls are golden brown. Fill the center of ring with lettuce, tomato, onions, olives, remaining cheese, sour cream, jalapenos and salsa if desired. **Yield:** 8 servings. ***Editor's Note:** When handling hot peppers, use rubber or plastic gloves to protect your hands. Avoid touching your face.

Dash pepper
    4 boneless skinless chicken breast halves
        (about 1 pound)
    1 cup (4 ounces) shredded Swiss cheese
1/2 teaspoon paprika
Hot cooked rice, optional

In a saucepan, melt 3 tablespoons butter. Stir in flour until smooth. Gradually stir in broth and milk. Bring to a boil; boil and stir for 2 minutes. Remove from the heat; set aside. In a skillet, saute onion in remaining butter until tender. Add the crab, mushrooms, cracker crumbs, parsley, salt, pepper and 2 tablespoons of the white sauce; heat through. Flatten chicken to 1/4-in. thickness. Spoon about 1/2 cup of the crab mixture on each chicken breast. Roll up and secure with a toothpick. Place in a greased 9-in. square baking dish. Top with remaining white sauce. Cover and bake at 350° for 30 minutes or until chicken juices run clear. Sprinkle with cheese and paprika. Bake, uncovered, 5 minutes longer or until cheese is melted. Remove toothpicks. Serve with rice if desired. **Yield:** 4 servings.

BEEF STROGANOFF MEATBALLS

Chris Duncan, Ellensburg, Washington

A rich sour cream and mushroom sauce gives this dish an elegant flavor. Yet it's so easy to prepare for a special occasion or for company. The meatballs can be made ahead and frozen to save time, which is often in short supply since we live on a hobby farm with our four active children!

    1 egg
1/4 cup milk
1/4 cup finely chopped onion
    2 teaspoons Worcestershire sauce
1-1/2 cups soft bread crumbs
    1 teaspoon salt
1/4 teaspoon pepper
1-1/2 pounds ground beef
SAUCE:
1-1/2 cups sliced fresh mushrooms
1/2 cup chopped onion
1/4 cup butter *or* margarine
    4 tablespoons all-purpose flour, *divided*
1/4 teaspoon salt
1-1/2 cups beef broth
    1 cup (8 ounces) sour cream
Hot cooked noodles
Paprika, optional

In a bowl, combine the egg, milk, onion and Worcestershire sauce. Stir in bread crumbs, salt and pepper. Add beef; mix well. Shape into 1-1/4-in.

CRAB-STUFFED CHICKEN BREASTS

Therese Bechtel, Montgomery Village, Maryland
(Pictured above)

Busy as an active-duty member of the Coast Guard and the mother of a young son, I prepare this elegant dish for guests and special occasions. The sauce is so versatile, though, I've used it on pork chops and baked potatoes, too.

    4 tablespoons butter *or* margarine, *divided*
1/4 cup all-purpose flour
    1 cup chicken broth
3/4 cup milk
1/4 cup chopped onion
    1 can (6 ounces) crabmeat, drained,
        flaked and cartilage removed
    1 can (4 ounces) mushroom stems and
        pieces, drained
1/3 cup crushed saltines (about 10 crackers)
    2 tablespoons minced fresh parsley
1/2 teaspoon salt

balls. Place in a lightly greased 15-in. x 10-in. x 1-in. baking pan. Bake, uncovered, at 350° for 15-20 minutes or until meat is no longer pink. In a saucepan, saute mushrooms and onion in butter until tender. Stir in 3 tablespoons flour and salt until blended. Gradually add broth. Bring to a boil over medium heat. Cook and stir for 2 minutes; reduce heat. Combine sour cream and remaining flour until smooth; stir into mushroom mixture. Add meatballs. Simmer, uncovered, for 4-5 minutes or until heated through, stirring occasionally. Serve over noodles. Sprinkle with paprika if desired. **Yield:** 6 servings.

SAUSAGE POTATO WRAPS

Julia Rathbun, Beggs, Oklahoma

With our busy schedule, we're always on the lookout for quick recipes. My husband came up with these mouth-watering wraps we frequently rely on in a morning rush.

    1 pound bulk hot pork sausage
    1 package (24 ounces) frozen O'Brien
       hash brown potatoes
    4 eggs
 1/2 cup milk
Salt and pepper to taste
   12 flour tortillas (8 inches)
Sour cream and salsa, optional

In a skillet, cook sausage until no longer pink; drain. Add potatoes; cook until lightly browned, about 15 minutes. Beat the eggs, milk, salt and pepper; add to the sausage mixture. Cook until eggs are completely set, stirring frequently. Divide mixture between tortillas; roll up tightly. Place in a greased 13-in. x 9-in. x 2-in. baking dish. Microwave, uncovered, on high for 3-5 minutes or until heated through, or microwave individually for 45 seconds. Serve with sour cream and salsa if desired. **Yield:** 6-8 servings. **Editor's Note:** This recipe was tested in an 850-watt microwave.

BLACK HILLS GOLDEN EGG BAKE

Sandra Giardino, Rapid City, South Dakota

(Pictured at right)

I developed this recipe when I was cooking for large groups of people. It's easy to make and gives you plenty of time to do other things while it's baking.

 1/2 cup sliced fresh mushrooms
 1/2 cup chopped green pepper

 1/4 cup butter *or* margarine
   10 eggs
 1/2 cup all-purpose flour
    1 teaspoon baking powder
 1/4 teaspoon salt, optional
    2 cups (16 ounces) small-curd cottage
       cheese
    2 cups (8 ounces) shredded cheddar
       cheese
    2 cups (8 ounces) shredded Monterey
       Jack cheese
 1/2 pound bulk pork sausage, cooked
       and drained
    6 bacon strips, cooked and crumbled
    1 can (2-1/4 ounces) sliced ripe olives,
       drained

In a skillet, saute mushrooms and green pepper in butter until tender. In a mixing bowl, combine eggs, flour, baking powder and salt if desired; mix well. Add mushroom mixture. Stir in remaining ingredients; mix well. Pour into a greased 13-in. x 9-in. x 2-in. baking dish. Bake, uncovered, at 400° for 15 minutes. Reduce heat to 350°; bake 25-35 minutes longer or until a knife inserted near the center comes out clean. **Yield:** 10-12 servings.

NO-FUSS MEATBALLS

L.M. Walton, Farmerville, Louisiana

I can always rely on these easy-to-make meatballs to feed my hungry family in a hurry. The simple yet savory sauce is made with just two ingredients I always have on hand, and it keeps the meatballs moist and tender.

    1 egg
1/4 cup milk
1/4 cup finely chopped onion
3/4 cup seasoned bread crumbs
1/2 teaspoon salt
Dash pepper
1-1/2 pounds lean ground beef
1-1/3 cups ketchup
    2 cups ginger ale
Hot cooked rice

In a bowl, combine the first six ingredients. Add beef; mix well. Shape into 1-1/4-in. balls. In a Dutch oven or large saucepan over medium heat, bring ketchup and ginger ale to a boil. Reduce heat. Add meatballs; cover and simmer for 30 minutes or until meat is no longer pink. Serve over rice. **Yield:** 6 servings.

CHICKEN WILD RICE CASSEROLE

Elizabeth Tokariuk, Lethbridge, Alberta

(Pictured below)

While this special dish is perfect for a company dinner, it's also just too good not to make often for everyday family meals. We think it is very nice served with some crusty rolls or French bread.

    1 small onion, chopped
1/3 cup butter or margarine
1/3 cup all-purpose flour
1-1/2 teaspoons salt
1/2 teaspoon pepper
    1 can (14-1/2 ounces) chicken broth
    1 cup half-and-half cream
    4 cups cubed cooked chicken
    4 cups cooked wild rice
    2 jars (4-1/2 ounces *each*) sliced
        mushrooms, drained
    1 jar (4 ounces) diced pimientos, drained
    1 tablespoon minced fresh parsley
1/3 cup slivered almonds

In a large saucepan, saute onion in butter until tender. Stir in flour, salt and pepper until blended. Gradually stir in broth; bring to a boil. Boil and stir for 2 minutes or until thickened and bubbly. Stir in the cream, chicken, rice, mushrooms, pimientos and parsley; heat through. Transfer to a greased 2-1/2-qt. baking dish. Sprinkle with almonds. Bake, uncovered, at 350° for 30-35 minutes or until bubbly. **Yield:** 6-8 servings.

POPEYE'S FAVORITE MEATBALLS

Cheryl Miller, Fort Collins, Colorado

As you probably guessed by the name of this recipe, spinach is the star of these hearty meatballs. Even folks who say they don't normally care for spinach can't get enough of them. And I don't mind serving them often since they're good for you, too.

✓ **Uses less fat, sugar or salt. Includes Nutritional Analysis and Diabetic Exchanges.**

Egg substitute equivalent to 1 egg
    1 tablespoon water
    1 cup low-fat cottage cheese
1/4 cup dry bread crumbs
    2 tablespoons dried minced onion
1/2 teaspoon garlic powder
    1 package (10 ounces) frozen chopped
        spinach, thawed and well drained
1-1/2 pounds lean ground beef

In a bowl, combine the first six ingredients. Add spinach and beef; mix well. Shape into 1-in. balls. Place on an ungreased baking sheet. Broil 4-6 in. from the heat for 8 minutes. Turn and broil 3-5 minutes longer or until meat is no longer pink. **Yield:** 8 servings. **Nutritional Analysis:** One serving equals 176 calories, 198 mg sodium, 44 mg cholesterol, 6 gm carbohydrate, 18 gm protein, 9 gm fat. **Diabetic Exchanges:** 2 meat, 1 vegetable.

Making Better Meatballs

• For a pretty presentation, skewer your favorite meatballs and serve them over rice, then top with sauce.
—Connie Richison
Winnebago, Minnesota

• Try experimenting with ground pork, turkey, lamb, sausage or a mixture of meats as a substitute for ground beef.
—Sharon Mancuso, Smyrna, Georgia

• Meatballs will bake evenly and keep their shape as the fat drips away if you bake them on a broiler pan.
—Gloria McCutcheon
Rocanville, Saskatchewan

• To make meatballs of equal size, pat meat mixture into a 1-inch-thick rectangle. With a knife, cut rectangle into the same number of squares as meatballs needed. Gently roll each square into a ball.
—Artha Dunk
Sunburst, Montana

• Crushed potato chips are a flavorful change from bread or cracker crumbs in meatballs.
—Mary Beaney
Bourbonnais, Illinois

• Add the ground meat to your meatball mixture after all other ingredients are thoroughly blended to avoid overmixing and ending up with tough meatballs.
—Ellen Grose
Lacombe, Alberta

• When making ground beef or ham meatballs, I combine the ingredients just before cooking them so that the meat does not take on a pink color during cooking.
—Jennifer Shauger
Bryan, Texas

• Try mixing shredded carrots into your favorite meatballs for added moistness, color, flavor and nutrition.
—Arlene Bartley
Roland, Manitoba

• For a little extra zip, substitute salsa for tomato sauce in your meatball recipe.
—Teresia Husk
Henderson, Kentucky

• To prevent the meat mixture from sticking, try chilling your meatballer before using.
—Edna Hoffman
Hebron, Indiana

• I always double the amount of sauce for my meatball recipe and serve the extra over spaghetti or rice.
A small ice cream scoop works well for shaping meatballs uniformly.
—Mrs. R.M. Page
Tahlequah, Oklahoma

• For a quick sandwich, top a hoagie bun with several sliced meatballs and sauce. Layer with cheese and bake or broil until the cheese is melted.
—Susan Pendergast
Monroe, New York

• When taking meatballs to a community supper, use your slow cooker to transport them and keep them warm.
—Dawn Johnson
Bloomsburg, Pennsylvania

• Vary your favorite porcupine meatball recipe by substituting brown rice for white rice or V8 juice for regular tomato juice.
—Linda Keery
Newburgh, New York

at 350° for 1-1/2 hours or until bean mixture reaches desired thickness. **Yield:** 14-16 servings. **Editor's Note:** This recipe can also be prepared in a slow cooker. Prepare as directed, transferring to a slow cooker instead of a baking dish. Cover and cook on low for 6-8 hours or until heated through.

HONEY BAKED RIBS

Marge Tubbs, Raleigh, North Carolina

Here's a delicious recipe that's easy to make. All the preparation is done the day before, so it's perfect for those busy days.

    1 can (10-1/2 ounces) beef consomme, undiluted
  1/2 cup ketchup
  1/2 cup soy sauce
  1/2 cup honey
    4 garlic cloves, minced
    4 pounds country-style spareribs, cut into serving-size pieces

Combine the first five ingredients in a bowl. Pour half into a large resealable plastic bag or shallow glass container; add ribs. Cover and refrigerate overnight, turning once. Refrigerate remaining marinade. Remove ribs to a greased roasting pan; discard marinade. Cover and bake at 425° for 10 minutes. Reduce heat to 325°. Cover and bake 30 minutes longer; drain. Pour reserved marinade over ribs. Bake, uncovered, for 45 minutes or until meat is tender, basting frequently. **Yield:** 6 servings.

MICHIGAN BEANS AND SAUSAGE

Janice Lass, Dorr, Michigan

(Pictured above)

I got this recipe from a church cookbook years ago. Bean casseroles like this one are a big hit at potlucks, picnics and other get-togethers.

    1 pound fully cooked kielbasa *or* Polish sausage, halved lengthwise and thinly sliced
    1 medium onion, chopped
    1 cup ketchup
  3/4 cup packed brown sugar
  1/2 cup sugar
    2 tablespoons vinegar
    2 tablespoons molasses
    2 tablespoons prepared mustard
    3 cans (15-1/2 ounces *each*) great northern beans, rinsed and drained

In a saucepan, cook sausage and onion in boiling water for 2 minutes; drain. In a bowl, combine the ketchup, sugars, vinegar, molasses and mustard. Stir in the beans and sausage mixture. Transfer to a greased 2-1/2-qt. baking dish. Cover and bake

SAVORY CHICKEN VEGETABLE STRUDEL

Michele Barneson, Washburn, Wisconsin

If you're looking for a way to "sneak" vegetables into a dish, try this one that looks fancy without the fuss. Now that our two sons are grown, I make it for my husband and me. It is definitely a recipe for company as well, though.

    2 cups diced cooked chicken
  1/2 cup shredded carrots
  1/2 cup finely chopped fresh broccoli
  1/3 cup finely chopped sweet red pepper
    1 cup (4 ounces) shredded sharp cheddar cheese
  1/2 cup mayonnaise
    2 garlic cloves, minced
  1/2 teaspoon dill weed
  1/4 teaspoon salt
  1/4 teaspoon pepper

    2 tubes (8 ounces *each*) refrigerated
      crescent rolls
    1 egg white, beaten
    2 tablespoons slivered almonds

In a bowl, combine the first 10 ingredients; mix well. Unroll crescent dough and place in a greased 15-in. x 10-in. x 1-in. baking pan; press seams and perforations together, forming a 15-in. x 12-in. rectangle (dough will hang over edges of pan). Spread filling lengthwise down the center of dough. On each long side, cut 1-1/2-in.-wide strips 3-1/2 in. into center. Starting at one end, alternate strips, twisting twice and laying at an angle across filling. Seal ends. Brush dough with egg white; sprinkle with almonds. Bake at 375° for 30-35 minutes or until golden brown. Cut into slices; serve warm. **Yield:** 12 servings.

MEATBALLS WITH GRAVY

Mary Stifflemire, Lexington, Texas

I love experimenting in the kitchen. These tasty meatballs made with turkey were a family-pleasing result the first time I made them. They're so good, people don't always realize they're good for you as well.

✓ **Uses less fat, sugar or salt. Includes Nutritional Analysis and Diabetic Exchanges.**

Egg substitute equivalent to 1 egg
    1/4 cup seasoned bread crumbs
      1 teaspoon garlic powder
      1 teaspoon onion powder
    1/4 to 1/2 teaspoon rubbed sage
    1/4 teaspoon pepper
    1/4 teaspoon dried basil
    1/4 teaspoon dried rosemary, crushed
      1 pound ground turkey breast
      1 medium onion, sliced
      1 can (4 ounces) mushroom stems and
        pieces, drained
      1 jar (12 ounce) fat-free turkey gravy
Hot cooked rice

In a bowl, combine the first eight ingredients. Add turkey; mix well. Shape into 1-1/2-in. balls. In a skillet coated with nonstick cooking spray, brown meatballs, turning frequently. Add onion and mushrooms; cook until onion is tender. Add gravy; bring to a boil. Reduce heat; simmer, uncovered, for 15-20 minutes or until meat is no longer pink, stirring frequently. Serve over rice. **Yield:** 4 servings. **Nutritional Analysis:** One serving (calculated without rice) equals 232 calories, 958 mg sodium, 63 mg cholesterol, 20 gm carbohydrate, 33 gm protein, 2 gm fat. **Diabetic Exchanges:** 4 very lean meat, 1 vegetable, 1 starch.

LEMON-BATTER FISH

Jackie Hannahs, Muskegon, Michigan
(Pictured below)

My husband ranks this recipe as one of his favorites. A lot of fishing takes place in our area, and this dish is a delicious way to put this "catch" to good use.

1-1/2 cups all-purpose flour, *divided*
      1 teaspoon baking powder
    3/4 teaspoon salt
    1/2 teaspoon sugar
      1 egg, beaten
    2/3 cup water
    2/3 cup lemon juice, *divided*
      2 pounds perch *or* walleye fillets, cut into
        serving-size pieces
Vegetable oil
Lemon wedges, optional

In a bowl, combine 1 cup flour, baking powder, salt and sugar; set aside. Combine egg, water and 1/3 cup lemon juice; add to the dry ingredients and mix until smooth. Dip fillets in remaining lemon juice and flour, then coat with the batter. Heat 1 in. of oil in a skillet. Fry fish, a few fillets at a time, over medium-high heat for 2-3 minutes on each side or until the fish flakes easily with a fork. Drain on paper towels. Garnish with lemon if desired. **Yield:** 6-8 servings.

SAVORY STUFFED PUMPKIN

Patricia Sacheck, Wasilla, Alaska

(Pictured below)

As soon as pumpkins are available in October, I stock up on them for making this special dish. The beefy mixture is filling and tastes good the next day—that is, if there are any leftovers!

        1-1/2 pounds ground beef
            1 medium onion, chopped
            1 can (10-3/4 ounces) condensed cream of
               mushroom soup, undiluted
            1 jar (4 ounces) sliced mushrooms,
               drained
            3 tablespoons soy sauce
            2 tablespoons brown sugar
        1-1/2 cups cooked rice
            1 can (8 ounces) sliced water chestnuts,
               drained
            1 large pie pumpkin (8 to 9 pounds)
      Vegetable oil

In a skillet over medium heat, cook beef and onion until meat is no longer pink; drain. Add soup, mushrooms, soy sauce and brown sugar. Simmer, uncovered, for 10 minutes, stirring occasionally. Stir in the rice and water chestnuts. Wash pump-

kin; cut a 6-in. circle around stem. Remove top and set aside. Discard seeds and loose fibers from the inside. Spoon beef mixture into pumpkin; replace top. Place on a greased 15-in. x 10-in. x 1-in. baking pan. Rub oil over outside of pumpkin. Bake, uncovered, at 350° for 1-1/2 hours or until pumpkin is tender. Scoop out some pumpkin with each serving of beef mixture. **Yield:** 6 servings.

SOUTHWEST BARLEY STEW

Add zip to supper by serving your family this Southwestern-style stew shared by the National Barley Foods Council. It's a zesty change of pace from the traditional beef stew.

            1 cup chopped onion
            1 cup chopped celery
            1 garlic clove, minced
            3 tablespoons vegetable oil
            2 quarts beef or chicken broth
            2 cans (14-1/2 ounces *each*) diced
               tomatoes, undrained
            1 cup medium pearl barley
            1 cup lentils
            1 can (4 ounces) chopped green chilies
            1 tablespoon chili powder
            2 teaspoons ground cumin
            1 teaspoon ground coriander
        1/8 teaspoon cayenne pepper

In a soup kettle or Dutch oven, saute onion, celery and garlic in oil until tender. Add the remaining ingredients. Bring to a boil. Reduce heat; cover and simmer for 1 hour or until barley is tender, stirring occasionally. **Yield:** 12 servings (3 quarts).

POT ROAST WITH CRANBERRY SAUCE

Elinor Muller, Vineyard Haven, Massachusetts

My friends rave about the different taste the cranberry sauce gives to this roast, and I couldn't agree more. I've made the sauce ahead of time and frozen it, which saves preparation time on a busy schedule.

        1/2 cup all-purpose flour
            1 garlic clove, minced
            1 teaspoon salt
        1/2 teaspoon pepper
            1 boneless rump *or* chuck roast (about
               3-1/2 pounds)
            3 tablespoons vegetable oil
            2 cups beef broth
            1 medium onion, grated

Pinch ground cinnamon
Pinch ground cloves
CRANBERRY SAUCE:
    2 cups fresh *or* frozen cranberries
    1 small navel orange, peeled and diced
    1/2 cup sugar
    1 tablespoon cider *or* red wine vinegar

Combine flour, garlic, salt and pepper; rub over the roast. In a Dutch oven, brown roast in oil. Add broth, onion, cinnamon and cloves. Cover and simmer for 2-1/2 hours or until the meat is tender. Meanwhile, combine the cranberries, orange and sugar in a saucepan. Cover and cook over low heat for 5 minutes. Uncover and simmer until the berries burst and the mixture is thickened, about 20 minutes. Remove roast and keep warm. Skim fat from pan juices, reserving 2 cups. Stir vinegar and reserved pan juices into the cranberry sauce. Slice roast; serve with the cranberry sauce. **Yield:** 8 servings.

▗▖▗▖▗▖▗▖▗▖▗▖▗▖▗▖

TURKEY POTATO MEATBALLS

Kathy Rusert, Mena, Arkansas

This hearty "meat-and-potatoes" dish is one of my husband's favorite meals. We like them better than traditional ground beef meatballs. Topped with a mushroom soup-based sauce, they're very savory and satisfying.

> ✓ Uses less fat, sugar or salt. Includes Nutritional Analysis and Diabetic Exchanges.

    2 medium potatoes, peeled and shredded
    1 small onion, grated
    2 medium carrots, grated
    1/2 cup dry bread crumbs
Egg substitute equivalent to 1 egg
    1/8 teaspoon pepper
1-1/2 pounds ground turkey
    1 tablespoon shortening
    1 can (10-3/4 ounces) low-fat condensed cream of mushroom soup, undiluted
1-1/3 cups skim milk
    1/2 cup uncooked instant rice

In a large bowl, combine the first six ingredients. Add turkey; mix well. Shape into 1-in. balls. In a skillet, brown meatballs in shortening; set aside. In an ungreased 13-in. x 9-in. x 2-in. baking dish, combine soup, milk and rice; stir in meatballs. Cover and bake at 350° for 30-35 minutes or until meatballs are no longer pink. **Yield:** 10 servings.
Nutritional Analysis: One serving equals 218 calories, 263 mg sodium, 55 mg cholesterol, 20 gm carbohydrate, 16 gm protein, 8 gm fat. **Diabetic Exchanges:** 1-1/2 meat, 1 starch, 1 vegetable.

▗▖▗▖▗▖▗▖▗▖▗▖▗▖▗▖

SKILLET BOW TIE LASAGNA

Arleta Schurle, Clay Center, Kansas

(Pictured above)

This quick recipe tastes just like lasagna, but you make it on the stove. It's very tasty and is always a hit with my hungry family.

    1 pound ground beef
    1 small onion, chopped
    1 garlic clove, minced
    1 can (14-1/2 ounces) diced tomatoes, undrained
1-1/2 cups water
    1 can (6 ounces) tomato paste
    1 tablespoon dried parsley flakes
    2 teaspoons dried oregano
    1 teaspoon salt
2-1/2 cups uncooked bow tie pasta
    3/4 cup small-curd cottage cheese
    1/4 cup grated Parmesan cheese

In a large skillet, cook beef, onion and garlic until meat is no longer pink; drain. Add the tomatoes, water, tomato paste, parsley, oregano and salt; mix well. Stir in pasta; bring to a boil. Reduce heat; cover and simmer for 20-25 minutes or until pasta is tender, stirring once. Combine cheeses; drop by rounded tablespoonfuls onto pasta mixture. Cover and cook for 5 minutes. **Yield:** 4 servings.

Old-Fashioned Chicken Potpie

Marilyn Hockey, Lisle, Ontario
(Pictured above)

Although this uses leftover chicken, I serve it sometimes as a special company dinner. Actually, my husband and daughters may enjoy it more than they enjoyed the original roasted bird with all the fixings!

  1/3 cup butter *or* margarine
  1/3 cup all-purpose flour
    1 garlic clove, minced
  1/2 teaspoon salt
  1/4 teaspoon pepper
1-1/2 cups water
  2/3 cup milk
    2 teaspoons chicken bouillon granules
    2 cups cubed cooked chicken
    1 cup frozen mixed vegetables
PASTRY:
1-2/3 cups all-purpose flour
    2 teaspoons celery seed
    1 package (8 ounces) cream cheese, cubed
  1/3 cup cold butter *or* margarine

In a saucepan, melt butter. Stir in flour, garlic, salt and pepper until blended. Gradually stir in water, milk and bouillon. Bring to a boil; boil and stir for 2 minutes. Remove from the heat. Stir in chicken and vegetables; set aside. For pastry, combine flour and celery seed in a bowl. Cut in cream cheese and butter until crumbly. Work mixture by hand until dough forms a ball. On a lightly floured surface, roll two-thirds of dough into a 12-in.

square. Transfer to an 8-in. square baking dish. Pour filling into crust. Roll remaining dough into a 9-in. square; place over filling. Trim, seal and flute edges. Cut slits in pastry. Bake at 425° for 30-35 minutes or until crust is golden brown and filling is bubbly. **Yield:** 6 servings.

Pumpkin Sloppy Joes

Donna Musser, Pearl City, Illinois

Here's a "vine" version of an old standby—sloppy joes made with pumpkin! I also sprinkles cloves, nutmeg and chili powder into the mix while it cooks for extra zest. The sandwiches taste good with dill pickle slices on the side.

  2 pounds ground beef
  1 medium onion, finely chopped
  1 cup ketchup
1/2 cup tomato juice
  1 teaspoon chili powder
3/4 teaspoon salt
1/4 teaspoon *each* ground cloves,
    nutmeg and pepper
  2 cups cooked *or* canned pumpkin
Hamburger buns, split

In a large skillet over medium heat, cook beef and onion until meat is no longer pink; drain. Add ketchup, tomato juice, chili powder, salt, cloves, nutmeg and pepper; mix well. Bring to a boil. Stir in pumpkin. Reduce heat; cover and simmer for 15-20 minutes. Serve on buns. **Yield:** 6-8 servings.

Spinach Turkey Meatballs

Mimi Blanco, Bronxville, New York

Our children call these "Gramby Meatballs" because the recipe came from my dear mother-in-law. It's a great way to make spinach palatable. I usually make a triple batch, bake them all and freeze the extras for a quick meal later.

  1 package (10 ounces) frozen chopped
    spinach, thawed and squeezed dry
  1 egg, beaten
  1 cup soft bread crumbs
  2 tablespoons grated onion
  1 teaspoon seasoned salt
  1 pound ground turkey
Tomato wedges, optional

In a bowl, combine spinach, egg, bread crumbs, onion and seasoned salt. Add turkey and mix well. Shape into 2-in. balls. Place in a lightly greased 15-in. x 10-in. x 1-in. baking pan. Bake, uncovered, at 400° for 20 minutes or until the meat is no longer pink. Drain on paper towels. Garnish with tomato wedges if desired. **Yield:** 4 servings.

BROCCOLI FISH BUNDLES

Frances Quinn, Farmingdale, New York

(Pictured below right)

These bundles take a little time to assemble, but they're worth it! They're always popular at a shower or buffet…and they're great for an everyday dinner, too. This flavorful dish goes nicely with rice pilaf or a saucy pasta.

    18 fresh broccoli spears (about 1-1/2
       pounds)
     6 cubes Monterey Jack cheese (1-1/2 inches)
     6 sole *or* flounder fillets (about 2 pounds)
   1/8 teaspoon lemon-pepper seasoning,
       optional
   1/3 cup butter *or* margarine, melted
     2 teaspoons lemon juice
     1 garlic clove, minced
   1/4 teaspoon salt
   1/8 teaspoon pepper

In a saucepan, place broccoli in a small amount of water. Bring to a boil. Reduce heat; cover and simmer for 2-3 minutes or until crisp-tender. Rinse in cold water; drain. For each bundle, place a cheese cube on three broccoli spears. Wrap with a fish fillet and fasten with a toothpick if necessary. Place on a greased foil-lined baking sheet. Sprinkle with lemon-pepper if desired. Bake at 350° for 15-25 minutes or until fish flakes easily with a fork. Meanwhile, combine butter, lemon juice, garlic, salt and pepper. Transfer fish bundles to a serving platter; remove toothpicks. Drizzle with butter mixture. **Yield:** 6 servings.

SURPRISE MEATBALL SKEWERS

Kristen Wondra, Hudson, Kansas

I still remember the first time I served these colorful kabobs—my family was thrilled to find a surprise in the tasty meatballs. Since I make them often, I sometimes substitute different vegetables or cheeses.

   1/3 cup honey
     3 tablespoons Dijon mustard
     2 tablespoons finely chopped onion
     2 tablespoons apple juice *or* cider
Dash cayenne pepper
     1 egg
   1/4 cup dry bread crumbs
     1 tablespoon minced fresh parsley
     1 teaspoon Italian seasoning
   1/4 teaspoon salt
Pepper to taste
     1 pound ground beef
     1 block (1-1/2 ounces) Monterey
       Jack *or* Swiss cheese, cut into 12 cubes
    12 small mushrooms, stems removed
     1 medium green pepper, cut into pieces
     1 medium sweet yellow *or* red pepper, cut
       into pieces
     1 medium onion, cut into wedges

In a saucepan, combine the first five ingredients. Bring to a boil. Reduce heat; simmer, uncovered, for 5-7 minutes or until onion is tender and sauce is slightly thickened. Remove from the heat; set aside. In a large bowl, combine the egg, bread crumbs, parsley, Italian seasoning, salt and pepper. Add beef and mix well. Divide into 12 portions. Place a cube of cheese in each mushroom cap; shape each meat portion around a mushroom. On six metal or soaked bamboo skewers, alternate meatballs, peppers and onion wedges. Grill, uncovered, over medium heat for 3 minutes on each side. Grill 10-12 minutes longer or until meat juices run clear, turning occasionally. Brush kabobs with reserved glaze during the last 2 minutes. **Yield:** 6 servings.

HONEY FRENCH TOAST

Priscilla Weaver, Hagerstown, Maryland

According to my family, this French toast is suitable for any meal. We think it's especially delicious.

- 1/4 cup all-purpose flour
- 1 tablespoon sugar
- 1/8 teaspoon salt
- 1 cup milk
- 3 eggs, beaten
- 18 slices Texas toast bread *or* 1-inch-thick slices Italian bread
- 3 tablespoons butter *or* margarine

Warm honey

In a bowl, combine flour, sugar, salt, milk and eggs until smooth. Dip both sides of bread into egg mixture. In a skillet, melt butter. Fry French toast for 2-3 minutes on each side or until golden brown. Transfer to serving plates. Drizzle with honey. **Yield:** 18 slices.

SPAGHETTI 'N' MEATBALLS

Ann Rath, Mankato, Minnesota

(Pictured below)

Always a family favorite, these delectable meatballs take little time to prepare because they don't need to be browned before being added to the sauce. I have found that the meatballs taste best if they are mixed just until all the ingredients are blended.

- 1 cup chopped onion
- 1 tablespoon vegetable oil
- 1 can (28 ounces) stewed tomatoes
- 2 cans (6 ounces *each*) tomato paste
- 1 tablespoon sugar
- 1 teaspoon salt
- 1/2 teaspoon dried basil
- 1/4 teaspoon dried oregano
- 1/8 teaspoon dried marjoram
- 1/8 teaspoon paprika

Dash pepper

- 2 eggs
- 1 garlic clove, minced
- 2 teaspoons dried parsley flakes
- 1 pound lean ground beef
- 1 cup grated Parmesan cheese
- 1/2 cup dry bread crumbs

Hot cooked spaghetti

In a soup kettle or Dutch oven, saute onion in oil until tender. Stir in the tomatoes, tomato paste, sugar and seasonings. Bring to a boil. Meanwhile, in a large bowl, beat eggs, garlic and parsley. Add the beef and mix well. Sprinkle with cheese and bread crumbs; mix gently. Shape into 1-1/2-in. balls. Add to the sauce; reduce heat. Cover and simmer for 30 minutes or until meat is no longer pink. Serve meatballs and sauce over spaghetti. **Yield:** 4 servings.

CURRIED BARLEY CHICKEN

The sweet taste of orange marmalade tops off this nicely seasoned chicken and barley dish shared by the National Barley Foods Council.

- 1/2 cup chopped onion
- 1/2 cup chopped sweet red pepper
- 1/2 cup chopped green pepper
- 1 garlic clove, minced
- 1 tablespoon olive *or* vegetable oil
- 1 medium tart apple, chopped
- 1 to 2 tablespoons curry powder
- 2-1/2 cups chicken broth
- 1 cup medium pearl barley
- 4 boneless skinless chicken breast halves
- 1/4 teaspoon garlic salt
- 3 tablespoons orange marmalade *or* apricot jam

In a skillet, saute onion, peppers and garlic in oil until crisp-tender. Stir in apple and curry; cook 1-2 minutes. Add broth and barley; bring to a boil. Reduce heat; cover and simmer for 15 minutes. Transfer to a greased 9-in. square baking dish. Arrange chicken on top; sprinkle with garlic salt. Cover and bake at 375° for 45 minutes. Uncover; brush with the marmalade. Bake, uncovered, for 15 minutes or until chicken juices run clear and barley is tender. **Yield:** 4 servings.

Grade-A Poultry Pointers

• When making your favorite coating mix for chicken, double or triple the amount and store the extra in resealable plastic bags.
—Opal Bobo
Cincinnati, Ohio

• Instead of moistening chicken with water or milk before coating it, brush on barbecue sauce for added flavor.
—Cecile Kanis
Chilliwack, British Columbia

• Now that we're empty nesters, I divide my favorite chicken casserole into two 8-inch pans and freeze one for later use.
—Mary Lou Guth, Eureka, Illinois

• For a fun variation on chicken enchiladas, place chicken filling in large cooked pasta shells instead of tortillas.
—Suzanne Stoop, Salford, Ontario

• Put a foil pan under chicken when grilling to catch drips and keep the fire from flaring up. You can also add a little water to the pan to generate extra steam and moisture so the chicken will stay juicy.
—Terry Walz, Red Deer, Alberta

• Cube or slice any leftover grilled chicken breasts and add to your Caesar salad. Delicious!
—Darlene Bindle
Guernsey, Saskatchewan

• For a quick, always-on-hand coating for chicken, dip pieces in mayonnaise, then sprinkle with seasoned salt and paprika.
—Barbara Roggenbuck
Harbor Beach, Michigan

• When cutting up whole chickens for recipes, freeze the backs and necks until there are enough for homemade chicken soup or broth.
—Jocelyn Nahirnick
Bon Accord, Alberta

• For a quick, delicious marinade, pour bottled Italian dressing over the chicken.
—Lauri Thomasson
Indianapolis, Indiana

• When a recipe calls for one whole chicken, you can substitute two large chicken breasts.
—Pat Hecker
Salina, Kansas

• Refrigerated biscuits can be used to prepare quick dumplings or homemade noodles. Tear into small pieces and drop into the broth for dumplings…or roll and cut into 1/4-inch strips for noodles.
—Brenda Amyx, Robert Lee, Texas

• Chicken is easier to cut into strips if it's semi-frozen.
—Amy Wolfe
Kittanning, Pennsylvania

• A fresh lemon makes a nice rub for a whole chicken. Then simply add a dusting of sage.
—Anna Moore
Howell, New Jersey

• Always thaw your poultry in its unopened wrapping to avoid the skin drying out.
—Debbie Thaxton, Rhome, Texas

• After cleaning chicken, I put all of the scraps and waste into a freezer bag and freeze it until my trash pickup day. Odors aren't a bother, and stray dogs aren't attracted to my garbage cans.
—Sharon Mateja, Warsaw, Missouri

• If you are in a hurry for cooked chicken for a salad or a casserole, try this: Sprinkle boneless skinless chicken breasts with poultry seasoning and place in a microwave-safe dish with a small amount of water. Microwave 3-4 minutes. Cool, then cube chicken.
—Monica Vander Waal
Hull, Iowa

in a shallow dish. Drop 1/3 cup crab mixture into crumbs; shape into a 3/4-in.-thick patty. Carefully turn to coat. Repeat with remaining crab mixture. In a skillet, cook patties in butter for 3 minutes on each side or until golden brown. **Yield:** 6 patties.

BARLEY BELL PEPPERS

If you and your family like stuffed peppers, you're going to love this recipe from the National Barley Foods Council. Instead of the usual rice, these fresh green peppers are filled with barley and a nice blend of seasonings, along with ground beef.

        1 can (14-1/2 ounces) diced tomatoes
    2/3 cup medium pearl barley
    1/2 teaspoon ground cumin
        6 medium green peppers
        1 medium onion, finely chopped
        2 garlic cloves, minced
        1 tablespoon olive *or* vegetable oil
    1/2 pound lean ground beef
    3/4 teaspoon ground allspice
    1/4 cup minced fresh parsley
    3/4 teaspoon salt
    1/4 teaspoon pepper

Drain tomatoes, reserving juice. Set the tomatoes aside. Add water to juice to measure 2 cups; place in a saucepan. Add barley and cumin; bring to a boil. Reduce heat; cover and simmer for 45 minutes or until tender. Meanwhile, cut tops off peppers; remove seeds. Place peppers in a Dutch oven and cover with water. Bring to a boil; boil for 3 minutes. Drain; rinse in cold water and set aside. In a skillet, saute onion and garlic in oil until tender. Add beef and allspice. Cook until meat is no longer pink. Add the barley mixture, parsley, salt, pepper and tomatoes; mix well. Spoon into peppers. Place in a greased 13-in. x 9-in. x 2-in. baking dish. Cover and bake at 350° for 25-30 minutes or until the peppers are tender and the filling is heated through. **Yield:** 6 servings.

MARYLAND CRAB CAKES

Catherine Tocha, Silver Spring, Maryland

(Pictured above)

I've lived in Maryland for more than 50 years so I know how much folks around here love crab cakes. I came up with this recipe myself, and my family really likes it.

        1 egg
    1/4 cup milk
        3 tablespoons mayonnaise
        1 tablespoon all-purpose flour
        1 tablespoon Worcestershire sauce
        1 teaspoon prepared mustard
        1 teaspoon salt
    1/4 teaspoon pepper
        1 pound cooked crabmeat *or* 3 cans
            (6 ounces *each*) crabmeat, drained,
            flaked and cartilage removed
    1/2 cup dry bread crumbs
        2 tablespoons butter *or* margarine

In a large bowl, whisk together the first eight ingredients. Fold in crab. Place the bread crumbs

BEEF NOODLE BAKE

Evelyne Olechnowicz, Windsor, Vermont

My grandmother brought this recipe with her from Scotland many years ago. I like to make it for church suppers and picnics.

    1-1/2 pounds ground beef
        1 small onion, chopped
        2 cans (8 ounces *each*) tomato sauce
        1 cup (8 ounces) sour cream

1 package (3 ounces) cream cheese,
cubed and softened
1 teaspoon sugar
1/2 to 1 teaspoon garlic salt
7 cups uncooked wide egg noodles,
cooked and drained
1 cup (4 ounces) shredded cheddar cheese

In a skillet, cook beef and onion until meat is no longer pink; drain. Remove from the heat; stir in tomato sauce, sour cream, cream cheese, sugar and garlic salt; mix until blended. Place half of the noodles in a greased 13-in. x 9-in. x 2-in. baking dish; top with half of the beef mixture. Repeat layers. Cover and bake at 350° for 30-35 minutes or until heated through. Sprinkle with cheese; bake 3-5 minutes longer or until cheese is melted. **Yield:** 6 servings.

SALSA BEEF SKILLET

Jeanne Bennett, North Richland Hills, Texas

Here's a main dish that's delicious, attractive and economical. It's great with a guacamole salad.

1 boneless chuck roast (2 to 2-1/2
pounds), cut into 3/4-inch cubes
2 tablespoons vegetable oil
1 jar (16 ounces) chunky salsa
1 can (8 ounces) tomato sauce
2 garlic cloves, minced
2 tablespoons brown sugar
1 tablespoon soy sauce
2 tablespoons minced fresh cilantro *or*
parsley
2 tablespoons lime juice
Hot cooked rice

In a large skillet, brown beef in oil; drain. Add salsa, tomato sauce, garlic, brown sugar and soy sauce; bring to a boil. Reduce heat; cover and simmer for 2 hours or until meat is tender. Stir in cilantro and lime juice; heat through. Serve over rice. **Yield:** 4-6 servings.

FIESTA PORK SANDWICHES

Yvette Massey, La Luz, New Mexico

(Pictured at right)

This is an easy and flavorful dish that my family really enjoys. When I fix it for company, I usually prepare the meat the day before so I can concentrate on side dishes and relaxing with my friends.

1 boneless pork shoulder roast (3 to 4
pounds)

1/3 cup lime juice
2 tablespoons grapefruit juice
2 tablespoons water
1 bay leaf
6 garlic cloves, minced
1/2 teaspoon salt
1/2 teaspoon dried oregano
1/2 teaspoon chili powder
2 tablespoons olive *or* vegetable oil
1 large onion, thinly sliced
12 to 14 sandwich rolls, split

Cut the roast in half; pierce several times with a fork. Place in a large resealable plastic bag or shallow glass container. Combine the next eight ingredients; pour over roast. Cover and refrigerate overnight, turning occasionally. Drain, reserving marinade. In a skillet over medium heat, brown the roast in oil on all sides. Place onion, roast and marinade in a slow cooker. Cover and cook on high for 2 hours. Reduce heat to low; cook 6-8 hours longer or until the meat is tender. Remove roast; shred or thinly slice. Discard the bay leaf. Skim fat from cooking juices and transfer to a saucepan; bring to a rolling boil. Serve pork on rolls with juices as a dipping sauce. **Yield:** 12-14 servings.

SPECIAL SEAFOOD SKILLET

Donald Boyer, Newport News, Virginia

(Pictured below)

Since fresh seafood is so readily available here on the Atlantic Coast, seafood recipes are quite popular. This is a great combination that should satisfy even the heartiest of appetites.

1/4 cup *each* chopped carrot, celery, onion and sweet red pepper
1/4 cup whole kernel corn
1/4 cup sliced fresh mushrooms
2 tablespoons vegetable oil, *divided*
8 ounces fresh *or* frozen bay scallops, thawed
4 ounces uncooked medium shrimp, peeled and deveined
1 teaspoon seafood seasoning
1 teaspoon soy sauce
1 package (3 ounces) cream cheese, softened
1/2 cup milk
1/2 cup shredded mozzarella cheese
1/8 teaspoon ground nutmeg
Hot cooked pasta *or* rice

In a skillet or wok, stir-fry carrot, celery, onion, red pepper, corn and mushrooms in 1 tablespoon oil for 4-5 minutes or until crisp-tender. Remove to a bowl and keep warm. Add remaining oil to the skillet; stir-fry scallops, shrimp, seafood seasoning and soy sauce for 3-4 minutes or until shrimp turn pink. Using a slotted spoon, transfer seafood to the bowl with the vegetable mixture. In a small mixing bowl, beat cream cheese, milk, mozzarella cheese and nutmeg until smooth. Return seafood and vegetables to skillet; stir in cream cheese mixture and heat through. Serve over pasta or rice. **Yield:** 2 servings.

CHICKEN 'N' BEAN TACOS

Wendy Hines, Chesnee, South Carolina

These flavorful tacos are a wonderful change of pace from regular tacos. My family loves the combination of black beans, chicken and tomatoes.

✓ Uses less fat, sugar or salt. Includes Nutritional Analysis and Diabetic Exchanges.

1 pound boneless skinless chicken breasts, cut into bite-size pieces
1/2 cup chopped onion
2 garlic cloves, minced
1 can (15 ounces) black beans, undrained
1/4 cup minced fresh parsley
1 to 2 teaspoons ground cumin
1/4 teaspoon pepper
12 corn tortillas (6 inches), warmed
1/2 cup reduced-fat shredded cheddar cheese
1 cup chopped fresh tomatoes

In a nonstick skillet, saute chicken, onion and garlic until juices run clear. Stir in beans, parsley, cumin and pepper; heat through. Spoon 1/3 cup down the center of each tortilla; sprinkle with cheese and tomatoes. Fold in half; serve immediately. **Yield:** 1 dozen. **Nutritional Analysis:** One taco equals 146 calories, 228 mg sodium, 22 mg cholesterol, 20 gm carbohydrate, 13 gm protein, 2 gm fat. **Diabetic Exchanges:** 1 starch, 1 lean meat, 1 vegetable.

ITALIAN BROCCOLI BAKE

Carol Wilson, Chelsea, Oklahoma

There are several diabetics in my family, and I've enjoyed adapting dishes to meet their needs. This flavorful Italian recipe is such a dish.

✓ Uses less fat, sugar or salt. Includes Nutritional Analysis and Diabetic Exchanges.

2 cups (16 ounces) fat-free cottage cheese
2 egg whites
1/4 cup grated Parmesan cheese
3 tablespoons all-purpose flour

Main Dishes

1/2 teaspoon Italian seasoning
1 large bunch broccoli, sliced lengthwise
  into spears
1 cup reduced-sodium meatless spaghetti
  sauce
1 cup (4 ounces) shredded part-skim
  mozzarella cheese

In a blender or food processor, place cottage cheese, egg whites, Parmesan cheese, flour and Italian seasoning; cover and process until smooth. Set aside. Place broccoli and a small amount of water in a skillet; cover and cook for 5-8 minutes or until crisp-tender. Drain. Place half of the broccoli in a single layer in a 13-in. x 9-in. x 2-in. baking dish coated with nonstick cooking spray. Top with cottage cheese mixture and remaining broccoli. Pour spaghetti sauce over broccoli. Sprinkle with mozzarella cheese. Bake, uncovered, at 375° for 30-35 minutes or until the cheese is melted and bubbly. Let stand 5 minutes before serving. **Yield:** 9 servings. **Nutritional Analysis:** One serving equals 147 calories, 341 mg sodium, 13 mg cholesterol, 13 gm carbohydrate, 15 gm protein, 5 gm fat. **Diabetic Exchanges:** 1-1/2 meat, 1 vegetable, 1/2 starch.

BEEF AND BEAN STEW

Pam Miller, Farmington Hills, Michigan

A large bowl of this stew on a chilly autumn day will quickly warm you up. It's great with a thick slice of homemade bread.

1/2 cup all-purpose flour
  1 tablespoon paprika
  1 teaspoon salt
1/4 teaspoon cayenne pepper
2-1/2 to 3 pounds beef stew meat, cut into
  1-inch cubes
  3 tablespoons olive *or* vegetable oil, *divided*
  2 medium onions, thinly sliced
  2 cups water
  1 can (6 ounces) tomato paste
3/4 teaspoon rubbed sage
1/2 teaspoon dried thyme
  1 can (16 ounces) kidney beans, rinsed
  and drained

In a large resealable plastic bag, combine the flour, paprika, salt and cayenne. Add beef and shake to coat. In a Dutch oven over medium heat, brown beef in 2 tablespoons oil. Remove with a slotted spoon. In the same pan, saute onions in the remaining oil. Add water, tomato paste, sage and thyme; mix well. Return beef to pan. Bring to a boil; reduce heat. Cover and simmer for 1-1/4 hours, stirring occasionally. Add more water if

needed. Stir in beans. Cover and simmer 15 minutes or until meat is tender. **Yield:** 6-8 servings.

AUTUMN ACORN SQUASH

Paula Marchesi, Rocky Point, New York

(Pictured above)

This quick and easy dish is a meal in itself. I serve this quite often during the fall and winter months.

  2 medium acorn squash
1/2 pound ground turkey
  1 egg
1/2 cup cooked wild rice
1/2 cup chopped peeled tart apple
1/2 cup chopped fresh *or* frozen cranberries
1/4 cup chopped celery
1/2 teaspoon salt
1/2 teaspoon dried parsley flakes
1/4 teaspoon ground allspice
1/4 teaspoon ground cardamom

Cut squash in half and discard seeds; set squash aside. In a skillet over medium heat, cook turkey until no longer pink; drain. Add egg, rice, apple, cranberries, celery, salt, parsley, allspice and cardamom. Spoon into squash halves; place in an ungreased 13-in. x 9-in. x 2-in. baking dish. Fill dish with hot water to a depth of 1/2 in. Cover and bake at 350° for 25 minutes. Uncover; bake 20-25 minutes longer or until the squash is tender. **Yield:** 4 servings.

ZUCCHINI CON CARNE

Sharon Secrest, Tucson, Arizona

(Pictured above)

Living in the land of green chilies and hot peppers, my family has grown to love the flavors of the Southwest. We now have a tradition of buying 50 pounds of chilies every year and roasting them on the grill. It keeps us stocked for the year.

  1-1/2 pounds beef stew meat, cut into 1-inch
        cubes
    1/4 cup all-purpose flour
      2 tablespoons vegetable oil
  1-1/2 cups water
      2 garlic cloves, minced
      1 teaspoon salt
    1/2 teaspoon pepper
      4 large zucchini, cut into chunks
      2 cups whole kernel corn
      1 medium onion, cut into wedges
      2 cans (4 ounces *each*) chopped green
        chilies, undrained
Shredded Monterey Jack cheese
Warmed flour tortillas, optional

Toss beef with flour until coated. In a Dutch oven over medium heat, brown beef in oil. Add water, garlic, salt and pepper; bring to a boil. Reduce heat; cover and simmer for 1 hour and 15 minutes or until the meat is tender. Add zucchini, corn, onion and chilies; bring to a boil. Reduce heat; cover and simmer for 20-30 minutes or until the vegetables are tender. Sprinkle with cheese and serve with tortillas if desired. **Yield:** 8-10 servings.

MEATBALL HOAGIES

Cynthia Barnard, Augusta, Maine

Whenever I make these hearty meatball sandwiches, they disappear quickly.

      6 celery ribs, chopped
      2 small green peppers, chopped
      1 large onion, chopped
      2 garlic cloves, minced
      2 tablespoons olive *or* vegetable oil
      1 can (28 ounces) crushed tomatoes
      1 can (8 ounces) tomato sauce
    1/3 cup tomato paste
      1 cup water
      2 teaspoons minced fresh parsley
      4 teaspoons salt
    1/2 teaspoon pepper
    1/4 to 1/2 teaspoon crushed red pepper
        flakes
MEATBALLS:
      2 eggs
      1 cup dry bread crumbs
    1/2 cup milk
      2 tablespoons dried minced onion
      2 tablespoons dried parsley flakes
    1/2 teaspoon garlic salt
    1/2 teaspoon pepper
      2 pounds ground beef
    8 to 10 hot dog *or* sandwich buns, split
Grated Parmesan cheese, optional

In a large saucepan or Dutch oven, saute celery, green peppers, onion and garlic in oil until tender, about 4-5 minutes. Add the next eight ingredients; bring to a boil. Reduce heat; simmer, uncovered, for 1-2 hours. For meatballs, beat eggs in a large bowl. Add the next six ingredients. Add beef and mix well. Shape into 1-in. balls and place on ungreased baking sheets. Bake, uncovered, at 450° for 12-15 minutes or until no longer pink. Drain on paper towels. Add to sauce; heat through. Serve on buns; top with Parmesan cheese if desired. **Yield:** 8-10 servings.

CHICKEN WITH PINEAPPLE SAUCE

Mary Ealey, Smithfield, Virginia

Here's a sweet thick glaze that really dresses up plain chicken. We think it also tastes good over ham.

      2 tablespoons brown sugar
      1 tablespoon cornstarch
      2 cans (8 ounces *each*) crushed pineapple,
        undrained
    1/4 cup soy sauce
    1/4 teaspoon garlic salt

1/4 teaspoon ground ginger
6 boneless skinless chicken breast halves
Minced chives, optional

In a saucepan, combine the brown sugar and cornstarch. Stir in the pineapple, soy sauce, garlic salt and ginger. Cook and stir over low heat until thickened. Place the chicken in a greased 9-in. square baking dish. Pour half of the sauce over chicken. Bake, uncovered, at 350° for 15 minutes. Baste; bake 10 minutes longer or until chicken juices run clear, basting several times with the remaining sauce. Sprinkle with chives if desired. **Yield:** 6 servings.

PORK AND APPLE SUPPER

Sharon Root, Wynantskill, New York

Our part of upstate New York was settled by the Dutch, and this recipe originated there. This is also apple country, with at least 10 major orchards within a 15-mile radius of our home.

1-1/2 pounds boneless pork, cubed
1 tablespoon vegetable oil
4 cups water
1 tablespoon chicken bouillon granules
1 teaspoon dried thyme
1/4 teaspoon pepper
1 bay leaf
10 to 12 small red potatoes (about 2 pounds), quartered
4 medium tart apples, peeled and cut into wedges
2 tablespoons cornstarch
2 tablespoons cold water

In a Dutch oven, brown pork in oil. Add water, bouillon, thyme, pepper and bay leaf; bring to a boil. Reduce heat; cover and simmer for 1-1/2 to 2 hours or until pork is almost tender. Add potatoes; cover and cook for 15 minutes. Add apples; cover and cook for 10-12 minutes or until crisp-tender. Discard bay leaf. Combine cornstarch and cold water until smooth; stir into pork mixture. Bring to a boil; cook and stir for 2 minutes or until thickened. **Yield:** 6-8 servings.

STUFFED DUCKLING

Joanne Callahan, Far Hills, New Jersey

(Pictured at right)

I enjoy experimenting in the kitchen. I started with a basic bread stuffing, then began adding different ingredients I had on hand in my cupboard. This is the pleasing recipe I came up with. The stuffing usually disappears long before the bird is gone!

1 domestic duckling (4 to 5 pounds)
1 teaspoon salt, *divided*
1/2 cup chopped onion
1 garlic clove, minced
1 tablespoon butter *or* margarine
2 cups cubed day-old bread
1 cup cooked rice
1 teaspoon dried basil
1 teaspoon dried rosemary, crushed
1 teaspoon rubbed sage
1 teaspoon dried parsley flakes
1/8 teaspoon pepper
1/2 cup raisins
1/2 cup chopped pecans
1/4 to 1/3 cup chicken broth

Sprinkle inside duckling cavity with 1/2 teaspoon salt. Prick skin in several places; set aside. In a skillet, saute onion and garlic in butter until tender. In a bowl, combine bread cubes, rice, basil, rosemary, sage, parsley, pepper and remaining salt. Add raisins, pecans and enough broth to moisten; toss gently. Stuff into duckling. Place with breast side up on a rack in a shallow roasting pan. Bake, uncovered, at 350° for 1-3/4 to 2 hours or until a meat thermometer reads 180° for duck and 165° for stuffing. Drain fat several times during roasting. Cover and let stand for 20 minutes before removing stuffing and carving. **Yield:** 2-4 servings.

APPLE BEEF STEW

Paula Pelis, Rocky Point, New York

(Pictured below)

Just about everyone has a recipe they know by heart. Well, this scrumptious recipe for stew is mine. It's easy to remember and make because all the ingredients (except the salt) are in measurements of two. Bay leaves, allspice and cloves nicely season this satisfying dish.

    2 pounds boneless chuck roast, cut into
        1-1/2-inch cubes
    2 tablespoons butter *or* margarine
    2 medium onions, cut into wedges
    2 tablespoons all-purpose flour
  1/8 teaspoon salt
    2 cups water
    2 tablespoons apple juice
    2 bay leaves

    2 whole allspice
    2 whole cloves
    2 medium carrots, sliced
    2 medium apples, peeled and cut into
        wedges

In a large skillet or Dutch oven over medium heat, brown beef in butter. Add onions; cook until lightly browned. Sprinkle with flour and salt. Gradually add water and apple juice. Bring to a boil; cook and stir for 2 minutes. Place bay leaves, allspice and cloves in a double thickness of cheesecloth; bring up corners of cloth and tie with string to form a bag. Add to pan. Reduce heat; cover and simmer for 1-1/2 hours or until meat is almost tender. Add carrots and apples; cover and simmer 15 minutes longer or until meat, carrots and apples are tender. Discard spice bag. Thicken if desired. **Yield:** 4 servings.

FOUR-CHEESE CHICKEN FETTUCCINE

Rochelle Brownlee, Big Timber, Montana

As a cattle rancher, my husband's a big fan of beef. For him to comment on a poultry dish is rare. But he always tells me, "I love this casserole!" I first tasted it at a potluck. Now, I fix it for my family at least once or twice a month.

    8 ounces fettuccine
    1 can (10-3/4 ounces) condensed cream of
        mushroom soup, undiluted
    1 package (8 ounces) cream cheese, cubed
    1 jar (4-1/2 ounces) sliced mushrooms,
        drained
    1 cup whipping cream
  1/2 cup butter *or* margarine
  1/4 teaspoon garlic powder
  3/4 cup grated Parmesan cheese
  1/2 cup shredded mozzarella cheese
  1/2 cup shredded Swiss cheese
2-1/2 cups cubed cooked chicken
TOPPING:
  1/3 cup seasoned bread crumbs
    2 tablespoons butter *or* margarine, melted
    1 to 2 tablespoons grated Parmesan cheese

Cook fettuccine according to package directions. Meanwhile, in a large kettle, combine soup, cream cheese, mushrooms, cream, butter and garlic powder. Stir in cheeses; cook and stir until melted. Add chicken; heat through. Drain fettuccine; add to the sauce. Transfer to a shallow greased 2-1/2-qt. baking dish. Combine topping ingredients; sprinkle over chicken mixture. Cover and bake at 350° for 25 minutes. Uncover; bake 5-10 minutes longer or until golden brown. **Yield:** 6-8 servings.

THREE-MEAT STROMBOLI

Lorelei Hull, Luling, Louisiana

(Pictured at right)

I made this hearty bread for a golf outing my husband attended and received many compliments. Several men asked for the recipe.

- 2 loaves (1 pound *each*) frozen bread dough, thawed
- 2 tablespoons Dijon mustard
- 1/2 cup grated Parmesan cheese, *divided*
- 4 ounces pastrami, finely chopped
- 4 ounces pepperoni, finely chopped
- 4 ounces salami, finely chopped
- 1 cup (4 ounces) shredded Swiss cheese
- 1 egg, beaten

Roll each loaf of bread into a 12-in. x 7-in. rectangle. Spread mustard to within 1 in. of edges. Sprinkle each with 2 tablespoons of Parmesan cheese. Combine pastrami, pepperoni, salami and Swiss cheese; sprinkle over dough. Top with the remaining Parmesan. Brush edges of dough with egg. Roll up, jelly-roll style, beginning with a long side. Seal edge and ends. Place seam side down on a greased baking sheet; cut three slits in the top of each loaf. Bake at 350° for 35-40 minutes. Slice; serve warm. **Yield:** 2 loaves (12-16 servings each).

It's Good for Them—and Good, Too

MOST YOUNGSTERS don't like liver. Diane Murdock's three were no exception.

"I knew it was good for them," this Charlotte Courthouse, Virginia mom says. "But they turned up their noses at it. So I decided to hide it by substituting chicken livers in a sweet-and-sour pork recipe.

"The kids loved it...and they never knew the difference! Now, I make my Sweet-and-Sour Chicken Livers (recipe at right) for my grandchildren, too."

Next time you stir up a quick meal, why not toss some chicken livers into the skillet? Judging from Diane's experience, no one will guess how good you are at disguise!

SWEET-AND-SOUR CHICKEN LIVERS

- 3/4 pound chicken livers, drained
- 1 tablespoon vegetable oil
- 3 medium green peppers, cut into 1-inch pieces
- 1 can (8 ounces) pineapple chunks, drained
- 1/2 teaspoon salt
- 1/4 cup sugar
- 1 tablespoon cornstarch
- 1 cup chicken broth
- 1/4 cup vinegar
- 1 tablespoon soy sauce
- Hot cooked rice

In a saucepan, saute chicken livers in oil for 8-10 minutes or until juices run clear. Add green peppers, pineapple and salt; saute until peppers are tender. Meanwhile, in a saucepan, combine sugar, cornstarch, broth, vinegar and soy sauce until smooth. Bring to a boil; reduce heat. Cook and stir for 2 minutes or until thickened and bubbly. Pour over chicken livers. Serve over rice. **Yield:** 4 servings.

x 9-in. x 2-in. baking dish. Arrange meatballs over top, pressing lightly into mixture. Cover and bake at 350° for 45 minutes. Uncover; bake 15 minutes longer or until meat is no longer pink and potatoes are tender. **Yield:** 8 servings.

✦✦✦✦✦✦✦✦✦✦✦✦✦

LAYERED TURKEY CASSEROLE

Joyce Platfoot, Wapakoneta, Ohio

This creamy casserole is an excellent way to use up leftover turkey and rice. In fact, I won a newspaper recipe contest with it years ago. It's great for when you're expecting company, because it can be put together the night before. Then just top with the onions and bake.

> 3 cups cooked long grain rice
> 1 package (16 ounces) frozen chopped broccoli, cooked and well drained
> 4 cups cubed cooked turkey
> 1 jar (4-1/2 ounces) sliced mushrooms, drained
> 8 slices process American cheese
> 1/2 cup chicken broth
> 1 can (10-3/4 ounces) condensed cream of mushroom soup, undiluted
> 1/2 cup mayonnaise*
> 1 can (2.8 ounces) french-fried onions

In a greased 13-in. x 9-in. x 2-in. baking dish, layer rice, broccoli, turkey, mushrooms and cheese. Pour broth over top. Combine soup and mayonnaise; spread over top. Sprinkle with onions. Bake, uncovered, at 350° for 25 minutes or until golden brown. **Yield:** 8-10 servings. ***Editor's Note:** Light or fat-free mayonnaise may not be substituted for regular mayonnaise.

✦✦✦✦✦✦✦✦✦✦✦✦✦

🏅 SOUTHERN CHICKEN ROLL-UPS

Catherine Darr, Charlotte, Arkansas

This is one of my favorite ways to cook chicken because it tastes so good and it doesn't take long to prepare. Folks are always pleasantly surprised to find melted Swiss cheese rolled up inside. I sometimes like to serve these roll-ups over rice.

✓ **Uses less fat, sugar or salt. Includes Nutritional Analysis and Diabetic Exchanges.**

> 6 boneless skinless chicken breast halves (1-1/2 pounds)
> 6 slices Swiss cheese
> 3 tablespoons all-purpose flour
> 1/2 teaspoon pepper
> 2 tablespoons butter *or* margarine
> 3/4 cup chicken broth

✦✦✦✦✦✦✦✦✦✦✦✦✦

MEATBALL HASH BROWN BAKE

Jo Ann Fritzler, Belen, New Mexico

(Pictured above)

For a seniors potluck at our church, I wanted to create a recipe that would incorporate a meat dish and side dish in one. This convenient casserole proved to be a real crowd-pleaser, and I was asked by many to share my recipe.

> 2 eggs
> 3/4 cup crushed saltines (about 20 crackers)
> 6 to 8 garlic cloves, minced
> 2 teaspoons salt, *divided*
> 1-1/2 teaspoons pepper, *divided*
> 1 pound lean ground beef
> 1 can (10-3/4 ounces) condensed cream of chicken soup, undiluted
> 1 cup (8 ounces) sour cream
> 1 cup (4 ounces) shredded cheddar cheese
> 1 large onion, chopped
> 1 package (30 ounces) frozen shredded hash brown potatoes, thawed

In a bowl, lightly beat eggs. Stir in cracker crumbs, garlic, 1 teaspoon salt and 1/2 teaspoon pepper. Crumble beef over mixture; mix well. Shape into 1-in. balls. In a covered skillet over low heat, cook meatballs in a small amount of water until browned; drain. In a bowl, combine the soup, sour cream, cheese, onion and remaining salt and pepper. With paper towels, pat hash browns dry. Stir into the soup mixture. Transfer to a greased 13-in.

1/2 teaspoon dried oregano

Flatten chicken to 1/4-in. thickness. Place a cheese slice on each; roll up jelly-roll style. In a shallow bowl, combine flour and pepper; add chicken and roll to coat. In a skillet over medium heat, cook chicken in butter until browned, about 10 minutes, turning frequently. Add broth and oregano; bring to a boil. Reduce heat; simmer for 12-14 minutes or until chicken juices run clear. **Yield:** 6 servings. **Nutritional Analysis:** One serving (prepared with reduced-fat cheese, margarine and low-sodium broth) equals 284 calories, 157 mg sodium, 94 mg cholesterol, 4 gm carbohydrate, 36 gm protein, 13 gm fat. **Diabetic Exchanges:** 4 lean meat, 1/2 starch, 1/2 fat.

FRIED GREEN TOMATO LASAGNA

Alice Colgan Reitz, Stump Creek, Pennsylvania

(Pictured below right)

My family likes lasagna, so I usually make it at least once a week. This variation is one I created to use tomatoes that aren't quite ripe yet. My family and friends love the combination of ingredients.

- 4 large ripe tomatoes, peeled and chopped
- 1 can (6 ounces) tomato paste
- 2 tablespoons sugar
- 2 tablespoons Italian seasoning
- 1 garlic clove, minced
- 1/2 teaspoon garlic salt
- 1/8 teaspoon pepper
- 5 tablespoons butter *or* margarine
- 4 large green tomatoes, cut into 1/4-inch slices
- 1/2 cup all-purpose flour
- 6 tablespoons grated Parmesan cheese
- 2 cups (8 ounces) shredded mozzarella cheese

In a large saucepan, combine the ripe tomatoes, tomato paste, sugar, Italian seasoning, garlic, garlic salt and pepper. Bring to a boil over medium heat. Reduce heat; cover and simmer for 1 hour, stirring occasionally. Remove from the heat; set aside. In a large skillet over medium heat, melt the butter. Dip green tomato slices in flour; brown in skillet on both sides. Remove to paper towels to drain. Spoon 3/4 cup tomato mixture into a greased 13-in. x 9-in. x 2-in. baking dish. Top with a third of the green tomatoes; sprinkle with 2 tablespoons Parmesan cheese. Repeat layers twice. Top with remaining tomato mixture and mozzarella cheese. Bake, uncovered, at 350° for 15-20 minutes or until cheese is melted and sauce is bubbly. Let stand 5 minutes before serving. **Yield:** 6-8 servings.

GOLDEN PORK CHOPS

Betty Sparks, Windsor, Connecticut

I've had this recipe for several years and really don't remember where I first got it. I have a large family and am always looking for easy recipes that will please all of them. This is definitely one of them.

- 1 can (14-3/4 ounces) cream-style corn
- 1/2 cup finely chopped onion
- 1/2 cup finely chopped celery
- 1/2 teaspoon paprika
- 1-1/2 cups crushed corn bread stuffing
- 4 boneless pork loin chops (3/4 inch thick)
- 1 tablespoon brown sugar
- 1 tablespoon spicy brown mustard

In a bowl, combine the corn, onion, celery and paprika. Stir in stuffing. Transfer to a greased 11-in. x 7-in. x 2-in. baking dish. Arrange pork chops over stuffing. Combine the brown sugar and mustard; spread over chops. Bake, uncovered, at 400° for 35-40 minutes or until meat juices run clear. **Yield:** 4 servings.

CHICKEN WITH APPLE CREAM SAUCE

Victoria Casey, Coeur d'Alene, Idaho

(Pictured below)

Topping chicken with an apple cream sauce is a unique and delicious way to serve it. It's an impressive dish to serve to company. Family and friends think the sauce is absolutely wonderful.

> 4 boneless skinless chicken breast halves
> 1 tablespoon vegetable oil
> 1 cup apple juice
> 1 teaspoon lemon juice
> 1/4 to 1/2 teaspoon dried rosemary, crushed
> 1/2 teaspoon salt
> 1/8 teaspoon pepper
> 1 tablespoon cornstarch
> 1/2 cup whipping cream
> 1 tablespoon minced fresh parsley *or* 1 teaspoon dried parsley flakes

Hot cooked rice

In a skillet over medium heat, cook the chicken in oil for 4 minutes on each side or until browned. Combine the apple juice, lemon juice, rosemary, salt and pepper; pour over chicken. Reduce heat; cover and simmer for 10 minutes or until chicken juices run clear. Remove chicken and keep warm. Combine cornstarch and cream until smooth; stir into cooking liquid in skillet. Bring to a boil; cook and stir for 2 minutes or until thickened. Add parsley. Return chicken to skillet and heat through. Serve over rice. **Yield:** 4 servings.

SAUCY MICROWAVE MEATBALLS

Edna Denny, Pine Island, Minnesota

These moist meatballs are a speedy way to make an Italian-style meal. They're ready in just minutes in the microwave.

> 1 egg
> 1/4 cup finely chopped onion
> 1 teaspoon salt
> 1 pound ground beef
> 1 can (8 ounces) tomato sauce
> 1/3 cup packed brown sugar
> 3 tablespoons lemon juice
> 1/8 teaspoon garlic salt

Hot cooked spaghetti

In a bowl, combine egg, onion and salt. Add beef; mix well. Shape into 1-1/2-in. balls. Place half in a microwave-safe 2-qt. dish. Cover and microwave on high for 3 to 3-1/2 minutes or until meatballs are firm and no longer pink; drain. Repeat with remaining meatballs. In a microwave-safe bowl, combine the tomato sauce, brown sugar, lemon juice and garlic salt. Cook, uncovered, on high for 1 to 1-1/2 minutes or until sugar is dissolved, stirring every 30 seconds. Pour over meatballs. Cover and microwave at 50% power for 4-5 minutes or until heated through. Serve over spaghetti. **Yield:** 4 servings. **Editor's Note:** This recipe was tested in an 850-watt microwave.

BROCCOLI BEEF BRAIDS

Penny Lapp, North Royalton, Ohio

This filling sandwich looks fancy but is really simple to make. Each slice is packed with ground beef, broccoli and cheese. Served with a green salad, this beefy sandwich makes a terrific lunch or dinner.

> 1 pound ground beef
> 1/2 cup chopped onion
> 1 package (10 ounces) frozen chopped broccoli
> 1 cup (4 ounces) shredded mozzarella cheese
> 1/2 cup sour cream
> 1/4 teaspoon salt
> 1/4 teaspoon pepper

2 tubes (8 ounces *each*) refrigerated
crescent rolls

In a skillet over medium heat, cook beef and
onion until meat is no longer pink; drain. Add
broccoli, cheese, sour cream, salt and pepper; heat
through. Unroll one tube of dough on a greased
baking sheet; seal the seams and perforations,
forming a 12-in. x 8-in. rectangle. Spread half of
beef mixture lengthwise down the center. On
each side, cut 1-in.-wide strips 3 in. into center.
Starting at one end, fold alternating strips at an
angle across filling; seal ends. Repeat. Bake at
350° for 15-20 minutes or until golden brown.
Yield: 2 loaves (8 servings each).

PORK SANDWICHES

Sue Felton, Cascade, Iowa

*Tender pork in a sweet sauce makes these stick-to-
your-ribs sandwiches a tasty change from the same old
sloppy joes. My family can't get enough of the tangy
barbecue recipe.*

    5 pounds bone-in pork loin roast
    1 can (10-3/4 ounces) condensed tomato
      soup, undiluted
    1 cup packed brown sugar
  1/4 cup butter *or* margarine, melted
  1/4 cup ketchup
    2 tablespoons lemon juice
    2 tablespoons prepared mustard
    1 tablespoon Worcestershire sauce
    1 to 2 tablespoons liquid smoke, optional
    1 teaspoon onion powder
  1/4 teaspoon garlic powder
   12 hamburger buns, split

Place roast on a rack in a shallow roasting pan.
Bake, uncovered, at 350° for 2 to 2-1/2 hours or
until a meat thermometer reads 160°. Remove
roast; using two forks, shred the meat. Discard
bone. In a large saucepan, combine the tomato
soup, brown sugar, butter, ketchup, lemon juice,
mustard, Worcestershire sauce, liquid smoke if
desired, onion powder and garlic powder; cook
and stir until heated through. Add pork; heat
through. Serve on buns. **Yield:** 12 servings.

HAM AND SWEET POTATO CUPS

Carleen Mullins, Wise, Virginia

(Pictured above right)

*This recipe certainly represents our region, as our state
is famous for its ham and the South is known for sweet
potatoes. It's one of the best sweet potato recipes I've
ever tried. It makes a great light meal all by itself.*

    2 cups frozen California-blend vegetables
    1 egg
    2 tablespoons milk, *divided*
    3 tablespoons dry bread crumbs
  1/8 teaspoon pepper
  3/4 pound fully cooked ham, ground (about
      3 cups)
    1 can (15 ounces) cut sweet potatoes,
      drained
  1/2 cup condensed cheddar cheese soup,
      undiluted

In a saucepan, cook vegetables according to package directions; drain and set aside. In a bowl,
beat egg and 1 tablespoon milk. Stir in bread
crumbs and pepper. Add ham; mix well. In another bowl, mash sweet potatoes until smooth;
spread onto the bottom and up the sides of four
10-oz. baking cups. Place about 1/3 cup ham
mixture in each cup. Top with vegetables. Combine the soup and remaining milk; spoon over
vegetables. Cover and bake at 350° for 40 minutes
or until heated through. **Yield:** 4 servings.

two greased 13-in. x 9-in. x 2-in. baking dishes. Cover and bake at 350° for 35-40 minutes or until zucchini is tender. **Yield:** 6 servings.

MUSTARD-GLAZED PORK ROAST

Nancy Gleason, Port Arthur, Texas

Cooking is one of my favorite hobbies, especially when I make rewarding dishes like this pork roast. Everyone always comments how good the glaze is.

   1 rolled boneless pork loin roast (3 to 4 pounds), trimmed
   1 garlic clove, cut into lengthwise strips
   1 bottle (8 ounces) Italian salad dressing
1/4 cup cider *or* red wine vinegar
1/4 teaspoon onion salt
Salt and pepper to taste
1/4 cup apricot preserves
1/4 cup prepared mustard
   2 tablespoons brown sugar
   2 tablespoons butter *or* margarine, melted

Cut slits in top of roast and insert garlic strips. Place roast in a large resealable bag; add the salad dressing and vinegar. Seal and refrigerate overnight. Drain and discard marinade. Place roast on a rack in a shallow roasting pan. Season with onion salt, salt and pepper. Bake, uncovered, at 325° for 1-3/4 to 2 hours or until a meat thermometer reads 160°. Combine preserves, mustard, brown sugar and butter; brush over roast during the last 15 minutes of baking. **Yield:** 8-10 servings.

CHICKEN BROCCOLI LASAGNA

Lisa Reilly, Kingston, Massachusetts

My family prefers this tasty chicken dish over a more traditional lasagna.

   6 tablespoons butter *or* margarine, *divided*
1/4 cup all-purpose flour
   2 cups milk
   1 cup chicken broth
   3 eggs, beaten
3/4 cup grated Parmesan cheese, *divided*
   1 teaspoon salt, *divided*
Pinch ground nutmeg
Pinch cayenne pepper
   1 cup chopped onion
   1 garlic clove, minced
   2 cups diced cooked chicken
   1 package (16 ounces) frozen chopped broccoli, thawed and drained
1/2 cup shredded carrot
1/4 cup minced fresh parsley
1/4 teaspoon pepper

BARLEY ZUCCHINI BOATS

(Pictured above)

Barley is delightful paired with garden-fresh zucchini in this flavorful recipe shared by the National Barley Foods Council.

   1 can (14-1/2 ounces) diced tomatoes
2/3 cup medium pearl barley
1/2 teaspoon ground cumin
   6 medium zucchini (8 to 9 inches)
1/2 pound ground beef *or* turkey
   1 medium onion, finely chopped
   2 garlic cloves, minced
3/4 teaspoon ground allspice
   1 tablespoon olive *or* vegetable oil
1/4 cup minced fresh parsley
3/4 teaspoon salt
1/4 teaspoon pepper
1/4 cup dry bread crumbs
1/4 cup grated Parmesan cheese
   2 tablespoons butter *or* margarine, melted

Drain tomatoes, reserving juice. Set the tomatoes aside. Add water to juice to measure 2 cups; place in a saucepan. Add barley and cumin; bring to a boil. Reduce heat; cover and simmer for 45 minutes or until tender. Meanwhile, place zucchini in a Dutch oven and cover with water; bring to a boil. Cook for 6 minutes or until slightly tender. Drain; cool slightly. Slice zucchini in half lengthwise. Scoop out pulp, leaving a 1/4-in. shell. Chop pulp and set aside. In a skillet, cook beef, onion, garlic and allspice in oil until meat is no longer pink; drain. Add barley mixture, parsley, salt, pepper, tomatoes and zucchini pulp; mix well. Spoon into zucchini shells. Combine bread crumbs, Parmesan cheese and butter; sprinkle over zucchini. Place in

15 lasagna noodles, cooked and drained
4 cups (16 ounces) shredded mozzarella cheese

In a saucepan, melt 4 tablespoons butter; stir in flour until smooth. Gradually add milk and broth; bring to a boil. Boil and stir for 2 minutes. Whisk half into eggs; return all to pan. Cook and stir over low heat for about 1 minute or until mixture reaches at least 160°. Remove from heat; add 1/2 cup Parmesan, 1/2 teaspoon salt, nutmeg and cayenne. Set aside. In a skillet, saute onion and garlic in remaining butter until tender. Add chicken, broccoli, carrot, parsley, pepper and remaining salt; cook for 3 minutes. Spread 1/2 cup of the Parmesan custard mixture into an ungreased 13-in. x 9-in. x 2-in. baking dish. Layer with a third of the noodles, half of the chicken mixture, 1/2 cup Parmesan custard, a third of the mozzarella cheese and 1 tablespoon Parmesan cheese. Repeat layers. Top with remaining noodles, mozzarella and Parmesan custard. Sprinkle with remaining Parmesan cheese. Bake, uncovered, at 350° for 40-45 minutes or until bubbly. Let stand 10 minutes before serving. **Yield:** 12 servings.

▪▪▪▪▪▪▪▪▪▪▪▪▪
FRIED CHICKEN COATING MIX

Dawn Supina, Edmonton, Alberta

(Pictured on the front cover)

My family tells me they'd like me to fix chicken with this coating mix all of the time. It's that good! I've had the recipe for years.

2 cups all-purpose flour
2 tablespoons salt
2 tablespoons pepper
1 tablespoon dried thyme
1 tablespoon dried tarragon
1 tablespoon ground ginger
1 tablespoon ground mustard
1 teaspoon garlic salt
1 teaspoon dried oregano
2 eggs
1/2 cup milk
1 broiler/fryer chicken (2-1/2 to 3-1/2 pounds), cut up
Oil for frying

Combine the first nine ingredients; store in an airtight container. In a shallow bowl, beat eggs and milk. Place 3/4 cup coating mix in a large resealable plastic bag. Dip chicken into egg mixture, then add to the bag, a few pieces at a time; shake to coat. Heat 1/4 in. of oil in a skillet over medium-high heat. Brown chicken on all sides; transfer to an ungreased 15-in. x 10-in. x 1-in. baking pan. Bake, uncovered, at 350° for 45-55 minutes

or until juices run clear. **Yield:** 2-1/2 cups coating mix (enough for 3 batches of chicken, 4-6 servings per batch).

▪▪▪▪▪▪▪▪▪▪▪▪▪
ZIPPY SWISS STEAK

Janice Dyer, Henderson, Nevada

(Pictured below)

This recipe has been in my family so long I don't even remember where it came from. Mexican-style food has been a favorite of mine since I was a child. This easy dish is mild, but it can be made hotter if desired.

1 large onion, chopped
2 garlic cloves, minced
4 tablespoons vegetable oil, *divided*
1 can (28 ounces) diced tomatoes, undrained
1 can (4 ounces) chopped green chilies
2 teaspoons salt, *divided*
3 tablespoons all-purpose flour
Dash pepper
2 pounds boneless round steak (1/2 inch thick)

In a saucepan, saute onion and garlic in 2 tablespoons of oil. Add tomatoes, chilies and 1 teaspoon of salt. Simmer, uncovered, for 20-25 minutes or until slightly thickened. Meanwhile, in a shallow bowl, combine the flour, pepper and remaining salt. Cut steak into serving-size pieces; dredge in flour mixture. In a skillet, brown steak on both sides in remaining oil. Transfer to an ungreased 13-in. x 9-in. x 2-in. baking dish. Set aside half of the tomato mixture; pour remaining mixture over steak. Cover and bake at 325° for 2 hours or until meat is tender. Heat reserved tomato mixture and serve with steak. **Yield:** 6 servings.

PORK CHOP BARLEY BAKE

Dress up plain pork chops by preparing this delicious dish from the folks at the National Barley Foods Council.

    1 cup medium pearl barley
  1/2 cup chopped onion
  1/2 cup chopped celery
    1 garlic clove, minced
    4 tablespoons butter *or* margarine, *divided*
    2 cups chicken broth
    1 cup orange juice
    1 teaspoon grated orange peel
  1/2 teaspoon dried rosemary, crushed
  1/2 cup chopped pecans, toasted
    6 pork loin chops (1 inch thick)
Salt and pepper to taste
GLAZE:
    1 cup orange marmalade
    2 tablespoons orange juice
    1 tablespoon prepared mustard
  1/2 teaspoon ground ginger
Orange slices and fresh rosemary, optional

In a large saucepan, saute barley, onion, celery and garlic in 3 tablespoons butter until barley is golden brown and vegetables are tender. Add broth, orange juice, peel and rosemary; bring to a boil. Reduce heat; cover and simmer for 35 minutes or until barley is partially cooked. Add pecans. Transfer to a greased 13-in. x 9-in. x 2-in. baking dish. In a skillet, brown pork chops on both sides in remaining butter. Sprinkle with salt and pepper. Arrange over barley mixture. Combine glaze ingredients; brush half over chops. Cover and bake at 350° for 45 minutes. Uncover; brush with remaining glaze. Bake 15 minutes longer or until juices run clear. Garnish with orange and rosemary if desired. **Yield:** 6 servings.

TERIYAKI SALMON

Jeannette Henderson, Stayton, Oregon

(Pictured below left)

Salmon is special here in the Northwest, and we've often had the privilege of catching some in the Columbia River. This recipe never fails to be a hit, whether we broil the salmon in the oven or grill it outdoors.

  1/2 cup vegetable oil
  1/4 cup lemon juice
  1/4 cup soy sauce
    1 teaspoon ground mustard
    1 teaspoon ground ginger
  1/4 teaspoon garlic powder
    4 salmon steaks (6 ounces *each*)

In a large resealable plastic bag or shallow glass container, combine the first six ingredients; mix well. Set aside 1/2 cup for basting and refrigerate. Add salmon to remaining marinade; cover and refrigerate for 1-1/2 hours, turning once. Drain and discard marinade. Place the salmon on a broiler pan. Broil 3-4 in. from the heat for 5 minutes. Brush with reserved marinade; turn and broil for 5 minutes or until fish flakes easily with a fork. Brush with marinade. **Yield:** 4 servings.

RASPBERRY CHICKEN

Carol Cottrill, Rumford, Maine

The raspberry sauce adds a touch of elegance to this easy-to-make chicken dish. Three simple seasonings further add to the chicken's flavor.

> ✓ **Uses less fat, sugar or salt. Includes Nutritional Analysis and Diabetic Exchanges.**

  1/2 teaspoon dried thyme
  1/2 teaspoon rubbed sage
  1/4 teaspoon pepper
    4 boneless skinless chicken breast halves
      (1 pound)
  1/4 cup seedless raspberry jam
    2 tablespoons orange juice
    2 tablespoons cider *or* red wine vinegar

Combine thyme, sage and pepper; rub over chicken. Lightly brown chicken in a skillet coated with nonstick cooking spray. Transfer to a 9-in. square baking dish coated with nonstick cooking spray. Cover and bake at 375° for 15 minutes or until juices run clear. In a saucepan, combine jam, orange juice and vinegar. Bring to a boil; boil for 2 minutes. Serve with the chicken. **Yield:** 4 servings. **Nutritional Analysis:** One serving equals 174 calories, 65 mg sodium, 73 mg cholesterol, 9 gm carbohydrate, 27 gm protein, 3 gm fat. **Diabetic Exchanges:** 4 very lean meat, 1/2 fruit.

SPINACH CHICKEN ENCHILADAS

Joy Headley, Grand Prairie, Texas

My husband is a pastor, so I fix meals for large groups often. This one is a favorite and a nice change from the usual beef enchiladas.

✓ Uses less fat, sugar or salt. Includes Nutritional Analysis and Diabetic Exchanges.

  4 boneless skinless chicken breast halves, cut into thin strips
1/4 cup chopped onion
  1 package (10 ounces) frozen chopped spinach, thawed and well drained
  1 can (10-3/4 ounces) condensed cream of mushroom soup, undiluted
3/4 cup milk
  1 cup (8 ounces) sour cream
  1 teaspoon ground nutmeg
  1 teaspoon garlic powder
  1 teaspoon onion powder
  8 flour tortillas (8 inches)
  2 cups (8 ounces) shredded mozzarella cheese
Minced fresh parsley

In a large skillet coated with nonstick cooking spray, cook chicken and onion over medium heat for 6-8 minutes or until chicken is no longer pink. Remove from the heat; add spinach and mix well. In a bowl, combine soup, milk, sour cream and seasonings; mix well. Stir 3/4 cup into chicken and spinach mixture. Divide evenly among tortillas. Roll up and place, seam side down, in a 13-in. x 9-in. x 2-in. baking pan coated with nonstick cooking spray. Pour the remaining soup mixture over enchiladas. Cover and bake at 350° for 30 minutes. Uncover and sprinkle with cheese; bake 15 minutes longer or until cheese is melted and bubbly. Garnish with parsley. **Yield:** 8 servings. **Nutritional Analysis:** One serving (prepared with skim milk and low-fat soup, sour cream and cheese) equals 295 calories, 496 mg sodium, 58 mg cholesterol, 22 gm carbohydrate, 29 gm protein, 11 gm fat. **Diabetic Exchanges:** 3 lean meat, 1 vegetable, 1/2 fat.

FRY BREAD SANDWICHES

Sandra Cameron, Flagstaff, Arizona

(Pictured above)

It was traditional for Native American girls in our village to learn to cook at an early age. I made fry bread many times for my father and seven brothers, and after I perfected the recipe, Father said it was the best he'd ever eaten.

  3 cups all-purpose flour
  1 teaspoon baking powder
1/2 teaspoon salt
1-1/4 cups milk
Oil for deep-fat frying
 12 lettuce leaves
 12 slices fully cooked turkey *or* ham
  1 small onion, sliced and separated into rings
  6 slices cheddar cheese
 18 thin slices tomato
  1 can (4 ounces) chopped green chilies

In a large bowl, combine flour, baking powder and salt. Add milk and stir to form a soft dough. Cover and let rest for 1 hour. About 30 minutes before serving, divide dough into six portions. On a lightly floured surface, roll each portion into an 8-in. circle. In a deep-fat fryer, heat oil to 375°. Fry bread circles, one at a time, until golden, turning once; drain on paper towels. Keep warm in a 300° oven. To serve, cut each circle in half. On six halves, layer the lettuce, turkey, onion, cheese and tomato; sprinkle with chilies. Top with remaining bread. Serve immediately. **Yield:** 6 servings.

On-the-Fly Chicken

THERE'S no need to brood when time is tight and supper isn't even started. Just turn to the super-simple chicken recipes featured here that require only about half an hour to fix. Your family is sure to think they're worth crowing about!

PECAN CHICKEN

Bonnie Jean Lintick, Kathyrn, Alberta

(Pictured below)

A pecan coating adds a pleasant crunch to plain chicken. My family likes dipping the crispy chicken pieces in the easy-to-make sauce.

> 1/3 cup finely chopped pecans
> 1/3 cup dry bread crumbs
> 1/2 teaspoon dried thyme
> 1/2 teaspoon paprika
> 1/2 teaspoon salt
> 4 boneless skinless chicken breast halves
> 3 tablespoons Dijon mustard

MAPLE-DIJON SAUCE:
> 1/4 cup maple syrup
> 1 tablespoon Dijon mustard

In a shallow bowl, combine the pecans, bread crumbs, thyme, paprika and salt. Coat chicken with mustard, then with pecan mixture. Place in a greased 13-in. x 9-in. x 2-in. baking dish. Bake, uncovered, at 375° for 30-35 minutes or until juices run clear. Meanwhile, combine the maple syrup and mustard in a small bowl; serve with chicken. **Yield:** 4 servings.

CHICKEN ENCHILADAS

Peggy Hoffman, Longview, Washington

This chicken dish has a nice zippy flavor, and it's a welcome change of pace from beef enchiladas.

> 4 cups shredded cooked chicken
> 2 cups (8 ounces) shredded cheddar cheese, *divided*

1 can (10-3/4 ounces) condensed cream
   of mushroom soup, undiluted
1/3 cup chopped onion
1 teaspoon salt
1/4 teaspoon pepper
3 cans (8 ounces *each*) tomato sauce
1 tablespoon chili powder
1/4 teaspoon ground cumin
1 can (2-1/4 ounces) sliced ripe olives,
   drained
10 flour tortillas (7 inches)
1/2 cup shredded Monterey Jack cheese

In a bowl, combine chicken, 1 cup cheddar cheese, soup, onion, salt and pepper; set aside. In a saucepan, combine tomato sauce, chili powder, cumin and olives. Simmer, uncovered, for 5-10 minutes. Meanwhile, spoon 1/3 to 1/2 cup chicken mixture down the center of each tortilla. Roll up; place seam side down in a greased 13-in. x 9-in. x 2-in. baking dish. Top with the tomato sauce mixture; sprinkle with Monterey Jack cheese and remaining cheddar cheese. Bake, uncovered, at 350° for 20-25 minutes or until heated through. **Yield:** 4-6 servings.

RANCH CHICKEN BITES

Ann Brunkhorst, Masonville, Iowa

These zesty bites are a fun and easy way to serve chicken. Only two simple ingredients make the savory ranch coating.

1 pound boneless skinless chicken breasts
1/2 cup ranch salad dressing
2-1/2 cups finely crushed sour cream and
   onion potato chips

Cut chicken into bite-size pieces; place in a bowl. Add salad dressing and stir to coat. Let stand for 10 minutes. Add potato chips and toss well. Place on a greased baking sheet. Bake, uncovered, at 350° for 18-20 minutes or until juices run clear. **Yield:** 4 servings.

CASHEW CHICKEN BAKE

Ruth Olson, Brooklyn Park, Minnesota

I first tasted this easy chicken dish at the home of a good friend years ago. I've made it many times since for my husband, who likes it as much as I do.

3 cups cubed cooked chicken
1-1/2 cups chopped celery

1-1/2 cups cooked small pasta
1 cup mayonnaise*
1/2 cup shredded cheddar cheese
1 jar (2 ounces) diced pimientos, drained
1 tablespoon grated onion
1/2 teaspoon salt
Dash pepper
1 cup salted cashew halves

In a bowl, combine the first nine ingredients. Chop 1/4 cup cashews; set aside. Stir the remaining cashews into chicken mixture. Transfer to a greased 8-in. square baking dish. Sprinkle with chopped cashews. Bake, uncovered, at 375° for 20-25 minutes or until heated through. **Yield:** 4-6 servings. ***Editor's Note:** Light or fat-free mayonnaise may not be substituted for regular mayonnaise.

CHOW MEIN CHICKEN

Debbie Franzen, Sewickley, Pennsylvania

Whenever I get the craving for Chinese food, I look no further than my own kitchen! This easy-to-make entree is ready in a matter of minutes.

2 celery ribs, chopped
1 medium onion, chopped
1/4 cup butter *or* margarine
1 can (10-3/4 ounces) condensed cream of
   mushroom soup, undiluted
1/2 cup chicken broth
1 tablespoon soy sauce
3 cups cubed cooked chicken
1/2 cup sliced fresh mushrooms
1 can (3 ounces) chow mein noodles
1/3 cup salted cashew halves

In a saucepan, saute celery and onion in butter until tender. Stir in soup, broth and soy sauce. Add the chicken and mushrooms; heat through. Transfer to a greased 2-qt. baking dish. Sprinkle with chow mein noodles and cashews. Bake, uncovered, at 350° for 15-20 minutes or until heated through. **Yield:** 4 servings.

PURCHASING POULTRY
- Select poultry well within the "sell by" date on the packaging.
- Packages should be well-sealed and free of tears.
- Frozen poultry should be solidly frozen.

Soups & Salads

Grandma's Sweet-Sour Veggies

Jeanne Schuyler, Wauwatosa, Wisconsin

(Pictured at left)

Every year when summer approaches, we look forward to a bonanza of fresh vegetables. There's nothing like a large bowl of fresh veggies to perk up a summer meal. This is one of our favorites.

> ✓ **Uses less fat, sugar or salt. Includes Nutritional Analysis and Diabetic Exchanges.**

    3 cups cauliflowerets
    3 cups broccoli florets
    2 medium carrots, thinly sliced
    1 medium zucchini, quartered and thinly
      sliced
    1 small red onion, julienned
  3/4 cup cider vinegar
  1/4 cup sugar
  1/2 teaspoon salt, optional
    2 tablespoons vegetable oil
Sunflower kernels, optional

In a bowl, combine the cauliflower, broccoli, carrots, zucchini and onion; set aside. In a saucepan over medium heat, bring vinegar, sugar and salt if desired to a boil. Remove from the heat; stir in oil. Pour over vegetables and toss to coat. Cover and refrigerate overnight. Just before serving, sprinkle with sunflower kernels if desired. **Yield:** 12-14 servings. **Nutritional Analysis:** One 3/4-cup serving (prepared without salt and sunflower kernels) equals 60 calories, 17 mg sodium, 0 cholesterol, 10 gm carbohydrate, 1 gm protein, 2 gm fat. **Diabetic Exchanges:** 1-1/2 vegetable, 1/2 fat.

Lettuce with Hot Bacon Dressing

Myra Innes, Auburn, Kansas

(Pictured at left)

I plant lettuce in my garden, so this is a recipe I make often. Served with the hot dressing, it's a nice change from a regular tossed salad.

    5 bacon strips
    8 cups torn salad greens
    2 hard-cooked eggs, chopped
    2 green onions, sliced
  1/2 cup sugar
  1/2 cup vinegar
  1/2 teaspoon seasoned salt
  1/2 teaspoon garlic powder
  1/4 teaspoon ground mustard

In a skillet, cook bacon until crisp. Remove the bacon; crumble and set aside. Drain, reserving 1/4 cup drippings. In a large bowl, combine the greens, eggs, onions and bacon. Add remaining ingredients to the drippings; bring to a boil. Drizzle over the salad and toss to coat. Serve immediately. **Yield:** 8 servings.

Hearty Chicken Vegetable Soup

Willie Jo Bond, Newton, Alabama

I've made this soup many times for my husband and four sons. Even though they're married and have homes of their own, my sons still like to come to our house to eat. This recipe is always a hit with them.

    3 large green peppers, chopped
    3 large onions, chopped
    2 tablespoons vegetable oil
    3 cans (two 28 ounces, one 14-1/2
      ounces) whole tomatoes, undrained
    4 cups fresh or frozen corn
    3 cups cubed cooked chicken
    3 large potatoes, diced
    1 can (16 ounces) butter beans, drained
    2 cups water
    1 cup frozen peas
    1 cup frozen chopped okra
  1/2 cup sugar
    3 jalapeno peppers, chopped*
  1/4 cup vinegar
    3 to 4 tablespoons salt

In a soup kettle, saute green peppers and onions in oil until tender. Add the remaining ingredients. Bring to a boil. Reduce heat; cover and simmer for 40 minutes or until potatoes are tender, stirring occasionally. **Yield:** 20 servings (5 quarts). ***Editor's Note:** When handling hot peppers, use rubber or plastic gloves to protect your hands. Avoid touching your face.

10 whole garlic heads
3/4 cup olive *or* vegetable oil
4 cans (one 14-1/2 ounces, three 28 ounces) diced tomatoes, undrained
1 medium onion, diced
3 cans (14-1/2 ounces *each*) stewed tomatoes
2/3 cup whipping cream
1 to 3 tablespoons chopped pickled jalapeno peppers
2 teaspoons sugar
1-1/2 teaspoons salt
1 teaspoon pepper
Croutons and shredded Parmesan cheese, optional

Remove papery outer skin from garlic (do not peel or separate cloves). Cut tops off garlic heads; place cut side up in an ungreased 8-in. square baking dish. Pour oil over garlic. Bake, uncovered, at 375° for 45-55 minutes or until softened. Cool for 10-15 minutes. Squeeze softened garlic into a blender or food processor. Add the 14-1/2-oz. can of diced tomatoes; cover and process until smooth. Set aside. Transfer 1/4 cup of oil from the baking dish to a Dutch oven or soup kettle (discard the remaining oil or save for another use). Saute onion in oil over medium heat until soft. Stir in the stewed tomatoes, cream, jalapenos, sugar, salt, pepper, pureed tomato mixture and remaining diced tomatoes. Bring to a boil. Reduce heat; cover and simmer for 1 hour. Garnish with croutons and cheese if desired. **Yield:** 18-20 servings (4-1/2 quarts).

***

PICANTE BROCCOLI CHICKEN SALAD

Krista Shumway, Billings, Montana

(Pictured above)

Our family likes things spicy, so I often add a fresh jalapeno pepper to this colorful salad. It's a simple, savory way to use up leftover chicken. Plus, it's very eye-catching!

1/2 cup mayonnaise
1/4 cup picante sauce
1 garlic clove, minced
1/2 to 1 teaspoon chili powder
2 cups cubed cooked chicken
2 cups broccoli florets
1 cup diced fresh tomato
1/2 cup shredded cheddar cheese
1/2 cup chopped onion
1/4 cup julienned green pepper
1/4 cup julienned sweet red pepper
Flour tortillas, warmed

In a large bowl, combine the first four ingredients; mix well. Add chicken, broccoli, tomato, cheese, onion and peppers; toss to coat. Refrigerate for at least 30 minutes before serving. Serve with tortillas. **Yield:** 6-8 servings.

***

TOMATO GARLIC SOUP

Lynn Thompson, Reston, Virginia

(Pictured on page 46)

I like to make this satisfying soup when I'm expecting a lot of people for dinner. My guests enjoy it, too.

***

CRUNCHY TURKEY SALAD

Brenda Moore James, Livermore, California

Adding a refreshing salad to a spread is a snap with this recipe. The water chestnuts, almonds, celery and chow mein noodles provide lots of crunch. Topping it all is a sweet-sour dressing my family loves.

1/4 cup sugar
1/4 cup vegetable oil
1/4 cup cider *or* red wine vinegar
1/2 teaspoon salt
1/2 teaspoon garlic salt
1/2 teaspoon pepper
5 cups cubed cooked turkey, chicken *or* ham
6 cups shredded lettuce
1 can (8 ounces) sliced water chestnuts, drained
2 celery ribs, sliced
4 green onions, sliced
2 tablespoons sesame seeds, toasted

2 tablespoons sliced almonds, toasted
1 can (3 ounces) chow mein noodles

In a jar with tight-fitting lid, combine sugar, oil, vinegar, salt, garlic salt and pepper; shake well. In a large bowl, combine remaining ingredients. Just before serving, add the dressing and toss to coat. **Yield:** 16 servings.

MOM'S CHICKEN 'N' BUTTERMILK DUMPLINGS

Ellen Proefrock, Brodhead, Wisconsin

I serve this—with a tossed or cucumber salad—to friends dining with us or on visits by our two sons and their families.

      1 stewing chicken (about 5 pounds),
        cut up
    10 cups water
      1 large onion, chopped
      2 medium carrots, sliced
      3 celery ribs, chopped
      4 garlic cloves, minced
      1 teaspoon salt
    1/4 cup butter *or* margarine
      6 tablespoons all-purpose flour
    1/8 teaspoon paprika
    1/8 teaspoon pepper
    1/2 cup half-and-half cream
DUMPLINGS:
      2 cups all-purpose flour
      4 teaspoons baking powder
      4 teaspoons sugar
      1 teaspoon salt
      2 eggs
    1/2 cup buttermilk
    1/4 cup butter *or* margarine, melted

In a soup kettle or Dutch oven, combine the first seven ingredients. Bring to a boil; skim foam from broth. Reduce heat; cover and simmer for 1-1/2 hours or until chicken is tender. Remove chicken; when cool enough to handle, debone and dice. Strain broth, reserving broth and vegetables. In the same kettle, melt butter. Stir in flour, paprika and pepper until smooth. Gradually stir in 6 cups reserved broth (save remaining broth for another use). Bring to a boil; boil and stir for 2 minutes. Reduce heat; stir in the cream, reserved vegetables and chicken. Cover and bring to a boil; reduce the heat to simmer. For dumplings, combine flour, baking powder, sugar and salt in a bowl. Combine eggs, buttermilk and butter; stir into dry ingredients to form a stiff batter. Drop by tablespoonfuls onto simmering mixture. Cover and simmer for 20 minutes or until a toothpick inserted in a dumpling comes out clean (do not lift cover while simmering). Serve immediately. **Yield:** 6-8 servings.

CREAMY POTATO SOUP

Michelle Wollenburg, Beatrice, Nebraska

(Pictured below)

My mother-in-law shared this recipe with me shortly after my husband and I were married. A bowl of the hot and creamy soup is perfect on a cold winter day.

      1 medium onion, chopped
      1 celery rib, chopped
      1 medium carrot, grated
    1/2 cup butter *or* margarine
      2 tablespoons all-purpose flour
      4 cups milk
      1 can (10-3/4 ounces) condensed cream
        of mushroom soup, undiluted
    1/2 cup cubed process American cheese *or*
        shredded cheddar cheese
      6 large potatoes, peeled, diced and cooked
        (about 8 cups)
      1 teaspoon seasoned salt

In a Dutch oven, saute onion, celery and carrot in butter until tender. Stir in flour until blended. Gradually add milk. Bring to a boil; cook and stir for 2 minutes or until thickened. Add soup, cheese, potatoes and seasoned salt; mix well. Cook and stir until cheese is melted and soup is heated through. **Yield:** 10-12 servings (3 quarts).

BARBECUE BEAN SALAD

Judith Saeugling, Dubuque, Iowa

(Pictured below)

I love to cook and try new recipes. I've been collecting cookbooks for years and have picked up some very old cookbooks at estate sales. This bean salad is a bit zestier than more traditional recipes. Chili powder, cumin and hot pepper sauce add a nice zip.

> 1 pound dry pinto beans
> 1/4 cup cider vinegar
> 1/4 cup vegetable oil
> 1/4 cup ketchup
> 1/4 cup packed brown sugar
> 1 tablespoon Dijon mustard
> 1 tablespoon Worcestershire sauce
> 2 teaspoons chili powder
> 3/4 teaspoon ground cumin
> 1 teaspoon salt
> 1/4 teaspoon pepper
> 1/4 teaspoon hot pepper sauce
> 1 can (15-1/4 ounces) whole kernel corn, drained
> 1 medium sweet red pepper, chopped
> 1 medium green pepper, chopped
> 1 medium onion, chopped
> 2 cups tortilla chips, coarsely crushed, *divided*

Place beans in a Dutch oven or soup kettle; add water to cover by 2 in. Bring to a boil; boil for 2 minutes. Remove from the heat; cover and let stand for 1 hour. Drain and discard liquid. Add water to cover beans by 2 in. Bring to a boil. Reduce heat; cover and simmer for 1 to 1-1/2 hours or until tender. Rinse, drain and set aside. For dressing, in a saucepan, combine the vinegar, oil, ketchup, brown sugar, mustard, Worcestershire sauce, chili powder, cumin, salt, pepper and hot pepper sauce. Bring to a boil. Reduce heat; cover and simmer for 10 minutes. Cool slightly. In a large salad bowl, combine the beans, corn, peppers and onion. Just before serving, stir in dressing and half of the chips. Sprinkle with remaining chips. **Yield:** 14-16 servings.

CREAMY CRANBERRY SALAD

Alexandra Lypecky, Dearborn, Michigan

One of my piano students shared this recipe with me many years ago. She told me it's the perfect salad for the holidays, and she was right.

> 3 cups fresh *or* frozen cranberries, coarsely chopped
> 1 can (20 ounces) crushed pineapple, drained
> 1 medium apple, peeled and chopped
> 2 cups miniature marshmallows
> 2/3 cup sugar
> 1/8 teaspoon salt
> 1/4 cup chopped walnuts, optional
> 2 cups whipping cream, whipped

In a bowl, combine cranberries, pineapple, apple, marshmallows, sugar, salt and walnuts if desired; mix well. Cover and refrigerate overnight. Just before serving, fold in whipped cream. **Yield:** 10-12 servings.

BACON CORN SOUP

Sheri Cartwright, Greenspring, West Virginia

Our church eats together every Sunday, and that's where I got this recipe. Everyone loves the flavorful combination of vegetables so much, we have this soup often.

> 4 bacon strips
> 1 cup chopped onion
> 2 cups water
> 1-1/2 cups diced peeled potatoes
> 1 teaspoon chicken bouillon granules
> 1/4 cup all-purpose flour
> 2 cups milk, *divided*
> 1 cup half-and-half cream

1 package (16 ounces) frozen corn
8 ounces process American cheese, cubed
Salt and pepper to taste

In a large saucepan, cook bacon until crisp. Remove bacon; crumble and set aside. In the drippings, saute onion until tender. Add water, potatoes and bouillon; cover and simmer until potatoes are tender. In a small bowl, combine flour and 1/4 cup milk until smooth. Add flour mixture, cream, corn and remaining milk to soup; bring to a boil. Cook and stir for 2-3 minutes or until thickened. Reduce heat; add cheese and bacon. Cook and stir until cheese is melted. Season with salt and pepper. **Yield:** 6-8 servings (about 2 quarts).

TOSSED SALAD WITH SPINACH DRESSING

Diane Hixon, Niceville, Florida

Here's a delicious tossed salad that's perfect to serve at cookouts. The spinach dressing adds wonderful flavor to the fresh vegetables.

4 cups cauliflowerets
4 cups torn lettuce
1 small onion, sliced and separated into rings
1 jar (3-1/2 ounces) stuffed olives, drained
1/4 cup crumbled blue cheese

DRESSING:
1/3 cup finely chopped fresh spinach
1/4 cup vegetable oil
2 tablespoons finely chopped onion
1 tablespoon plus 1 teaspoon lemon juice
2 teaspoons minced fresh parsley
3/4 teaspoon sugar

In a bowl, combine the cauliflower, lettuce, onion, olives and blue cheese. In a jar with a tight-fitting lid, combine the dressing ingredients; shake well. Pour over salad and toss to coat; serve immediately. **Yield:** 8 servings.

NORTHWEST SALMON CHOWDER

Josephine Parton, Granger, Washington

(Pictured above right)

I've lived on a farm in the Yakima Valley all my life. I have a big garden, and by the end of fall, my cellar shelves are full of canned fruits and vegetables. This recipe uses some of the root vegetables I grow...along with the delicious salmon that is so plentiful here.

1/2 cup *each* chopped celery, onion and green pepper

1 garlic clove, minced
3 tablespoons butter *or* margarine
1 can (14-1/2 ounces) chicken broth
1 cup uncooked diced peeled potatoes
1 cup shredded carrots
1-1/2 teaspoons salt
1/2 teaspoon pepper
1/4 to 3/4 teaspoon dill weed
1 can (14-3/4 ounces) cream-style corn
2 cups half-and-half cream
1-3/4 to 2 cups fully cooked salmon chunks *or* 1 can (14-3/4 ounces) salmon, drained, flaked, bones and skin removed

In a large saucepan, saute celery, onion, green pepper and garlic in butter until the vegetables are tender. Add broth, potatoes, carrots, salt, pepper and dill; bring to a boil. Reduce heat; cover and simmer for 40 minutes or until the vegetables are nearly tender. Stir in the corn, cream and salmon. Simmer for 15 minutes or until heated through. **Yield:** 8 servings (2 quarts).

SOUTHERN CHICKEN RICE SOUP

Rosalie Biar, Thorndale, Texas

(Pictured at left)

A favorite at soup night at our church, this recipe's one my husband concocted after he retired. I frequently find it on the table when I get home from work. This satisfying soup is a meal in itself along with some fresh bread.

      1 broiler/fryer chicken (about 3 pounds)
     10 cups water
      2 teaspoons salt
    1/2 cup uncooked long grain rice
    1/2 cup chopped onion
    1/2 cup chopped celery
    1/2 cup thinly sliced carrots
    1/2 cup sliced fresh *or* frozen okra
      1 can (14-1/2 ounces) stewed tomatoes, diced
      1 tablespoon chopped green chilies
      1 garlic clove, minced
  1-1/2 teaspoons chili powder
      1 teaspoon seasoned salt

Meaty Spheres Add Zest to Salads

TO "dress up" an ordinary lettuce salad, Le Ane Wohlgemuth of Rimbey, Alberta tosses in an unusual ingredient folks are sure to gobble right up—tangy turkey meatballs!

"I often top salads with strips of just-cooked chicken. Doing something similar with meatballs seemed ideal," says the busy country wife and mother of two. "I especially like how quick this dish is to prepare."

Le Ane shares her zippy recipe below so it can star at your family's salad bar, too!

TURKEY MEATBALL SALAD

      1 egg
      6 teaspoons soy sauce, *divided*
      1 can (8 ounces) water chestnuts, drained and chopped
    1/3 cup thinly sliced green onions
    1/4 cup dry bread crumbs
      1 pound ground turkey
DRESSING:
      1 tablespoon cornstarch
      1 teaspoon sugar
  1-1/2 cups chicken broth
    1/2 teaspoon vinegar
      1 medium head iceberg lettuce, finely shredded
  Additional green onions, optional
      1 medium lemon, cut into wedges, optional

In a large bowl, beat egg and 4 teaspoons soy sauce; add water chestnuts, green onions and bread crumbs. Add turkey and mix well. Shape into 1-in. balls. Place in a single layer in a greased 15-in. x 10-in. x 1-in. baking pan. Bake, uncovered, at 400° for 10-12 minutes or until meat is no longer pink. Meanwhile, for dressing, combine cornstarch and sugar in a saucepan. Whisk in broth, vinegar and remaining soy sauce until smooth. Bring to a boil; cook and stir for 2 minutes or until thickened. To serve, arrange meatballs over lettuce; garnish with onions and lemon if desired. Serve with the dressing. **Yield:** 4 servings.

1/2 teaspoon lemon-pepper seasoning
1/2 teaspoon Creole seasoning

Place chicken, water and salt in a soup kettle or Dutch oven. Bring to a boil; skim foam from broth. Reduce heat; cover and simmer for 1 to 1-1/2 hours or until the chicken is tender. Remove chicken; when cool enough to handle, debone and dice. Skim fat from broth. Add rice, vegetables and seasonings. Cook, uncovered, over medium heat for 30 minutes. Add the chicken. Simmer for 30 minutes or until vegetables are tender. **Yield:** 10 servings (about 2-1/2 quarts).

ALMOND CHICKEN SALAD

Brenda Nickerson, Clymer, New York

I rely on this refreshing chicken salad often for lunch or a light supper. It can be made ahead of time and popped in the refrigerator, which is perfect for my busy schedule.

> ✓ Uses less fat, sugar or salt. Includes Nutritional Analysis and Diabetic Exchanges.

4 cups cubed cooked chicken
1 cup chopped celery
1 cup seedless green grapes, halved
1/2 cup fat-free mayonnaise
1/2 cup nonfat plain yogurt
1/4 teaspoon pepper
1/4 cup chopped almonds, toasted

In a large bowl, combine chicken, celery, grapes, mayonnaise, yogurt and pepper; mix well. Cover and refrigerate for several hours. Stir in almonds just before serving. **Yield:** 8 servings. **Nutritional Analysis:** One serving (3/4 cup) equals 126 calories, 138 mg sodium, 43 mg cholesterol, 8 gm carbohydrate, 13 gm protein, 4 gm fat. **Diabetic Exchanges:** 2 lean meat, 1/2 fruit.

MACARONI SALAD

Edie DeSpain, Logan, Utah

Put this colorfully creamy combination into the mix of dishes at your next get-together—and watch it disappear fast! Chopped radishes, cucumber, green pepper and onion lend fresh garden flavor to the macaroni mixture.

1 package (7 ounces) elbow macaroni, cooked and drained
1 cup chopped cucumber
1/2 cup chopped green pepper
1/2 cup chopped radishes
2 tablespoons chopped onion
1/2 teaspoon salt

1 package (8 ounces) cream cheese, softened
1/4 cup mayonnaise
1/4 cup sweet pickle relish
1 tablespoon prepared mustard
Lettuce leaves and additional radishes

In a bowl, combine the first six ingredients; set aside. In a mixing bowl, beat cream cheese; add mayonnaise, relish and mustard. Fold into macaroni mixture. Press into a 6-cup ring mold coated with nonstick cooking spray. Refrigerate for several hours or overnight. Just before serving, unmold onto a lettuce-lined serving platter. Garnish with radishes. **Yield:** 12-16 servings.

CAULIFLOWER SPINACH SALAD

Marjorie Carey, Freeport, Florida

(Pictured below)

Cauliflower, mandarin oranges, green pepper and radishes flavorfully dress up plain fresh spinach in this quick-and-easy salad.

2 cups cauliflowerets
1 can (11 ounces) mandarin oranges, well drained
1/4 cup chopped green pepper
2 large radishes, sliced
4 cups torn fresh spinach
1 can (5 ounces) evaporated milk
1/3 cup orange juice concentrate

In a large bowl, combine the first five ingredients. Pour milk in a small bowl; gradually whisk in orange juice concentrate. Drizzle over salad and toss to coat. Refrigerate leftovers. **Yield:** 8-10 servings.

MEATBALL MINESTRONE

Sue Murray, Hershey, Pennsylvania

I came across this soup recipe years ago when I was looking for restricted diet foods. It's as good tasting as it is good for you.

✓ Uses less fat, sugar or salt. Includes Nutritional Analysis and Diabetic Exchanges.

   1 egg white
   2 tablespoons quick-cooking oats
   2 tablespoons nonfat Parmesan cheese topping
 1/8 teaspoon Italian seasoning
 1/8 teaspoon garlic powder
 1/2 pound ground turkey breast
   1 cup chopped onion
   1 cup chopped celery
   2 garlic cloves, minced
   3 cans (14-1/2 ounces *each*) low-sodium chicken broth
   1 can (28 ounces) no-salt-added whole tomatoes, undrained and chopped
   1 can (6 ounces) tomato paste
   1 cup chopped carrots
   1 cup diced peeled potatoes
 1/2 cup minced fresh parsley
   1 teaspoon dried basil
   1 teaspoon dried thyme
   1 cup uncooked spiral pasta

In a bowl, combine the first five ingredients. Crumble turkey over mixture; mix well. Shape in- to 3/4-in. balls. Place on a baking sheet coated with nonstick cooking spray. Bake, uncovered, at 350° for 20 minutes or until meat is no longer pink. In a large saucepan coated with nonstick cooking spray, saute onion, celery and garlic until crisp-tender. Add broth, tomatoes, tomato paste, vegetables and seasonings. Bring to a boil. Reduce heat; cover and simmer for 30 minutes. Stir in pasta and meatballs. Cook, uncovered, over medium heat for 10-12 minutes or until vegetables and pasta are tender. **Yield:** 12 servings. **Nutritional Analysis:** One 1-cup serving equals 118 calories, 128 mg sodium, 11 mg cholesterol, 19 gm carbohydrate, 9 gm protein, 1 gm fat. **Diabetic Exchanges:** 1 starch, 1 very lean meat.

CAULIFLOWER PEA SALAD

Marilyn Armstrong, Monticello, Illinois

A light dressing really lets the fresh flavor of the vegetables shine through in this salad. It's great for potlucks or other get-togethers.

✓ Uses less fat, sugar or salt. Includes Nutritional Analysis and Diabetic Exchanges.

   5 cups cauliflowerets
   2 cups frozen peas, thawed
   1 cup diced celery
 1/2 cup chopped onion
 1/2 cup plain nonfat yogurt
 1/3 cup fat-free mayonnaise
1-1/2 teaspoons dill weed
   1 teaspoon salt-free herb blend

In a bowl, combine the first four ingredients. In a small bowl, combine yogurt, mayonnaise, dill and herb blend; mix well. Add to cauliflower mixture; toss to coat. Refrigerate until serving. **Yield:** 16 servings. **Nutritional Analysis:** One serving equals 33 calories, 77 mg sodium, trace cholesterol, 6 gm carbohydrate, 2 gm protein, trace fat. **Diabetic Exchange:** 1 vegetable.

GOLDEN GLOW GELATIN MOLD

Aline Savoie, Edmonton, Alberta

(Pictured at left)

Bursting with sunshiny citrus flavor, this sweet-and-creamy gelatin mold will brighten the table and delight guests. I make it for many a party, and not one bite is ever left.

   2 cans (8 ounces *each*) crushed pineapple
 30 large marshmallows
   1 package (6 ounces) lemon gelatin
   2 cups boiling water

1 package (3 ounces) cream cheese,
    softened
1 cup cold water
1-1/2 cups shredded carrots
Leaf lettuce and lemon slices, optional

Drain pineapple, reserving juice; set the pineapple aside. In a saucepan, combine pineapple juice and marshmallows; cook and stir over low heat until marshmallows are melted. Remove from the heat. Dissolve gelatin in boiling water. Add cream cheese; stir until mixture is thoroughly blended. Stir in cold water and marshmallow mixture. Chill until partially set. Fold in carrots and pineapple. Pour into a 6-cup mold coated with nonstick cooking spray. Refrigerate until set. Unmold onto a lettuce-lined serving plate. Garnish with lemon if desired. **Yield:** 12-16 servings.

GOLDEN PUMPKIN SALAD

Janell Burrell, Cornelia, Georgia

This delicious salad is the result of a bumper crop of pumpkins. I had so many on hand one fall, I started experimenting with different ways of preparing them. This sweet dish I came up with is one the whole family really enjoys.

2 cups shredded uncooked fresh pie
    pumpkin
1 can (8 ounces) crushed pineapple,
    undrained
1/2 cup raisins
1 tablespoon mayonnaise
1/2 teaspoon sugar
Leaf lettuce, optional

Place pumpkin in a 1-qt. microwave-safe bowl. Cover and microwave on high for 3 minutes; cool. Stir in pineapple, raisins, mayonnaise and sugar. Refrigerate overnight. Serve on lettuce if desired. **Yield:** 4 servings. **Editor's Note:** This recipe was tested in an 850-watt microwave.

GRILLED CHICKEN PASTA SALAD

Lori Thon, Basin, Wyoming

(Pictured above right)

During the warmer summer months, my family often requests this recipe. It's a wonderful way to serve grilled chicken that puts the fresh vegetables of the season to good use. Simply add garlic bread for a great meal.

1-1/2 cups Italian salad dressing
1/2 cup cider vinegar
1/3 cup honey

2 teaspoons dried oregano
1 teaspoon dried basil
1/2 teaspoon pepper
6 boneless skinless chicken breast halves
    (1-1/2 pounds)
1 package (12 ounces) fettuccine
1-1/2 cups broccoli florets
3 medium carrots, thinly sliced
2 celery ribs, thinly sliced
1 cup chopped green pepper
2 cans (2-1/4 ounces *each*) sliced ripe
    olives, drained
DRESSING:
1-1/2 cups Italian salad dressing
1 teaspoon garlic salt
1 teaspoon dried oregano
1 teaspoon Italian seasoning

In a large resealable plastic bag or shallow glass container, combine the first six ingredients. Cut each chicken breast into four strips; add to dressing mixture. Seal or cover and refrigerate for 2-3 hours. Drain and discard marinade. Grill chicken, uncovered, over medium heat for 4-5 minutes on each side or until juices run clear. Meanwhile, cook fettuccine according to package directions; drain and cool. Cut chicken into bite-size pieces; set aside. In a large bowl, combine vegetables, olives and fettuccine. Combine dressing ingredients in a jar with a tight-fitting lid; shake well. Pour over salad and toss to coat. Top with chicken. **Yield:** 6 servings.

4 medium tomatoes, chopped
3 large cucumbers, seeded and chopped
1 medium onion, chopped
10 radishes, sliced
2 cups (16 ounces) sour cream
1/4 cup lemon juice
1 teaspoon seasoned salt
1/2 teaspoon pepper
3/4 teaspoon celery seed, optional

In a large bowl, combine tomatoes, cucumbers, onion and radishes. In a small bowl, combine the remaining ingredients. Add to vegetables and toss to coat. Cover and refrigerate for at least 2 hours. Serve with a slotted spoon. **Yield:** 16 servings.

CRUNCHY DILLED SLAW

Dorothy De Hart, Bradley, California

(Pictured on the front cover)

This colorful coleslaw is good with just about any kind of meat. I've taken it to many potluck dinners, where it's always well received.

1 small head cabbage, shredded
2 medium green peppers, thinly sliced
1 medium sweet red pepper, thinly sliced
1 small onion, chopped
1 celery rib, thinly sliced
1 cup vinegar
3/4 cup sugar
2 teaspoons dill seed
1 teaspoon ground mustard
1 teaspoon salt
3/4 cup vegetable oil

In a large bowl, toss the first five ingredients. In a small saucepan, combine vinegar, sugar, dill seed, mustard and salt; bring to a boil. Remove from the heat; add oil. Pour over cabbage mixture; toss to coat. Cover and refrigerate for at least 1 hour. **Yield:** 10-12 servings.

STUFFED SWEET PEPPER SOUP

Joseph Kendra, Coraopolis, Pennsylvania

Tomatoes, peppers, garlic and onions are the mainstays of my garden. Being the oldest of seven children, I acquired a knack for cooking from my mom.

1 pound ground beef
2 quarts water
1 quart tomato juice
3 medium sweet red *or* green peppers, diced
1-1/2 cups chili sauce

IDAHO POTATO SALAD

Rhonda Munk, Boise, Idaho

(Pictured above)

Mom used to make this potato salad without a recipe. When I got married, she and I made it one afternoon and wrote down the ingredients so I could make it at home. Of course, we use our famous Idaho potatoes.

4 pounds potatoes, cooked and peeled
3/4 cup sliced peeled cucumber
2 hard-cooked eggs, chopped
2 green onions, sliced
4-1/2 teaspoons chopped dill pickle
1 cup mayonnaise *or* salad dressing
1-1/2 teaspoons dill pickle juice
1-1/2 teaspoons prepared mustard
3/4 cup sliced radishes

Cut potatoes into 1/4-in.-thick slices; place in a large bowl. Add cucumber, eggs, onions and pickle. In a small bowl, combine the mayonnaise, pickle juice and mustard; pour over potato mixture and toss gently to coat. Cover and refrigerate. Fold in radishes just before serving. **Yield:** 10-12 servings.

CREAMY SUMMER VEGETABLE SALAD

Barbara Arneson, Creston, Washington

Mother made this salad whenever we barbecued. It's easy to fix, goes well with meat or chicken and is a good way to utilize garden vegetables.

1 cup uncooked long grain rice
2 celery ribs, diced
1 large onion, diced
2 teaspoons browning sauce, optional
3 chicken bouillon cubes
2 garlic cloves, minced
1/2 teaspoon salt

In a large kettle or Dutch oven over medium heat, cook beef until no longer pink; drain. Add the remaining ingredients; bring to a boil. Reduce heat; simmer, uncovered, for 1 hour or until the rice is tender. **Yield:** 16 servings (4 quarts).

HEARTY CHICKEN SALAD

Lisa Buese, Olathe, Kansas

When I was first married, I experimented with a lot of recipes. I guess I got carried away. My husband told me that although he enjoyed trying new recipes, sometimes he'd like to have something familiar. I've arrived at a happy medium since then. This is one "test" that's become a favorite!

1/3 cup vegetable oil
1/4 cup cider *or* white wine vinegar
2 tablespoons honey
2 tablespoons sesame seeds, toasted
2 tablespoons soy sauce
1 teaspoon dried parsley flakes
1/2 teaspoon ground ginger
1/2 teaspoon ground mustard
3 cups coarsely chopped cooked chicken
2 cups shredded green *or* Chinese cabbage
1 cup fresh snow peas, halved
1 cup sliced carrots
1/2 cup sliced green onions
1/2 cup sliced radishes
Salted peanuts, optional

In a large bowl, combine the oil, vinegar, honey, sesame seeds, soy sauce, parsley, ginger and mustard; mix well. Stir in the chicken. Cover and refrigerate for at least 1 hour. Just before serving, toss cabbage, peas, carrots, onions and radishes in a serving bowl; top with the chicken mixture. Sprinkle with peanuts if desired. **Yield:** 6-8 servings.

CREAM OF CAULIFLOWER SOUP

Carol Reaves, San Antonio, Texas

(Pictured at right)

Generally, my husband isn't a soup fan—but his spoon's poised and ready for this version. I adapted this rich and creamy concoction from a recipe I tasted at a local restaurant...and it's since become a popular item on my "menu".

2 medium onions, chopped
2 medium carrots, grated
2 celery ribs, sliced
2 garlic cloves, minced
1/4 cup plus 6 tablespoons butter *or* margarine, *divided*
1 medium head cauliflower, chopped
5 cups chicken broth
1/4 cup minced fresh parsley
1 teaspoon salt
1 teaspoon coarsely ground pepper
1/2 teaspoon dried basil
1/2 teaspoon dried tarragon
6 tablespoons all-purpose flour
1 cup milk
1/2 cup whipping cream
1/4 cup sour cream
Fresh tarragon, optional

In a soup kettle or Dutch oven, saute the onions, carrots, celery and garlic in 1/4 cup butter until tender. Add cauliflower, broth, parsley, salt, pepper, basil and tarragon. Cover and simmer for 30 minutes or until the vegetables are tender. Meanwhile, in a saucepan, melt the remaining butter. Stir in flour until smooth. Gradually stir in the milk and whipping cream. Bring to a boil; cook and stir for 2 minutes or until thickened. Add to cauliflower mixture. Cook for 10 minutes or until thickened, stirring frequently. Remove from the heat; stir in sour cream. Garnish with tarragon if desired. **Yield:** 8 servings.

▰▰▰▰▰▰▰▰▰▰▰▰
BAKED GERMAN POTATO SALAD

Julie Myers, Lexington, Ohio

What makes this German potato salad so different is that it's sweet instead of tangy. The first time I took this salad to work, people kept coming out of their offices to find out what smelled so good. By lunch, it was gone. Now, I make a double batch to take to work!

        12 medium red potatoes (about 3 pounds)
         8 bacon strips
         2 medium onions, chopped
       3/4 cup packed brown sugar
       1/3 cup vinegar
       1/3 cup sweet pickle juice
       2/3 cup water, *divided*
         2 teaspoons dried parsley flakes
         1 teaspoon salt
   1/2 to 3/4 teaspoon celery seed
     4-1/2 teaspoons all-purpose flour

In a saucepan, cook potatoes until just tender; drain. Peel and slice into an ungreased 2-qt. baking dish; set aside. In a skillet, cook bacon until crisp; drain, reserving 2 tablespoons drippings. Crumble bacon and set aside. Saute onions in drippings until tender. Stir in brown sugar, vinegar, pickle juice, 1/2 cup water, parsley, salt and celery seed. Simmer, uncovered, for 5-10 minutes. Meanwhile, combine flour and remaining water until smooth; stir into onion mixture. Bring to a boil. Cook and stir for 2 minutes or until thickened. Pour over potatoes. Add bacon; gently stir

to coat. Bake, uncovered, at 350° for 30 minutes or until heated through. **Yield:** 8-10 servings.

▰▰▰▰▰▰▰▰▰▰▰▰
CHEESY POTATO SOUP

Doris Self, Greensboro, North Carolina

We like to eat hot bowlfuls of this cheesy soup often throughout the winter. It sure warms you through on a cold and dreary day.

✓ **Uses less fat, sugar or salt. Includes Nutritional Analysis and Diabetic Exchanges.**

         1 cup diced peeled potato
       1/2 cup shredded carrot
       1/4 cup chopped onion
       1/4 cup chopped celery
     1-3/4 cups low-sodium chicken broth
         3 tablespoons cornstarch
     1-3/4 cups evaporated skim milk
         1 cup (4 ounces) finely shredded
           reduced-fat cheddar cheese

In a large saucepan, combine the potato, carrot, onion, celery and chicken broth. Cover and simmer until potato is tender, about 12 minutes. Mash mixture with a potato masher. Combine the cornstarch and milk until smooth; gradually add to vegetable mixture. Bring to a boil; cook and stir for 2 minutes or until thickened. Stir in the cheese until melted. **Yield:** 5 servings. **Nutritional Analysis:** One 1-cup serving equals 199 calories, 153 mg sodium, 20 mg cholesterol, 24 gm carbohydrate, 16 gm protein, 5 gm fat. **Diabetic Exchanges:** 1 skim milk, 1 meat, 1/2 starch.

▰▰▰▰▰▰▰▰▰▰▰▰
TERIYAKI BARLEY SALAD

(Pictured at left)

Bring a taste of the Orient to your own dinner table with this recipe shared by the National Barley Foods Council. It's a salad that tastes like a stir-fry! Try it and see if it doesn't perk up your next dinner.

     1-1/2 cups water
       1/2 cup medium pearl barley
       1/4 teaspoon salt
         2 medium carrots, thinly sliced
         8 ounces fresh *or* frozen snow peas
         2 cups cubed cooked chicken
         1 can (8 ounces) sliced water chestnuts,
           drained
         4 green onions, thinly sliced
       1/4 cup vegetable oil
       1/4 cup teriyaki *or* soy sauce
         1 tablespoon cider *or* white wine vinegar
       1/2 teaspoon garlic powder

1/4 teaspoon ground ginger *or* 1 teaspoon grated fresh gingerroot

In a saucepan, combine the water, barley and salt; bring to a boil. Reduce heat; cover and simmer for 45 minutes or until tender. Meanwhile, place carrots and a small amount of water in a pan; cover and cook for 2-3 minutes. Add peas; cook 1 minute longer or until crisp-tender. Drain. Combine barley, carrots, peas, chicken, water chestnuts and onions. In a jar with a tight-fitting lid, combine remaining ingredients; shake well. Pour over warm barley mixture and toss to coat. Refrigerate until serving. **Yield:** 6 servings.

WARM BEAN AND CHARD SALAD

Sandra Louth, Burlingame, California

This is one of those dishes I make when I'm bored with the usual fare. Chard is grown here, and it's delicious in this salad. It's nice to have a different kind of salad to share.

- 1 small red onion, chopped
- 1 tablespoon olive *or* vegetable oil
- 1/4 cup tomato paste
- 1 teaspoon honey
- 2 cans (15 ounces *each*) garbanzo beans, rinsed and drained
- 1 cup water
- 12 to 13 cups loosely packed julienned chard *or* spinach leaves (about 1-1/2 pounds)
- 1/2 teaspoon salt
- 1/4 teaspoon pepper

In a Dutch oven or a large saucepan, saute onion in oil until tender. Add tomato paste and honey; cook for 1 minute. Add the beans and water; bring to a boil. Add chard, salt and pepper; return to a boil. Reduce heat; cover and simmer for 15-25 minutes or until the greens are wilted. Serve immediately. **Yield:** 4-6 servings.

LEMONY CHICKEN FRUIT SALAD

Johnece Stuard, Mansfield, Texas

(Pictured above right)

Back in the 1950s, I was a home economist for the electric company, which is how I came across this recipe. My family especially likes it in summer months. I've also found it's good for potlucks and other gatherings since it's so different from other chicken salads.

- 2 cans (8 ounces *each*) pineapple chunks
- 1 medium apple, diced

- 3 cups cubed cooked chicken
- 1 cup seedless grapes, halved
- 3 tablespoons butter *or* margarine
- 3 tablespoons all-purpose flour
- 1/4 cup sugar
- 1 teaspoon salt
- 1/2 cup lemon juice
- 2 egg yolks, lightly beaten
- 1/2 cup whipping cream
Lettuce leaves
- 1/2 cup slivered almonds, toasted

Drain pineapple, reserving the juice. Set aside pineapple and 1/2 cup juice. Toss remaining juice with apple; drain. In a large bowl, combine chicken, grapes, pineapple and apple. Cover and refrigerate. In a saucepan, melt butter. Stir in flour, sugar and salt until smooth; gradually add lemon juice and the reserved pineapple juice. Bring to a boil; boil and stir for 2 minutes. Reduce heat. Add a small amount to egg yolks; return all to pan. Bring to a gentle boil; cook and stir for 2 minutes. Remove from the heat; chill for 10-15 minutes. Beat whipping cream until stiff peaks form; fold into cooled dressing. Pour over chicken mixture; gently stir to coat. Chill for 1 hour. Serve in a lettuce-lined bowl. Sprinkle with slivered almonds. **Yield:** 6-8 servings.

CHUNKY CHEESE SOUP

Gertrude Slabach, Virgilina, Virginia

Although winters in Virginia are not necessarily harsh, it still gets cold enough to chill you to the bone. This tasty soup warms you through and through. It's very cheesy and chock-full of ham and vegetables.

     2 cups water
     2 cups diced peeled potatoes
 1/2 cup diced carrot
 1/2 cup chopped celery
 1/4 cup chopped onion
 1-1/2 teaspoons salt
 1/4 teaspoon pepper
     1 cup cubed fully cooked ham*
 1/4 cup butter *or* margarine
 1/4 cup all-purpose flour
     2 cups milk
     2 cups (8 ounces) shredded cheddar cheese

In a large saucepan, combine the first seven ingredients; bring to a boil. Reduce heat; cover and simmer until the vegetables are tender. Add ham. In another saucepan, melt the butter; stir in flour until smooth. Gradually add milk. Bring to a boil; cook and stir for 2 minutes or until thickened. Stir in cheese until melted; add to the soup. **Yield:** 6-8 servings. ***Editor's Note:** In place of the ham, one of the following can be substituted—6 ounces of tuna or salmon; 1 cup of cooked ground beef or bulk pork sausage; or 1 pound of bacon, cooked and crumbled.

EASTERN SHORE SEAFOOD SALAD

Kimberly Brennan, Clear Spring, Maryland

(Pictured above)

We live just a short distance from the Chesapeake Bay area, so dishes featuring crabmeat are very popular here. This is a new recipe I came across that I think is extra special.

     1 pound cooked medium shrimp
     3 cups cooked *or* canned crabmeat,
        drained, flaked and cartilage removed
     1 small onion, chopped
     1 celery rib, thinly sliced
 1/2 cup mayonnaise
     2 teaspoons seafood seasoning
     1 teaspoon lemon juice
 1/2 teaspoon salt
 1/8 teaspoon pepper
Leaf lettuce, optional
     1 hard-cooked egg, sliced, optional

In a large bowl, combine shrimp, crab, onion and celery. In a small bowl, combine mayonnaise, seafood seasoning, lemon juice, salt and pepper; add to the shrimp mixture and mix gently. Cover and refrigerate for at least 1 hour. If desired, serve in a lettuce-lined bowl and garnish with egg. **Yield:** 6 servings.

GREEN BEAN POTATO SALAD

Bea Vrsaljko, Belle Chasse, Louisiana

I favor the flavor of green beans and find them a great companion to potatoes. A versatile side dish—add ham to make the salad a meal in itself—this one's among the recipes that I've invented myself. It's a delicious twist on ordinary potato salads.

 1-1/2 pounds small red potatoes, quartered
     1 garlic clove, peeled and halved
     2 cups cut fresh green beans (1-1/2-inch
        pieces)
     1 can (14-1/2 ounces) chicken broth
TARRAGON DRESSING:
     3 tablespoons olive *or* vegetable oil
     3 tablespoons cider vinegar
     1 garlic clove, minced
     1 tablespoon minced fresh parsley
     1 to 1-1/2 teaspoons minced fresh tarragon
        or 1/4 to 1/2 teaspoon dried tarragon
 1/2 teaspoon ground mustard
 1/2 teaspoon salt

1/4 teaspoon pepper
1/4 teaspoon Creole *or* Cajun seasoning
Lettuce leaves, optional

In a saucepan, cook potatoes and garlic in boiling salted water for 5 minutes. Add beans; cook 10-14 minutes longer or until vegetables are tender. Drain; discard garlic. Place vegetables in a bowl. Warm broth; pour over vegetables. Cover and refrigerate for at least 2 hours, stirring several times. In a small bowl, combine oil, vinegar and seasonings; mix well. Drain vegetables; add dressing and toss to coat. Serve in a lettuce-lined bowl if desired. **Yield:** 6-8 servings.

BROCCOLI CAULIFLOWER SALAD
Linda Kangas, Outlook, Saskatchewan

This salad has been to as many family gatherings as I have! It holds well…and leftovers are still tasty a day later. When I'm not trying out new recipes, I enjoy being an at-home mom to our nine children.

- 1 medium head cauliflower, broken into florets (about 7-1/2 cups)
- 1 medium bunch broccoli, cut into florets (about 4 cups)
- 2 cups seedless red grapes
- 6 green onions with tops, sliced
- 2 cups (8 ounces) shredded mozzarella cheese
- 2 cups mayonnaise
- 1/4 cup grated Parmesan cheese
- 2 tablespoons sugar
- 2 tablespoons vinegar
- 1/2 to 1 pound sliced bacon, cooked and crumbled

Leaf lettuce
Additional red grapes, optional

In a large bowl, combine the cauliflower, broccoli, grapes, onions and mozzarella cheese. Combine the mayonnaise, Parmesan cheese, sugar and vinegar; pour over vegetable mixture and toss to coat. Cover and refrigerate for at least 2 hours. Just before serving, stir in bacon. Transfer to a lettuce-lined bowl. Garnish with grapes if desired. **Yield:** 15-20 servings.

NEW ENGLAND POTATO SOUP
Priscilla Beaujon, Canandaigua, New York

(Pictured at right)

While on our honeymoon in New England, my husband and I walked into an old country store and were immediately swept off our feet by the aroma of soup that was cooking. We each ordered a bowl and found it to be absolutely delicious! We tried to persuade the cook to give us the recipe, but she said it was a secret. Upon returning home, I experimented until I came up with this recipe, which is very close.

- 1 medium onion, chopped
- 1 celery rib, thinly sliced
- 2 tablespoons butter *or* margarine
- 1 can (14-1/2 ounces) chicken broth
- 3 medium potatoes, peeled and cubed
- 1-1/2 teaspoons sugar
- 1/2 to 1 teaspoon salt
- 1/2 teaspoon dried rosemary, crushed
- 1/2 teaspoon dried thyme
- 1/8 to 1/4 teaspoon pepper
- 1/3 cup all-purpose flour
- 2-1/2 cups milk, *divided*
- 1-1/2 cups cubed fully cooked ham
- 1 cup frozen peas

In a saucepan, saute onion and celery in butter until tender. Add broth, potatoes, sugar, salt, rosemary, thyme and pepper; bring to a boil. Reduce heat; cover and simmer for 15-20 minutes or until potatoes are tender. Combine flour and 1/2 cup milk until smooth; gradually stir into soup. Bring to a boil; cook and stir for 2 minutes. Stir in ham, peas and remaining milk; heat through. **Yield:** 6-7 servings.

Side Dishes & Condiments

CHEDDAR-MUSHROOM STUFFED POTATOES

Jenean Schuetz, Longmont, Colorado

(Pictured at left)

To come up with this recipe, I just put together three of my family's favorite ingredients—potatoes, mushrooms and bacon. I prepare it as a quick-and-easy party dish. It's also a natural contribution to a potluck. And I serve it as an entree at times with a side vegetable.

6 large russet potatoes
2/3 cup whipping cream
1 cup (4 ounces) shredded cheddar cheese, *divided*
1/4 cup chopped fresh mushrooms
1/2 to 1 teaspoon garlic salt
1/2 teaspoon dried basil
1/2 teaspoon dried oregano
4 bacon strips, cooked and crumbled, *divided*

Bake potatoes at 375° for 1 hour or until tender. When cool enough to handle, cut a thin slice off the top of each potato and discard. Scoop out pulp, leaving a 1/4-in. shell; set shells aside. Place pulp in a mixing bowl; add cream and mash. Blend in 3/4 cup cheese, mushrooms, garlic salt, basil and oregano. Reserve 2 tablespoons bacon; stir the remaining bacon into potato mixture. Spoon into potato shells. Top with remaining cheese and bacon. Microwave on high for 5-8 minutes or bake, uncovered, at 375° for 25-30 minutes or until potatoes are heated through. **Yield:** 6 servings. **Editor's Note:** This recipe was tested in an 850-watt microwave.

GOLDEN MASHED POTATOES

Cindy Stith, Wickliffe, Kentucky

(Pictured at left)

When there's no gravy with the meat, this is great to serve in place of regular mashed potatoes. I make it often to take to picnics and church socials. My husband even made it for his family's reunion one year when I couldn't go!

9 large potatoes (about 4 pounds), peeled and cubed
1 pound carrots, cut into 1/2-inch chunks
8 green onions, thinly sliced
1/2 cup butter *or* margarine
1 cup (8 ounces) sour cream
1-1/2 teaspoons salt
1/8 teaspoon pepper
3/4 cup shredded cheddar cheese

In a soup kettle or Dutch oven, cook the potatoes and carrots in boiling salted water until tender; drain. Place in a mixing bowl; mash and set aside. In a skillet, saute onions in butter until tender. Add to potato mixture. Add sour cream, salt and pepper; mix until blended. Transfer to a greased 13-in. x 9-in. x 2-in. baking dish. Sprinkle with cheese. Bake, uncovered, at 350° for 30-40 minutes or until heated through. **Yield:** 10-12 servings.

HERBED GARLIC POTATOES

Sherry DesJardin, Fairbanks, Alaska

(Pictured at left)

My mom cooks from scratch and rarely uses a recipe. But it was actually my dad who invented this dish. The potatoes fit any kind of meal—fancy or burgers.

15 small red potatoes (about 2 pounds)
1/3 cup butter *or* margarine
1/4 cup minced fresh parsley
2 tablespoons minced fresh *or* dried chives
1-1/2 teaspoons minced fresh tarragon *or* 1/2 teaspoon dried tarragon
2 to 3 garlic cloves, minced
1/2 to 1 teaspoon salt
1/4 teaspoon pepper
3 bacon strips, cooked and crumbled, optional

Cut the potatoes in half and place in a saucepan; cover with water. Cover and bring to a boil; cook until tender, about 15 minutes. Drain well. In a large skillet, melt butter. Add the parsley, chives, tarragon and garlic; cook and stir over low heat for 1-2 minutes. Add the potatoes, salt, pepper and bacon if desired; toss to coat. Cook until heated through, about 5 minutes. **Yield:** 6-8 servings.

CHURCH SUPPER POTATOES

Michelle Grigsby, Beavercreek, Ohio

(Pictured on page 62)

As a pastor's wife, I cook for crowds often. This dish's always a hit. The recipe is very adaptable, and the results disappear.

  3 pounds russet potatoes (about 9 medium), peeled and cut into 1/2-inch cubes
  2 garlic cloves, peeled
  2 packages (3 ounces *each*) cream cheese, softened
  2 tablespoons butter *or* margarine
1/2 cup sour cream
  2 cups (8 ounces) shredded cheddar cheese, *divided*
  1 teaspoon garlic salt
  1 teaspoon onion salt
  1 package (10 ounces) frozen chopped spinach, thawed and squeezed dry

Place the potatoes and garlic in a large saucepan; cover with water. Cover and bring to a boil; cook for 20-25 minutes or until very tender. Drain well. In a mixing bowl, mash potatoes and garlic with the cream cheese and butter. Add sour cream, 1 cup of cheddar cheese, garlic salt, onion salt and spinach. Stir just until mixed. Spread into a greased 2-qt. baking dish. Bake, uncovered, at 350° for 30-35 minutes or until heated through. Top with remaining cheese; bake 5 minutes longer or until the cheese is melted. **Yield:** 10-12 servings.

COLORFUL OVEN VEGETABLES

Grace Ammann, Richfield, Minnesota

(Pictured below left)

As a party planner for a catering company, I often serve this attractive side dish with a steak dinner or at a brunch. Our two grown sons and their families often request these fresh-tasting, oven-roasted vegetables, too.

1/3 cup butter *or* margarine
1/2 teaspoon dried thyme
1/4 to 1/2 teaspoon salt
1/4 teaspoon pepper
  3 cups cauliflowerets
  2 cups broccoli florets
  6 medium carrots,* julienned
  3 small onions, quartered

Place butter in a shallow 3-qt. baking dish; place in a 400° oven for 5 minutes or until melted. Stir in thyme, salt and pepper. Add the vegetables and toss to coat. Cover and bake for 25-30 minutes or until the vegetables are crisp-tender. **Yield:** 10-12 servings. *****Editor's Note:** 2 cups baby carrots may be substituted; cut into julienne strips.

BREADED CAULIFLOWER

Sandra Furman-Krajewski, Amsterdam, New York

My mother gets the credit for this delicious dish, which is a mainstay at our house. It's wonderful served with turkey, roast beef or ham.

  1 small head cauliflower, broken into florets (about 5 cups)
  4 egg yolks
  1 teaspoon garlic powder
  1 teaspoon onion powder
  1 teaspoon minced fresh parsley
1/2 teaspoon sugar
1/2 teaspoon salt
1/4 teaspoon pepper
  1 cup seasoned bread crumbs
  3 tablespoons grated Parmesan cheese
3/4 cup butter *or* margarine
Minced fresh parsley, optional

Place cauliflower and a small amount of water in a skillet. Bring to a boil. Reduce heat; cover and

simmer until crisp-tender, about 8 minutes. Drain and set aside. In a bowl, whisk egg yolks and seasonings. Place bread crumbs and Parmesan cheese in a large resealable plastic bag. Add a few florets at a time to the egg mixture; toss to coat. Using a slotted spoon, transfer cauliflower to crumb mixture; toss to coat. In a skillet, melt the butter over medium-high heat. Cook cauliflower in batches until golden brown, about 4 minutes. Sprinkle with parsley if desired. **Yield:** 4-6 servings.

SPINACH ARTICHOKE PIE

Lori Coleman, Glassboro, New Jersey

Spinach is an abundant vegetable here in our state. I make this side dish often when spinach is in season.

    3 tablespoons vegetable oil, *divided*
    1/4 cup dry bread crumbs
    1/2 pound fresh mushrooms, sliced
    1 pound fresh spinach, chopped and
        cooked
    1 jar (6-1/2 ounces) marinated artichoke
        hearts, drained and quartered
    1 cup day-old bread cubes
    1-1/4 cups shredded cheddar cheese, *divided*
    1 jar (4 ounces) diced pimientos, drained
    2 eggs, beaten
    1/4 to 1/2 teaspoon garlic powder

Brush the bottom and sides of a 9-in. pie plate with 2 tablespoons oil; sprinkle with bread crumbs. Set aside. In a skillet, saute mushrooms in remaining oil; drain. Remove from the heat. Squeeze spinach dry; add to mushrooms. Stir in artichokes, bread cubes, 1 cup of cheese, pimientos, eggs and garlic powder; stir well. Spoon into the prepared pie plate. Bake, uncovered, at 350° for 30 minutes. Sprinkle with remaining cheese. Bake 5-10 minutes longer or until the cheese is melted. Let stand for 10 minutes before cutting. **Yield:** 6-8 servings.

BACON POTATO PANCAKES

Linda Hall, Hazel Green, Wisconsin

(Pictured above right)

Potatoes are something I can eat any time of day and almost any way. This recipe's one I came up with to go along with pigs in blankets several years ago.

5 to 6 medium uncooked red potatoes, peeled
        and shredded (3 cups)
    5 bacon strips, cooked and crumbled
    1/2 cup chopped onion

    2 eggs, beaten
    2 tablespoons all-purpose flour
Salt and pepper to taste
Dash ground nutmeg
Oil for frying

Rinse and thoroughly drain potatoes. In a bowl, combine the potatoes, bacon, onion, eggs, flour, salt, pepper and nutmeg. In an electric skillet, heat 1/8 in. of oil to 375°. Drop batter by 2 heaping tablespoonfuls into hot oil. Flatten to form patties. Fry until golden brown; turn and cook the other side. Drain on paper towels. **Yield:** 2 dozen.

PICKLED PUMPKIN

Myra Innes, Auburn, Kansas

Cubes of pickled pumpkin make a tasty addition to any meal. We like to have this side dish as part of our Thanksgiving feast. The recipe's a great way to use up any extra pumpkins you might have on hand.

    2 cups water
    1 cup sugar
3-1/2 cups cubed peeled pie pumpkin
    1/2 cup cider vinegar
    1 teaspoon whole cloves

In a saucepan, bring water and sugar to a boil; cook and stir for 5 minutes. Add pumpkin, vinegar and cloves. Reduce heat; simmer, uncovered, for 1 hour and 15 minutes or until pumpkin is tender. Discard cloves. Store in the refrigerator for up to 3 weeks. **Yield:** 4 cups.

CRABBY POTATOES

Suzanne Rawlings, Jacksonville, Florida

We have potato and crab festivals near our home. I combined the two ingredients into a recipe that gives potatoes a surprise taste.

> 3 large baking potatoes
> 1/2 cup butter *or* margarine, melted
> 2 tablespoons milk
> 1 tablespoon mayonnaise
> Salt and pepper to taste
> 2 cans (6 ounces *each*) crabmeat, drained, flaked and cartilage removed
> 3/4 cup shredded cheddar cheese, optional

Bake potatoes at 375° for 1 hour or until tender. Cool. Cut potatoes in half lengthwise. Scoop out the pulp and place in a mixing bowl; set shells aside. Add butter to pulp and mash. Beat in milk, mayonnaise, salt and pepper until smooth. Fold in crab. Spoon into potato shells. Place in an ungreased 11-in. x 7-in. x 2-in. baking dish. Sprinkle with cheese if desired. Bake, uncovered, at 350° for 30 minutes or until heated through. **Yield:** 6 servings.

SAVORY CAULIFLOWER PIE

Debbie Hart, Ft. Wayne, Indiana

(Pictured above)

If you're looking for a hearty side dish to take to a church potluck or family gathering, this pie is the perfect choice. It's a family favorite.

> 3 cups seasoned croutons, crushed
> 1/2 cup butter *or* margarine, melted, *divided*
> 1 small head cauliflower, cut into small florets (about 5 cups)
> 1 cup chopped onion
> 1/2 cup thinly sliced carrot
> 1 garlic clove, minced
> 1/2 teaspoon salt
> 1/4 to 1/2 teaspoon dried oregano
> 1 cup (4 ounces) shredded cheddar cheese, *divided*
> 2 eggs
> 1/4 cup milk

In a bowl, combine croutons and 1/4 cup butter. Press onto the bottom and up the sides of an ungreased 9-in. pie plate. Bake at 375° for 8 minutes or until lightly browned; set aside. In a large skillet, saute the cauliflower, onion, carrot, garlic, salt and oregano in remaining butter over medium heat for 10 minutes, stirring frequently. Sprinkle 1/2 cup cheese into prepared crust. Top with the cauliflower mixture and remaining cheese. In a bowl, beat the eggs and milk. Pour over pie. Bake, uncovered, at 375° for 30 minutes or until a knife inserted near the center comes out clean and the cauliflower is tender. **Yield:** 6-8 servings.

HOT PICANTE SAUCE

Diana Murphy, Black Earth, Wisconsin

It's hard to keep jars of this concoction in stock. My husband and I make the sauce from tomatoes and peppers we grow ourselves. It's so popular that we never seem to have enough.

> 18 cups quartered peeled fresh tomatoes (about 20 medium)
> 6 cups chopped onions (about 6 large)
> 2-1/4 cups chopped green peppers (about 2 medium)
> 2 cups sliced jalapeno peppers* (about 9)
> 2 cups vinegar
> 1-1/3 cups sliced sweet banana peppers* (about 6)
> 1/4 cup salt
> 1/4 cup sugar
> 2 tablespoons lemon juice
> 1 tablespoon dried oregano
> 1 teaspoon ground cumin
> 2 cans (12 ounces *each*) tomato paste

In a large kettle, combine the first 11 ingredients. Bring to a boil; reduce heat. Simmer, uncovered, for 2 hours, stirring occasionally. Stir in tomato paste. Simmer for 20 minutes, stirring frequently. Ladle hot mixture into hot jars, leaving 1/4-in. headspace. Adjust caps. Process for 20 minutes in a boiling-water bath. **Yield:** 10 pints. ***Editor's Note:** When handling hot peppers, use rubber or plastic gloves to protect your hands. Avoid touching your face.

Fresh Ideas for Florets

• When cooking broccoli, add the thicker stems to the boiling water first and cook for a couple of minutes before putting in the florets. —*Marilyn Janssen Dawson Creek, British Columbia*

• For an impressive presentation, surround a whole cauliflower head with broccoli florets on a large platter. Serve with cheese sauce alongside.
—*Helen Jones, Booneville, Mississippi*

• Plastic milk containers with bottoms removed act as a "greenhouse" when placed around young broccoli or cauliflower plants. —*Florence Lee Yankton, South Dakota*

• To reduce fat and calories in a broccoli salad, dress it with light mayonnaise thinned with cider vinegar and sweetened with a sugar substitute.
—*C. Anne Nielsen Lake Wylie, South Carolina*

• Serve your favorite broccoli or cauliflower soup in bread bowls made from frozen bread dough. Roll out thawed dough and shape over aluminum foil balls, then bake until golden brown.
—*Linda Martin, Central City, Iowa*

• A teaspoon of sugar added to the water when you're steaming broccoli will act as a flavor enhancer and help keep its bright green color. —*Sharon Bloom New Philadelphia, Ohio*

• For a different appearance and flavor, add some chopped fresh parsley or pimientos to your favorite cheese sauce before pouring it over cooked broccoli or cauliflower. —*Jnell Willford Piedmont, Missouri*

• Your broccoli harvest will last longer if you cut only open florets. You'll get several cuttings from each plant.
—*Tammy Vass, Hillsville, Virginia*

• To help cauliflower retain its color while cooking, add a small amount of nonfat dry milk to the cooking water.
—*Catherine Funk, Andover, Minnesota*

• In our area, broccoli planted for fall harvesting does not seem to have the aphid problems that spring-planted broccoli does. —*Dorcas Hauser Winston-Salem, North Carolina*

• Soak broccoli and cauliflower in a sinkful of salt water before cooking to bring out any insects.
—*Ann Rachel Hamelryck Westcliffe, Colorado*

• Add freshly ground nutmeg to your favorite cheese sauce for a different twist when making broccoli or cauliflower au gratin. —*Diane Halferty Corpus Christi, Texas*

• To give a nutty flavor to broccoli and cauliflower, drizzle melted butter over the hot cooked vegetables and sprinkle with toasted slivered almonds.
—*Kristy Deloach Hot Springs, Arkansas*

• When transplanting broccoli in your garden, wrap a strip of newspaper around each stem to keep the cutworms away.
—*Carolyn Manz, Tiffin, Ohio*

• Instead of cheese, add shredded carrots to your cauliflower or broccoli salad. They're colorful and low-calorie!
—*Ann Mlodzik, Ripon, Wisconsin*

ROSEMARY JELLY

Margaret Dumire, Carroll, Ohio

This deliciously different green jelly gets its flavor from an unusual source—savory rosemary. The herb adds a refreshing zip to the otherwise sweet spread.

> 1-1/4 cups boiling water
> 2 tablespoons minced fresh rosemary
> 3 cups sugar
> 1/4 cup vinegar
> 1 pouch (3 ounces) liquid fruit pectin
> 2 to 3 drops green food coloring

In a large saucepan, combine boiling water and rosemary; cover and let stand for 15 minutes. Strain, reserving liquid. If necessary, add water to measure 1-1/4 cups. Return liquid to pan; add sugar and vinegar. Bring to a full boil over high heat, stirring constantly. Add pectin, stirring until mixture boils. Boil and stir for 1 minute. Remove from the heat; skim off foam. Add food coloring if desired. Pour hot mixture into hot jars, leaving 1/4-in. headspace. Adjust caps. Process for 10 minutes in a boiling-water bath. **Yield:** 3-1/2 pints.

CORN STUFFING BALLS

Audrey Groe, Lake Mills, Iowa

(Pictured below)

My mom had many "winning" recipes, and this was one of our family's favorites. I can still picture these stuffing balls encircling the large meat platter piled high with one of her delicious entrees.

> 6 cups herb-seasoned stuffing croutons
> 1 cup chopped celery

> 1/2 cup chopped onion
> 3/4 cup butter *or* margarine, *divided*
> 1 can (14-3/4 ounces) cream-style corn
> 1 cup water
> 1-1/2 teaspoons poultry seasoning
> 3/4 teaspoon salt
> 1/4 teaspoon pepper
> 3 egg yolks, beaten

Place croutons in a large bowl and set aside. In a skillet, saute celery and onion in 1/2 cup butter. Add corn, water, poultry seasoning, salt and pepper; bring to a boil. Remove from heat; cool for 5 minutes. Pour over croutons. Add egg yolks; mix gently. Shape 1/2 cupfuls into balls; flatten slightly. Place in a greased 15-in. x 10-in. x 1-in. baking pan. Melt remaining butter; drizzle over stuffing balls. Bake, uncovered, at 375° for 30 minutes or until lightly browned. **Yield:** 12 servings.

ORANGE SPICED CARROTS

Mary MacKie, Winnipeg, Manitoba

I made these carrots for some out-of-town guests, and they were still raving about them 2 years later! I prefer them over plain carrots.

> 2-1/2 cups sliced carrots
> 1 tablespoon brown sugar
> 1-1/2 teaspoons cornstarch
> 1/2 cup orange juice
> 1/8 teaspoon ground ginger
> 1/8 teaspoon ground nutmeg
> Minced fresh parsley, optional

Place carrots in a saucepan; add 1 in. of water. Bring to a boil. Reduce heat; cover and simmer until crisp-tender, about 7-9 minutes. Drain; set aside and keep warm. In the same pan, combine brown sugar, cornstarch, orange juice, ginger and nutmeg until smooth. Bring to a boil; boil and stir for 1 minute. Return carrots to the pan; cook and stir over low heat until heated through. Sprinkle with parsley if desired. **Yield:** 5 servings.

LOW-FAT STUFFED POTATOES

Marcia Mundell, Bennett, Colorado

These stuffed potatoes may be low in fat, but they're loaded with flavor! Two kinds of cheese make them extra-creamy.

> ✓ Uses less fat, sugar or salt. Includes Nutritional Analysis and Diabetic Exchanges.

> 4 medium russet potatoes
> 1 cup fat-free cottage cheese
> 1/2 cup shredded light cheddar cheese

3 tablespoons nonfat yogurt
2 tablespoons snipped fresh dill *or* 2
   teaspoons dill weed
1 tablespoon light mayonnaise
1 tablespoon prepared mustard
1 tablespoon snipped chives
Pepper and cayenne pepper to taste
Paprika

Bake potatoes at 375° for 1 hour or until tender. When cool enough to handle, halve potatoes lengthwise. Scoop out the pulp, leaving a thin shell; set shells aside. In a mixing bowl, mash pulp, cottage cheese, cheddar cheese, yogurt, dill, mayonnaise, mustard, chives, pepper and cayenne. Spoon into the shells; sprinkle with paprika. Place in an ungreased shallow baking pan. Bake, uncovered, at 375° for 25-30 minutes or until heated through. **Yield:** 8 servings. **Nutritional Analysis:** One serving equals 120 calories, 140 mg sodium, 8 mg cholesterol, 17 gm carbohydrate, 8 gm protein, 2 gm fat. **Diabetic Exchanges:** 1 starch, 1 lean meat.

END OF SUMMER VEGETABLE BAKE

Judy Williams, Hayden, Idaho

(Pictured above right)

When my husband worked as a deputy ag commissioner, he'd bring me bushels of vegetables from area farms. This pretty side dish is the result—it's easy to fix but impressive enough for company.

1 small head cauliflower, broken into
   small florets (about 5 cups)
1 medium bunch broccoli, cut into small
   florets (about 4 cups)
1 medium onion, chopped
2 garlic cloves, minced
1 tablespoon butter *or* margarine
2 medium tomatoes, chopped
3/4 teaspoon dried basil
3/4 teaspoon dried oregano
3/4 teaspoon salt
1/4 teaspoon pepper
1/4 teaspoon hot pepper sauce
4 eggs
1/3 cup half-and-half cream
1-1/2 cups (6 ounces) shredded Swiss cheese,
   divided
1/4 cup shredded Parmesan cheese

Place the cauliflower and broccoli in a saucepan with a small amount of water. Bring to a boil. Reduce heat; cover and simmer for 5-10 minutes or until crisp-tender. Drain and set aside. In a large skillet, saute onion and garlic in butter until tender. Stir in tomatoes, seasonings, cauliflower and broccoli. Cook, uncovered, until heated through, about 4 minutes, stirring occasionally. Remove from the heat and set aside. In a large bowl, beat eggs and cream; stir in 1 cup Swiss cheese, Parmesan cheese and the vegetable mixture. Transfer to a greased shallow 2-qt. baking dish. Sprinkle with remaining Swiss cheese. Bake, uncovered, at 375° for 25-30 minutes or until a knife inserted near the center comes out clean. Let stand 10 minutes before serving. **Yield:** 12 servings.

CREAMY MUSTARD SAUCE

Estelle Harp, Shawnee, Oklahoma

Add extra zip to a ham dinner with this easy-to-fix sauce! The combination of mustard, mayonnaise and other ingredients nicely enhances the smoky flavor of ham.

1 tablespoon butter *or* margarine
1 tablespoon all-purpose flour
1 tablespoon ground mustard
1/3 cup water
1/3 cup vinegar
1/4 cup sugar
1/3 cup mayonnaise

In a saucepan, melt butter. Stir in flour and mustard until smooth. Add water, vinegar and sugar; mix well. Bring to a boil; cook and stir for 2 minutes or until slightly thickened. Remove from the heat; add mayonnaise and mix well. **Yield:** 1 cup.

Kids Open Wide for Crater 'Taters'!

YOU don't need to visit Mount St. Helens to "peak" at a volcano...just cook one up in your kitchen.

"Kids of all ages get a kick out of my Potato Volcano," reports Beatta Robben from Grinnell, Kansas. "I make it by mounding mashed potatoes into the shape of a mountain, putting a crater in the middle, and filling it with cheese sauce and drizzling some down the sides like lava. Then I broil it until it's bubbling and brown.

"It's such a curiosity—your family will ask for this deliciously different dish again and again."

And the compliments? They will come spewing forth!

POTATO VOLCANO

- 8 to 10 medium russet potatoes, peeled and cubed
- 1/4 to 1/2 cup milk
- 3 tablespoons butter *or* margarine
- 1/2 teaspoon salt

CHEESE SAUCE:
- 1 tablespoon butter *or* margarine
- 1 tablespoon all-purpose flour
- 3/4 cup milk
- 1-1/2 cups cubed process American cheese

Salt and pepper to taste

Place potatoes in a large saucepan and cover with water. Cover and bring to a boil; cook for 20-25 minutes or until very tender. Drain well; mash with milk. Add butter and salt; beat until fluffy. Mound potato mixture about 4 in. high on a 9-in. broiler-proof pan; set aside. In a saucepan, melt butter; stir in flour until smooth. Gradually add milk. Bring to a boil; cook and stir for 2 minutes or until thickened. Add cheese, salt and pepper; stir until the cheese is melted. With a large spoon, form a well 3 to 3-1/2 in. deep and 2 in. wide in the potato mixture. Pour cheese sauce into the well and drizzle down the sides. Broil 4 to 6 in. from the heat for 10 minutes or until the cheese sauce is browned and bubbling. **Yield:** 6 servings.

PIEROGI CASSEROLE

Margaret Popou, Kaslo, British Columbia

My husband never tires of this hearty casserole, no matter how many times I serve it. It's great for potlucks, too!

- 1 cup finely chopped onion
- 1/4 cup butter *or* margarine
- 2 cups (16 ounces) small-curd cottage cheese, drained
- 1 egg
- 1/4 teaspoon onion salt
- 2 cups mashed potatoes (prepared with milk and butter)
- 1 cup (4 ounces) shredded cheddar cheese
- 1/4 teaspoon salt
- 1/8 teaspoon pepper
- 9 lasagna noodles, cooked and drained

In a skillet, saute onion in butter until tender; set aside. In a bowl, combine cottage cheese, egg and onion salt. In another bowl, combine potatoes, cheddar cheese, salt and pepper. Place three noodles in a greased 13-in. x 9-in. x 2-in. baking dish. Top with cottage cheese mixture and three noodles. Top with potato mixture, remaining noodles and onion. Cover and bake at 350° for 25-30 minutes or until heated through. Let stand 10 minutes before serving. **Yield:** 12 servings.

EASY REFRIGERATOR PICKLES

Catherine Seibold, Elma, New York

This is a great way to use cucumbers and onions from the garden. Here in Upstate New York, we have an abundance of cucumbers.

- 6 cups thinly sliced cucumbers
- 2 cups thinly sliced onions
- 1-1/2 cups cider vinegar
- 1-1/2 cups sugar
- 1/2 teaspoon salt
- 1/2 teaspoon mustard seed
- 1/2 teaspoon celery seed
- 1/2 teaspoon ground turmeric
- 1/2 teaspoon ground cloves

Place cucumbers and onions in a large bowl; set aside. Combine remaining ingredients in a saucepan; bring to a boil. Cook and stir just until the sugar is dissolved. Pour over cucumber mixture; cool. Cover tightly and refrigerate for at least 24 hours before serving. **Yield:** 6 cups.

MUSHROOM WILD RICE BAKE

Lynn Kidder, Baxter, Minnesota

Wild rice is an important part of Minnesota history. This is an excellent-tasting dish and a very easy way to prepare wild rice.

    4 cups water
    4 beef bouillon cubes
    2 garlic cloves, minced
  1/2 cup uncooked wild rice, rinsed
  1/2 cup uncooked long grain rice
    1 jar (4-1/2 ounces) sliced mushrooms,
      drained
  1/4 cup butter *or* margarine

In a saucepan, combine water, bouillon, garlic and wild rice; bring to a boil over medium heat. Reduce heat; cover and simmer for 30 minutes. Add long grain rice; cover and simmer for 20-25 minutes or until the rice is tender. Stir in mushrooms and butter. Transfer to an ungreased 8-in. square baking dish. Bake, uncovered, at 350° for 30-40 minutes or until liquid is absorbed. **Yield:** 6-8 servings.

SWISS POTATO SQUARES

Nancy Foust, Stoneboro, Pennsylvania

(Pictured at right)

To vary these squares, you can substitute cheddar cheese for the Swiss or use Canadian bacon instead of ham. However you make them, they taste wonderful.

    8 medium russet potatoes (about 3
      pounds), peeled and cubed
  1/3 cup butter *or* margarine, melted
    1 tablespoon minced fresh parsley
  1-1/2 teaspoons salt
  1/4 teaspoon pepper
  1-1/2 cups cubed Swiss cheese
    1 cup cubed fully cooked ham
    1 small onion, grated
    1 teaspoon garlic powder
    3 eggs
  1/2 cup milk
Paprika

Place potatoes in a saucepan and cover with water. Cover and bring to a boil; cook for 20-25 minutes or until very tender. Drain well. Mash with butter, parsley, salt and pepper. Spread about 4

cups of the potato mixture onto the bottom and up the sides of a greased 8-in. square baking dish. Combine cheese, ham, onion and garlic powder; spoon into potato shell. Combine eggs and milk; pour over all. Top with remaining potato mixture. Sprinkle with paprika. Bake, uncovered, at 400° for 45-50 minutes or until golden. Let stand 5 minutes before cutting. **Yield:** 8-9 servings.

COTTAGE MASHED POTATOES

Veronica Teipel, Manchester, Missouri

These scrumptious spuds have pounds of meal appeal! They offer a rich texture and nutty taste that will have folks coming back for more.

    4 cups warm mashed potatoes
      (without added milk and butter)
    2 cups (16 ounces) small-curd cottage
      cheese
  3/4 cup sour cream
    1 to 2 tablespoons grated onion
  1-1/2 to 2 teaspoons salt
  1/2 teaspoon pepper
    2 tablespoons butter *or* margarine, melted
  1/4 cup sliced almonds, toasted

In a bowl, combine potatoes, cottage cheese, sour cream, onion, salt and pepper. Transfer to a greased 2-qt. baking dish. Drizzle with butter. Bake, uncovered, at 350° for 30 minutes. Sprinkle with almonds. Bake 5 minutes longer or until heated through. **Yield:** 6-8 servings.

1 tablespoon butter *or* margarine
1 can (10-3/4 ounces) condensed cream of celery soup, undiluted
1/2 cup milk
1 teaspoon Worcestershire sauce
1/8 teaspoon hot pepper sauce
2 packages (16 ounces *each*) frozen French-style green beans, thawed and drained
1 can (8 ounces) sliced water chestnuts, drained
1 cup (4 ounces) shredded cheddar cheese

In a skillet, saute the red pepper and onion in butter until tender. Add the soup, milk, Worcestershire sauce and hot pepper sauce; stir until smooth. Stir in the green beans and water chestnuts. Transfer to an ungreased 1-1/2-qt. baking dish. Sprinkle with cheese. Bake, uncovered, at 350° for 15 minutes or until heated through and cheese is melted. **Yield:** 6-8 servings.

CRISPY POTATO WEDGES

Gloria Mumm, Staples, Minnesota

These potatoes were an instant hit with my family and are requested often. I like that they're so quick and easy to prepare.

2 tablespoons vegetable oil
1 teaspoon salt
1/2 teaspoon *each* dried basil, oregano and thyme
1/4 teaspoon pepper
1/4 teaspoon paprika
6 medium potatoes, cut into wedges
1/4 cup grated Parmesan cheese

In a bowl, combine oil and seasonings. Add potato wedges and stir to coat. Arrange in a single layer in an ungreased 15-in. x 10-in. x 1-in. baking pan. Bake, uncovered, at 450° for 15 minutes. Sprinkle with cheese; bake 10-15 minutes longer or until potatoes are crisp-tender. **Yield:** 6 servings.

FESTIVE GREEN BEAN CASSEROLE

June Mullins, Livonia, Missouri
(Pictured above)

This recipe came from a cookbook my son gave to me over 20 years ago. It's a tasty dish that I make often for family get-togethers and potluck suppers.

1 cup chopped sweet red pepper
1 small onion, finely chopped

ORIENTAL CAULIFLOWER

Carol Krueger, Pewaukee, Wisconsin

Every time I make this simple Asian-style side dish starring cauliflower I get requests for the recipe. No one can believe how easy it is to make.

1 medium head cauliflower, broken into florets
3 tablespoons cold water, *divided*
1/2 cup diced celery
1 small onion, finely chopped
1/4 cup minced fresh parsley
1 tablespoon butter *or* margarine
1 cup hot water
1 tablespoon chicken bouillon granules
2 tablespoons cornstarch
1 tablespoon soy sauce
Dash pepper

Place cauliflower in a microwave-safe dish. Add 1 tablespoon cold water. Cover and microwave on high for 6-7 minutes or until tender; drain and set aside. In a 1-qt. microwave-safe bowl, combine celery, onion, parsley and butter. Cover and microwave on high for 1-2 minutes or until vegetables are tender. In a small bowl, combine hot water and bouillon until dissolved. In another small bowl, combine the cornstarch and remaining cold water until smooth. Add soy sauce, pepper and bouillon; mix well. Stir into celery mixture. Microwave, uncovered, at 70% power for 3-4 minutes or until sauce comes to a boil, stirring after each minute. Pour over cauliflower. **Yield:** 4-6 servings. **Editor's Note:** This recipe was tested in an 850-watt microwave.

Side Dishes & Condiments

A Handful of Hot Potato Hints

• For a different "crunch" in potato salad, add fresh cauliflower, broccoli or your favorite chopped nuts.
—*Bertha Dunbar, Lewiston, Maine*

• Leftover baked potatoes can make good potato salad or soup.
—*Elsie Keith, Trion, Georgia*

• Instant mashed potato flakes do a good job thickening soups and chowders. Just make sure the soup is hot before adding the flakes. —*Donna Bitz Swift Current, Saskatchewan*

• To prevent potatoes from darkening when boiling, add a small amount of milk to the water. —*Nancy Stratford Island Park, Idaho*

• A pinch of baking soda added to mashed potatoes makes them fluffier.
—*Johnnie Goodrich, Muldoon, Texas*

• Rather than bread crumbs or oatmeal, mix a handful or two of potato flakes into meatballs or meat loaf.
To add flavor and help thicken gravy, use the water from boiled potatoes.
—*Lillian Carlson, Richfield, Minnesota*

• Just a little dried minced garlic or garlic powder livens up mashed potatoes.
—*Alice Ewers, Portland, Oregon*

• For extra-nutritious potato soup, try adding a package of frozen mixed vegetables. —*Melissa Spratto Elmendorf AFB, Alaska*

• By adjusting the baking time, you can bake potatoes with other items at a range of heat from 325° to 450°.
—*Linda Bacon, Hancock, Wisconsin*

• To make a wonderful cream sauce for potatoes and veggies, use the potato water mixed with powdered milk, flour and butter. You can add seasonings, too!
—*Connie Reavie Fort St. John, British Columbia*

• Whenever you boil or steam potatoes, save the water and use it to replace the liquid that's called for in yeast bread recipes. The loaves always turn out more moist and flavorful. —*Melissa Hoehn Burnie, Tasmania*

• For a very smooth-textured potato soup, try pureeing potatoes (slightly cooled) with chicken broth in your blender. —*Carla Gagnon Kelowna, British Columbia*

• Give potato salad a beautiful presentation by serving individual portions in halved green or sweet red peppers.
—*Ruth Hewell, Porterdale, Georgia*

• If you buy potatoes at the grocery, take a bag from the bottom of the pile. It will have had the least exposure to light, which can cause greening.
Store potatoes where it's cool and dark—but not in the refrigerator.
—*Nancy Schlegel Valley View, Pennsylvania*

• To give potato soup "punch", add a couple chopped jalapeno peppers.
—*Pamela Winningham Byrdstown, Tennessee*

• When making cheesy potato dishes, coat your grater lightly with nonstick cooking spray beforehand. Cleanup is a breeze! —*Marjorie Dorscht Teeswater, Ontario*

GRILLED THREE-CHEESE POTATOES

Margaret Hanson-Maddox
Montpelier, Indiana
(Pictured below)

While this is delicious grilled, I've also cooked it in the oven at 350° for an hour. Add cubed ham to it and you can serve it as a full-meal main dish.

6 large potatoes, sliced 1/4 inch thick
2 medium onions, chopped
1/3 cup grated Parmesan cheese
1 cup (4 ounces) shredded sharp cheddar cheese, *divided*
1 cup (4 ounces) shredded mozzarella cheese, *divided*
1 pound sliced bacon, cooked and crumbled
1/4 cup butter *or* margarine, cubed
1 tablespoon minced fresh or dried chives
1 to 2 teaspoons seasoned salt
1/2 teaspoon pepper

Divide the potatoes and onions equally between two pieces of heavy-duty foil (about 18-in. square) that have been coated with nonstick cooking spray. Combine Parmesan cheese and 3/4 cup each cheddar and mozzarella; sprinkle over potatoes and onions. Top with bacon, butter, chives, seasoned salt and pepper. Bring opposite ends of foil together over filling and fold down several times. Fold unsealed ends toward filling and crimp tightly. Grill, covered, over medium heat for 35-40 minutes or until potatoes are tender. Remove from the grill. Open foil carefully and sprinkle with remaining cheeses. **Yield:** 6-8 servings.

WILD RICE FLORET BAKE

Donna Torgerson, Park Rapids, Minnesota

My mom used to make this hearty side dish for family get-togethers. Now I do the same when our five grown children come to visit.

1 medium onion, chopped
3 tablespoons butter *or* margarine
2 tablespoons all-purpose flour
1/2 teaspoon salt
Dash pepper
2 cups milk
1 cup (8 ounces) sour cream
1 cup (4 ounces) shredded cheddar cheese, *divided*
4 cups cooked wild rice, *divided*
6 cups chopped cooked broccoli (about 1 large bunch)
5 cups chopped cooked cauliflower (about 1 small head)
6 bacon strips, cooked and crumbled

In a saucepan, saute the onion in butter until tender. Stir in flour, salt and pepper until blended. Gradually add milk. Bring to a boil; cook and stir for 2 minutes or until thickened and bubbly. Remove from the heat; stir in sour cream and 1/2 cup cheese until smooth. Place 2 cups wild rice in a greased 13-in. x 9-in. x 2-in. baking dish. Top with broccoli and cauliflower. Place remaining wild rice lengthwise down the center of dish. Pour the sauce over all. Sprinkle with remaining cheese. Cover and bake at 350° for 20 minutes. Uncover; sprinkle with bacon. Bake 10-15 minutes longer or until bubbly. **Yield:** 8-10 servings.

CRISPY BAKED CAULIFLOWER

Elvera Dallman, Franklin, Nebraska

I make this simple side dish often. It's so tasty, no one ever realizes it's good for them as well.

✓ **Uses less fat, sugar or salt. Includes Nutritional Analysis and Diabetic Exchanges.**

4 cups cauliflowerets
6 tablespoons all-purpose flour
1/4 teaspoon garlic powder
1/4 teaspoon paprika

1/4 teaspoon pepper
2-1/2 cups cornflakes, crushed
2 egg whites

Place cauliflower in a saucepan with a small amount of water. Cover and cook for 5-10 minutes or until crisp-tender; drain. In a small resealable plastic bag, combine flour, garlic powder, paprika and pepper. Place cornflake crumbs in another resealable bag. Lightly beat egg whites in a shallow bowl. Toss the cauliflowerets one at a time in flour mixture, then roll in egg whites and coat with crumbs. Place on a baking sheet coated with nonstick cooking spray. Bake at 425° for 15-20 minutes or until golden brown. Serve immediately. **Yield:** 6 servings. **Nutritional Analysis:** One serving equals 92 calories, 145 mg sodium, 0 cholesterol, 19 gm carbohydrate, 4 gm protein, trace fat. **Diabetic Exchanges:** 1 starch, 1 vegetable.

RANCH POTATOES

Elaine Eavenson, Moselle, Massachusetts

I sometime substitute cream of chicken soup for the cream of mushroom. Even the "particular eaters" in my family love these potatoes.

    8 to 10 medium potatoes, peeled and cut into 1/2-inch cubes
    1 can (10-3/4 ounces) condensed cream of mushroom soup, undiluted
1-1/4 cups milk
    1 envelope ranch salad dressing mix
1-1/4 cups shredded sharp cheddar cheese, *divided*
Salt and pepper to taste
    6 bacon strips, cooked and crumbled

Place potatoes in a saucepan and cover with water. Bring to a boil; cook until almost tender, about 10 minutes. Drain; place in a greased 13-in. x 9-in. x 2-in. baking dish. Combine soup, milk, salad dressing mix, 1 cup cheese, salt and pepper; pour over potatoes. Top with bacon and remaining cheese. Bake, uncovered, at 350° for 25-30 minutes or until potatoes are tender. **Yield:** 10 servings.

HARVEST PUMPKIN BUTTER

Marlene Muckenhirn, Delano, Minnesota

Stir up a fresh alternative to traditional apple butter by making this scrumptious spread. It's yummy on English muffins or any kind of toasted bread.

    1 cup cooked *or* canned pumpkin
    1/2 cup honey

    1/4 cup molasses
    1 tablespoon lemon juice
    3/4 teaspoon ground cinnamon

In a small saucepan, combine all of the ingredients; mix well. Bring to a boil, stirring frequently. Reduce heat; simmer, uncovered, for 15 minutes or until thickened. Refrigerate for at least 1 hour. **Yield:** 1-1/4 cups.

BROCCOLI CORN CASSEROLE

Beverly Griggs, Roseburg, Oregon

(Pictured above)

Here's a wonderful vegetable dish that's a little different. Give it a try and see if your family likes it as much as mine does.

1-1/2 cups crushed cornflakes, *divided*
1-1/4 cups soft bread crumbs (about 2 slices), *divided*
    1/3 cup butter *or* margarine, melted, *divided*
    1 can (14-3/4 ounces) cream-style corn
    1 package (10 ounces) frozen chopped broccoli, thawed
    2 eggs
    2 tablespoons chopped onion
    1 teaspoon salt
    1/8 teaspoon pepper

In a bowl combine 1/4 cup of cornflake crumbs and 1/3 cup bread crumbs. Drizzle with 2 tablespoons butter and toss to coat; set aside. In a large bowl, combine the corn, broccoli, eggs, onion, salt, pepper and the remaining cornflakes, bread crumbs and butter. Transfer to a greased 1-1/2-qt. baking dish. Sprinkle with reserved crumb mixture. Bake, uncovered, at 350° for 45 minutes or until heated through. **Yield:** 4-6 servings.

IN "KNEAD" *of new bread and roll recipes? A basketful of these fresh-from-the-oven goodies is sure to please.*

FRESHLY BAKED BREAD. Clockwise from top: Bubble Bread Wreath (p. 78), Orange Banana Nut Bread (p. 78) and Mashed Potato Cinnamon Rolls (p. 77).

Breads & Rolls

MASHED POTATO CINNAMON ROLLS

Christine Duncan, Ellensburg, Washington

(Pictured at left)

A neighbor gave me the recipe for these yummy rolls. They're warm and wonderful to serve for breakfast or as a treat any time of day. I often make extra mashed potatoes with these cinnamon rolls in mind.

- 1/2 pound russet potatoes, peeled and quartered
- 2 packages (1/4 ounce *each*) active dry yeast
- 2 tablespoons sugar
- 2 cups warm water (110° to 115°)
- 3/4 cup butter *or* margarine, melted
- 2 eggs, beaten
- 3/4 cup sugar
- 2/3 cup instant nonfat dry milk powder
- 1 tablespoon salt
- 2 teaspoons vanilla extract
- 8 to 8-1/2 cups all-purpose flour

FILLING:

- 1/2 cup butter *or* margarine, melted
- 3/4 cup packed brown sugar
- 3 tablespoons ground cinnamon

ICING:

- 2 cups confectioners' sugar
- 1/4 cup milk
- 2 tablespoons butter *or* margarine, melted
- 1/2 teaspoon vanilla extract

Place potatoes in a saucepan and cover with water. Bring to a boil; cook until tender. Drain, reserving 1/2 cup cooking liquid; set aside. Mash potatoes; set aside 1 cup. (Save remaining potatoes for another use.) Heat reserved potato liquid to 110°-115°. In a mixing bowl, dissolve yeast and sugar in potato liquid; let stand 10 minutes. Add warm water, mashed potatoes, butter, eggs, sugar, milk powder, salt, vanilla and 5 cups flour; beat until smooth. Add enough remaining flour to form a soft dough. Turn onto a floured surface; knead until smooth and elastic, about 6-8 minutes. Place in a greased bowl, turning once to grease top. Cover and chill overnight. Punch dough down; divide into thirds. On a floured surface, roll each portion into a 12-in. x 8-in. rectangle; spread with butter. Combine brown sugar and cinnamon; sprinkle over the dough. Roll up from a long side; pinch seam to seal. Cut each into 12 slices; place cut side down in three greased 13-in. x 9-in. x 2-in. baking pans. Cover and let rise until almost doubled, 45 minutes. Bake at 350° for 25-30 minutes. Combine sugar, milk, butter and vanilla; drizzle over rolls. **Yield:** 3 dozen.

PUMPKIN STREUSEL MUFFINS

Denise Nebel, Wayland, Iowa

Tucked into the middle of each moist muffin is a tasty surprise—in the shape of a cube of cream cheese! The simple filling adds loads of creamy flavor, and the streusel topping is nice and crunchy.

- 1-3/4 cups all-purpose flour
- 1/2 cup sugar
- 1 tablespoon baking powder
- 1 teaspoon ground cinnamon
- 1/2 teaspoon salt
- 1/2 teaspoon ground nutmeg
- 1 egg
- 1/2 cup milk
- 1/2 cup cooked *or* canned pumpkin
- 1/3 cup vegetable oil
- 1 package (3 ounces) cream cheese, cut into 12 cubes

STREUSEL:

- 1/4 cup packed brown sugar
- 1/4 cup chopped pecans
- 1 teaspoon ground cinnamon
- 1 tablespoon cold butter *or* margarine

In a bowl, combine the first six ingredients. In another bowl, beat the egg; add milk, pumpkin and oil. Stir into dry ingredients just until moistened. Fill 12 greased or paper-lined muffin cups half full. Place a cream cheese cube in the center of each. Top with remaining batter. For streusel, combine the brown sugar, pecans and cinnamon in a small bowl. Cut in the butter until crumbly. Sprinkle over batter. Bake at 400° for 18-22 minutes or until muffins test done. Cool for 5 minutes before removing from pan to a wire rack to cool completely. **Yield:** 1 dozen.

POPPY SEED ROLLS

Dottie Miller, Jonesborough, Tennessee

(Pictured below)

I've made these often for Sunday dinner, and they are delicious! There's nothing like homemade rolls to top off a meal.

    1 package (1/4 ounce) active dry yeast
    1/4 cup warm water (110° to 115°)
    1/4 cup plus 1 teaspoon sugar, *divided*
    1 cup warm milk (110° to 115°)
    1/2 cup shortening
    1-1/2 teaspoons salt
    1 egg, beaten
    3-3/4 to 4 cups all-purpose flour
Butter *or* margarine, melted
Poppy seeds

In a mixing bowl, dissolve yeast in water. Add 1 teaspoon of sugar; let stand for 5 minutes. Beat in milk, shortening, salt, egg and remaining sugar. Add enough flour to form a soft dough. Turn onto a floured surface; knead until smooth and elastic, about 6-8 minutes. Place in a greased bowl, turning once to grease top. Cover and let rise in a warm place until doubled, about 1 hour. Punch the dough down. Divide into 18 portions; shape into balls. Place in greased muffin cups. Cover and let rise until doubled, about 30 minutes. Brush tops with but-

ter; sprinkle with poppy seeds. Bake at 375° for 11-13 minutes or until golden brown. Remove from pans to wire racks. **Yield:** 1-1/2 dozen.

ORANGE BANANA NUT BREAD

Barbara Roethlisberger, Shepherd, Michigan

(Pictured on page 76)

I like this recipe because the orange juice gives the bread such a unique flavor and makes it moist. It's a tasty twist on regular banana bread.

    1-1/2 cups sugar
    3 tablespoons vegetable oil
    2 eggs
    3 medium ripe bananas, mashed (about
        1-1/4 cups)
    3/4 cup orange juice
    3 cups all-purpose flour
    1-1/2 teaspoons baking powder
    1-1/2 teaspoons baking soda
    1/2 teaspoon salt
    1 cup chopped walnuts

In a mixing bowl, combine the sugar, oil and eggs; mix well. Stir in bananas and orange juice. Combine the dry ingredients; add to banana mixture, beating just until moistened. Stir in walnuts. Pour into two greased 8-in. x 4-in. x 2-in. loaf pans. Bake at 325° for 50-60 minutes or until a toothpick inserted near the center comes out clean. Cool for 10 minutes; remove from pans to a wire rack to cool completely. **Yield:** 2 loaves.

BUBBLE BREAD WREATH

Sylvia Petker, Port Rowan, Ontario

(Pictured on page 76)

Every year, I bake about 20 of these wreaths to give as gifts and more for our family Christmas brunch. The bread pulls apart easily, so it's a cinch to serve.

    2 tablespoons active dry yeast
    1 tablespoon plus 1/2 cup sugar, *divided*
    1 cup warm water (110° to 115°)
    2 cups warm milk (110° to 115°)
    1-2/3 cups butter *or* margarine, softened,
        divided
    2 eggs, beaten
    1 tablespoon salt
    8 cups all-purpose flour
    1 cup chopped red and green candied
        cherries, *divided*
    1-1/3 cups chopped pecans, *divided*
SYRUP:
    1 cup light corn syrup

6 tablespoons butter *or* margarine
2 teaspoons vanilla extract

In a large mixing bowl, dissolve yeast and 1 tablespoon sugar in water. Let stand for 10 minutes. Add milk, 2/3 cup butter, eggs, salt and remaining sugar. Stir in enough flour to form a soft dough. Turn onto a floured surface; knead until smooth and elastic, about 6-8 minutes. Place in a greased bowl, turning once to grease top. Cover and let rise in a warm place until doubled, about 45 minutes. Punch dough down; shape into 1-1/2-in. balls. Divide half of the balls between two greased 10-in. fluted tube pans. In each pan, arrange 1/4 cup cherries in spaces between balls; sprinkle with about 1/3 cup pecans. Melt the remaining butter; drizzle 1/4 cup over each pan. Repeat the layers once. Cover and let rise until nearly doubled, about 20 minutes. Bake at 350° for 40-45 minutes or until golden brown. Cool 10 minutes before inverting onto wire racks. Meanwhile, in a saucepan, heat syrup ingredients. Brush over warm loaves. **Yield:** 2 loaves. **Editor's Note:** For easiest removal, cool loaves in pans for only 10 minutes.

ROSEMARY APRICOT LOAVES

Audrey Thibodeau, Mesa, Arizona

You'll love the herby fragrance that rosemary gives to these deliciously different apricot loaves as they're baking in the oven.

1-1/2 cups apricot nectar
1-1/2 cups chopped pitted dates
1/2 cup chopped dried apricots
1 tablespoon grated orange peel
1-1/4 teaspoons dried rosemary, crushed
1/2 cup butter *or* margarine, softened
1 cup sugar
1 egg
1/3 cup evaporated milk
2-1/4 cups all-purpose flour
1-1/2 teaspoons baking soda

In a saucepan, combine apricot nectar, dates and apricots. Bring to a boil. Reduce heat; cover and simmer for 5 minutes. Remove from the heat. Stir in orange peel and rosemary; cool for 10-15 minutes. In a mixing bowl, cream butter and sugar. Add egg and milk. Combine flour and baking soda; add to creamed mixture alternately with date mixture, beating just until combined. Pour into two greased and floured 8-in. x 4-in. x 2-in. loaf pans. Bake at 375° for 35-45 minutes or until a toothpick inserted near the center comes out clean. Cool for 10 minutes; remove from pans to wire racks. **Yield:** 2 loaves.

CHIVE-CHEESE CORN BREAD

Sybil Eades, Gainesville, Georgia

(Pictured above)

This corn bread goes well with any main dish. The chives and cheddar cheese give it a special flavor.

1 cup cornmeal
1 cup all-purpose flour
1/4 cup sugar
4 teaspoons baking powder
2 eggs
1 cup milk
1/4 cup butter *or* margarine, melted
1 cup (4 ounces) shredded sharp cheddar cheese
3 tablespoons minced chives

In a large bowl, combine cornmeal, flour, sugar and baking powder. In another bowl, whisk the eggs, milk and butter. Stir into dry ingredients just until moistened. Gently fold in cheese and chives. Pour into a greased 13-in. x 9-in. x 2-in. baking pan. Bake at 400° for 18 minutes or until golden brown. Cut into strips; serve warm. **Yield:** 12-15 servings.

and place on greased baking sheets. Bake at 400° for 15 minutes or until golden brown. Combine sugar and cinnamon in a small bowl. Brush pretzels with butter, then dip in cinnamon-sugar. Serve warm. **Yield:** 14 pretzels.

BABY BASIL-ZUCCHINI MUFFINS

Marion Lowery, Medford, Oregon

These delicious treats make the most of the basil and zucchini I grow. The aroma during baking is so tempting, my family flocks to the kitchen to grab muffins for snacking. I've learned to always mix up a double batch so I have enough for dinner!

2-1/2 cups all-purpose flour
1/4 cup sugar
3 tablespoons minced fresh basil *or* 1 tablespoon dried basil
1 tablespoon baking powder
1 teaspoon salt
2 eggs
3/4 cup milk
2/3 cup vegetable oil
2 cups finely shredded peeled zucchini
1/2 cup grated Parmesan cheese

In a bowl, combine the first five ingredients. In another bowl, beat eggs, milk and oil; stir into dry ingredients just until moistened. Fold in zucchini. Fill greased or paper-lined miniature muffin cups two-thirds full. Sprinkle with cheese. Bake at 400° for 12-15 minutes or until the muffins test done. Cool for 5 minutes before removing from pans to wire racks to cool completely. **Yield:** about 4-1/2 dozen.

CINNAMON-RAISIN SOFT PRETZELS

Susie King, Quarryville, Pennsylvania

(Pictured above)

I came up with this recipe after sampling pretzels at a Pennsylvania Dutch farmer's market. They're quicker than cinnamon rolls and easy for kids to eat.

1 package (1/4 ounce) active dry yeast
1-1/2 cups warm water (110° to 115°)
2 tablespoons brown sugar
1 teaspoon salt
2 cups cake flour
2 to 2-1/4 cups all-purpose flour
3/4 cup raisins
2 tablespoons baking soda
2 cups hot water (120° to 130°)
3 tablespoons butter *or* margarine, melted
3/4 cup sugar
1 teaspoon ground cinnamon

In a large bowl, dissolve yeast in warm water. Stir in brown sugar and salt. Add cake flour; stir well. Add enough all-purpose flour to form a soft dough. Stir in raisins. Turn onto a floured surface; knead until smooth and elastic, about 6-8 minutes. Place in a greased bowl, turning once to grease top. Cover and let rise in a warm place until dough has risen slightly, about 30 minutes. Punch dough down; divide into 14 balls. Roll each ball into a 15-in. rope. In a bowl, dissolve baking soda in hot water. Dip each rope in baking soda mixture; drain on paper towels. Form into pretzel shapes

WALNUT CREAM BRAID

Jean Erickson, North Pole, Alaska

I make this pretty plaited bread each December for family and friends. It's become a tasty tradition we all look forward to. The nutty cheese filling is so good!

1 package (1/4 ounce) active dry yeast
1/4 cup warm water (110° to 115°)
1/2 cup butter *or* margarine, softened
2 tablespoons sugar
1/2 teaspoon salt
1 egg
2 to 2-1/2 cups all-purpose flour
FILLING:
2 packages (3 ounces *each*) cream cheese, softened
3/4 cup sugar
1/2 cup finely chopped walnuts
Confectioners' sugar, optional

In a mixing bowl, dissolve yeast in water. Add butter, sugar, salt, egg and 1-1/2 cups flour; beat on low for 3 minutes, scraping bowl occasionally. Add enough remaining flour to form a soft dough. Turn onto a floured surface; knead until smooth and elastic, about 6-8 minutes. Place in a greased bowl, turning once to grease top. Cover and let rise in a warm place until doubled, about 1 hour. Meanwhile, in a small mixing bowl, beat the cream cheese and sugar; set aside. Punch dough down; divide in half. On a floured surface, roll each portion into a 12-in. x 8-in. rectangle and place on greased baking sheets. Spread half of the filling down the center third of each rectangle. Sprinkle with walnuts. On each long side, cut 1-in.-wide strips about 2-1/2 in. into center. Starting at one end, fold alternating strips at an angle across filling. Seal ends. Cover and let rise for 30 minutes. Bake at 375° for 15-20 minutes or until browned. Cool on wire racks. Dust with confectioners' sugar if desired. **Yield:** 2 loaves.

▪▪▪▪▪▪▪▪▪▪▪▪▪▪
PEACH COBBLER BREAD

Amy Maindelle, Jonesboro, Georgia

(Pictured below right)

I developed this recipe to take advantage of our wonderful Georgia peaches. My husband says it tastes just like peach cobbler.

    1/3 cup butter *or* margarine, softened
      1 cup sugar
      2 eggs
    1/3 cup water
      1 teaspoon vanilla extract
    1/8 teaspoon almond extract
      1 cup diced peeled peaches
  1-2/3 cups all-purpose flour
      1 teaspoon baking soda
    1/2 teaspoon salt
    1/4 teaspoon baking powder
    1/2 cup chopped pecans
TOPPING:
      2 tablespoons chopped pecans
      2 tablespoons brown sugar

In a mixing bowl, cream butter and sugar. Add the eggs, one at a time, beating well after each addition. Beat in water and extracts. Stir in peaches. Combine flour, baking soda, salt and baking powder; gradually add to the creamed mixture. Stir in pecans. Pour into a greased 9-in. x 5-in. x 3-in. loaf pan. Combine topping ingredients; sprinkle over batter. Bake at 350° for 50-55 minutes or until a toothpick inserted near the center comes out clean. Cool for 10 minutes before removing from pan to a wire rack. **Yield:** 1 loaf.

▪▪▪▪▪▪▪▪▪▪▪▪▪▪
CHEESE BATTER BREAD

Shirley Ramsey, Wymore, Nebraska

Hearty breads are very much a part of our Midwest heritage. This bread has a unique flavor and is a family favorite.

      1 package (1/4 ounce) active dry yeast
      1 cup warm chicken broth (110° to 115°)
      1 tablespoon butter *or* margarine
      2 tablespoons sugar
    1/2 teaspoon salt
    1/2 teaspoon poultry seasoning
      1 egg, beaten
      3 cups all-purpose flour, *divided*
  1-1/4 cups finely shredded cheddar cheese, *divided*
Onion salt, optional

In a mixing bowl, dissolve yeast in broth. Add butter, sugar, salt, poultry seasoning, egg and 1 cup of flour; beat until smooth, about 1 minute. Add 1 cup of cheese and the remaining flour; stir for 1 minute. Cover and let rise in a warm place until doubled, about 30 minutes. Stir the batter about 25 strokes. Spread evenly into a greased 9-in. x 5-in. x 3-in. loaf pan. Cover and let rise until doubled, about 20 minutes. Sprinkle with the remaining cheese and onion salt if desired. Bake at 375° for 25-30 minutes or until golden brown. Remove from the pan and serve warm. **Yield:** 1 loaf.

THESE rapid breads provide home-baked goodness in record time without all the hassle.

QUICK BREADS. Clockwise from top right: Blueberry Orange Bread (p. 84), Bacon Cheddar Round (p. 84), Fruit 'n' Nut Mini Loaves (p. 84), Raisin Banana Bread (p. 85) and Spiced Pumpkin Bread (p. 84).

▞▞▞▞▞▞▞▞▞▞▞
BLUEBERRY ORANGE BREAD

Donna Smith, Victor, New York

(Pictured on page 83)

Plump ripe blueberries and orange juice bring a refreshing and fruity flavor to this special golden loaf. One slice is never enough!

      2 cups all-purpose flour
      1 cup sugar
      1 teaspoon baking powder
    1/2 teaspoon baking soda
    1/2 teaspoon salt
      1 egg
    1/2 cup orange juice
    1/3 cup water
      2 tablespoons butter *or* margarine, melted
      2 tablespoons grated orange peel
    3/4 cup fresh *or* frozen blueberries

In a large bowl, combine the first five ingredients. In another bowl, combine egg, orange juice, water, butter and orange peel. Add to dry ingredients just until combined. Fold in the blueberries. Pour into a greased and floured 8-in. x 4-in. x 2-in. loaf pan. Bake at 350° for 65-70 minutes or until a toothpick inserted near the center comes out clean. Cool for 10 minutes; remove from pan to a wire rack. **Yield:** 1 loaf.

▞▞▞▞▞▞▞▞▞▞▞
SPICED PUMPKIN BREAD

Ruby Williams, Bogalusa, Louisiana

(Pictured on page 82)

Cloves, cinnamon and molasses add plenty of spice to this appealing pumpkin bread. You needn't wait 'til autumn to make it—you can use convenient canned pumpkin any time of year!

    3/4 cup butter *or* margarine, softened
      2 cups sugar
      4 eggs
      2 cups cooked *or* canned pumpkin
    2/3 cup orange juice
      2 tablespoons molasses
  1-1/2 teaspoons vanilla extract
  3-1/3 cups all-purpose flour
      1 teaspoon baking powder
      1 teaspoon baking soda
      1 teaspoon salt
      1 teaspoon ground cinnamon
    3/4 to 1 teaspoon ground cloves
      1 cup raisins
      1 cup chopped pecans

In a mixing bowl, cream butter and sugar. Add the eggs, one at a time, beating well after each addition. Add pumpkin, orange juice, molasses and vanilla. Combine dry ingredients; add to creamed mixture and mix until blended. Stir in remaining ingredients. Pour into two greased and floured 9-in. x 5-in. x 3-in. loaf pans. Bake at 350° for 65-75 minutes or until a toothpick inserted near the center comes out clean. Cool for 10 minutes; remove from pans to wire racks. **Yield:** 2 loaves.

▞▞▞▞▞▞▞▞▞▞▞
FRUIT 'N' NUT MINI LOAVES

Judi Oudekerk, Buffalo, Minnesota

(Pictured on page 82)

Every slice of these pretty mini loaves is loaded with fruit and nuts. Use red and green maraschino cherries at Christmas for added color.

  1-1/2 cups all-purpose flour
  1-1/2 cups sugar
      1 teaspoon baking powder
    1/2 teaspoon salt
      1 pound dried apricots *or* dates, halved
      1 pound Brazil nuts
      1 cup pecan halves
      1 jar (10 ounces) maraschino cherries, drained
      5 eggs
      1 teaspoon vanilla extract

In a large bowl, combine the first four ingredients. Add apricots, nuts and cherries; mix well. Beat eggs and vanilla; stir into the dry ingredients just until moistened. Spoon into eight greased and floured 4-1/2-in. x 2-1/2-in. x 1-1/2-in. loaf pans (pans will be full). Bake at 325° for 40-50 minutes or until a toothpick inserted near the center comes out clean. Cool for 10 minutes; remove from the pans to wire racks. Cool completely before slicing. **Yield:** 8 mini loaves.

▞▞▞▞▞▞▞▞▞▞▞
BACON CHEDDAR ROUND

Dorothy Collins, Winnsboro, Texas

(Pictured on page 83)

I often stir up a "round" of this cheesy bread. With just six ingredients, the moist bread mixes up in minutes. Of course, it gets gobbled up quickly, too!

  3-1/2 cups biscuit/baking mix
    1/4 cup sugar
  1-1/2 cups (6 ounces) shredded cheddar cheese

6 bacon strips, cooked and crumbled
1 egg
1-1/3 cups milk

In a large bowl, combine the biscuit mix and sugar. Stir in cheese and bacon. Beat egg and milk; add to cheese mixture just until moistened. Pour into a greased and floured 9-in. springform pan. Bake at 350° for 35-40 minutes or until a toothpick inserted near the center comes out clean. Cool for 10 minutes; remove sides of pan and serve warm. **Yield:** 1 loaf.

RAISIN BANANA BREAD

Margaret Hinman, Burlington, Iowa

(Pictured on page 82)

Grated carrots and zucchini, plus raisins and walnuts, bring a wonderful blend of flavors to this out-of-the-ordinary banana bread.

 3 cups all-purpose flour
 2 cups sugar
 1 teaspoon baking powder
 1 teaspoon salt
 1 teaspoon pumpkin pie spice
1/2 teaspoon baking soda
1/2 teaspoon ground cinnamon
 3 eggs
 1 cup vegetable oil
 2 teaspoons vanilla extract
 1 cup grated zucchini
 1 cup grated carrot
1/2 cup mashed ripe banana

1/2 cup raisins
1/2 cup chopped walnuts

In a mixing bowl, combine the first seven ingredients. Add eggs, oil and vanilla; mix well. Stir in zucchini, carrot, banana, raisins and nuts. Pour into four greased and floured 5-3/4-in. x 3-in. x 2-in. loaf pans. Bake at 350° for 45-48 minutes or until a toothpick inserted near the center comes out clean. Cool for 10 minutes; remove from the pans to wire racks. **Yield:** 4 loaves.

SHAMROCK BISCUITS

(Pictured below)

Just the right mix of seasonings flavors these simple-to-fix biscuits baked by the Reiman Publications test kitchen staff. Garlic, Parmesan cheese and oregano add a tasty twist to standard refrigerated dough. Using a cookie cutter to form shamrocks gives them a festive flair for gatherings all through spring.

 1 tube (17.3 ounces) large refrigerated
     biscuits
1/4 cup butter or margarine, melted
 2 tablespoons grated Parmesan cheese
 1 garlic clove, minced
1/4 teaspoon dried oregano

Cut biscuits into shamrock shapes with a 2-in. cookie cutter or knife; discard trimmings. Place biscuits on an ungreased baking sheet. Bake at 375° for 11-15 minutes or until golden brown. Combine remaining ingredients; brush over warm biscuits. **Yield:** 10 biscuits.

These Easter Bunnies Are on a Roll

EVEN the Easter Bunny's bound to be impressed by a basketful of these funny bunnies brightening your dinner table!

Bonnie Myers of Callaway, Nebraska shared the scrumptious recipe for Herb Dinner Rolls. Then our Reiman Publications test kitchen staff came up with the clever idea of shaping the dough into rabbits.

So if you're planning an Easter feast, why not hop to it and roll out a bevy of bunnies? They'll multiply quicker than you think...and your hearty eaters will "cotton" to them!

HERB DINNER ROLLS

1 package (1/4 ounce) active dry yeast
1/4 cup warm water (110° to 115°)
3/4 cup warm milk (110° to 115°)
2 tablespoons sugar
2 tablespoons shortening
1 egg, beaten
2 teaspoons celery seed
1 teaspoon rubbed sage
1 teaspoon salt
1/2 teaspoon ground nutmeg
3 to 3-1/2 cups all-purpose flour
Melted butter *or* margarine

In a mixing bowl, dissolve yeast in water. Add milk, sugar, shortening, egg, celery seed, sage, salt, nutmeg and 3 cups flour; beat until smooth. Add enough remaining flour to form a soft dough. Turn onto a floured surface; knead until smooth and elastic, about 6-8 minutes. Place in a greased bowl, turning once to grease top. Cover and let rise in a warm place until doubled, about 1-1/2 hours. Punch dough down; let rest 10 minutes. Shape into 30 balls; place on greased baking sheets. Cover and let rise until doubled, about 45 minutes. Brush tops with butter. Bake at 375° for 10-12 minutes or until lightly browned. Cool on wire racks. **Yield:** 2-1/2 dozen.

EASTER BUNNY ROLLS

Prepare the dough for Herb Dinner Rolls. Divide dough into 24 pieces. For each bunny, roll one piece of dough into an 18-in. rope. Cut rope into one 10-in. piece, one 5-in. piece and three 1-in. pieces. Coil 10-in. piece for body; place on a greased baking sheet. Coil 5-in. piece for head; place next to body. Form ears from two 2-in. pieces; place next to head. Form tail from third 1-in. piece; place next to body. Pinch and seal pieces together. Repeat, placing bunnies 2 in. apart on the baking sheet. Cover and let rise until doubled, about 45 minutes. Bake at 375° for 10-12 minutes or until lightly browned. Cool on wire racks. **Yield:** 2 dozen.

BROCCOLI CORN BREAD

Lois Triplet, Springhill, Louisiana

This recipe was inspired by my husband's love of corn bread. It's so moist and tasty, he and folks who dine with us (like our two children) eat it plain, though it's also good alongside soups and stews.

    1 cup plus 1 tablespoon cornmeal, *divided*
    1/3 cup all-purpose flour
  1-1/2 teaspoons baking powder
    3/4 teaspoon salt
    1/4 teaspoon baking soda
      5 eggs, beaten
      1 package (10 ounces) frozen chopped
        broccoli, thawed and drained
  1-1/2 cups (6 ounces) shredded cheddar
        cheese
  1-1/2 cups (12 ounces) small-curd cottage
        cheese
      1 medium onion, chopped
    3/4 cup butter *or* margarine, melted

In a bowl, combine 1 cup of cornmeal, flour, baking powder, salt and baking soda. In another bowl, combine the eggs, broccoli, cheeses, onion and butter. Add to cornmeal mixture; mix just until moistened. Sprinkle remaining cornmeal in a greased 13-in. x 9-in. x 2-in. baking pan. Pour batter into pan. Bake at 350° for 30-40 minutes or until a toothpick inserted near the center comes out clean. Serve warm. **Yield:** 12-15 servings.

CHOCOLATE ZUCCHINI BREAD

Charlotte McDaniel, Williamsville, Illinois

You'd never guess zucchini is the "secret ingredient" in this easy-to-assemble bread—it has such big chocolate taste! I freeze extra zucchini from my garden in summer and make this bread to give as gifts all winter long.

      3 cups all-purpose flour
      3 cups sugar
    1/2 cup baking cocoa
  1-1/2 teaspoons baking powder
  1-1/2 teaspoons baking soda
      1 teaspoon salt
    1/4 teaspoon ground cinnamon
      4 eggs
  1-1/2 cups vegetable oil
      2 tablespoons butter *or* margarine, melted
  1-1/2 teaspoons vanilla extract
  1-1/2 teaspoons almond extract
      3 cups grated zucchini
      1 cup chopped pecans
    1/2 cup raisins

In a large bowl, combine the first seven ingredients. Combine the eggs, oil, butter and extracts; mix well. Stir into dry ingredients just until moistened. Fold in zucchini, pecans and raisins. Pour into three greased and floured 8-in. x 4-in. x 2-in. loaf pans. Bake at 350° for 55-60 minutes or until a toothpick inserted near the center comes out clean. Cool for 10 minutes; remove from the pans to wire racks. **Yield:** 3 loaves.

CARAWAY CLOVERLEAF ROLLS

Ruth Reid, Jackson, Minnesota

(Pictured below)

I've taken these rolls to numerous get-togethers and have received many compliments. Folks around here love to bake, so there's always good eating at our socials.

      2 packages (1/4 ounce *each*) active dry
        yeast
  1-1/2 cups warm water (110° to 115°)
      1 cup whole wheat flour
    1/2 cup sugar
    1/2 cup vegetable oil
      2 teaspoons caraway seeds
  1-1/2 teaspoons salt
  3-1/2 to 4 cups all-purpose flour

In a mixing bowl, dissolve yeast in water. Add whole wheat flour, sugar, oil, caraway, salt and 2 cups all-purpose flour; beat until smooth. Add enough of the remaining all-purpose flour to form a soft dough. Turn onto a floured surface; knead until smooth and elastic, about 6-8 minutes. Place in a greased bowl, turning once to grease top. Cover and let rise in a warm place until doubled, about 1 hour. Punch dough down. Divide in half, then divide each half into 36 pieces. Shape into balls; place three balls each in greased muffin cups. Cover and let rise until doubled, about 30 minutes. Bake at 375° for 15-18 minutes or until golden brown. **Yield:** 2 dozen.

PARMESAN CHEESE STICKS

Katherine Goss, Wildomar, California

I love to share with guests these buttery, cheesy sticks, which melt in your mouth. They always receive plenty of compliments. It's such an easy way to liven up simple slices of bread.

    2 eggs
1/2 cup milk
  12 slices bread, crusts removed
1-1/2 cups grated Parmesan cheese
    1 tablespoon dried parsley flakes
1/2 cup butter *or* margarine, melted

In a bowl, beat eggs and milk. Dip four slices of bread into egg mixture; place each between two plain slices. Cut each stack into three strips. Combine Parmesan cheese and parsley. Dip all sides of each strip in butter; roll in cheese mixture. Place 2 in. apart on an ungreased baking sheet. Bake at 375° for 10-12 minutes or until lightly browned. Serve warm. **Yield:** 1 dozen. **Editor's Note:** Unbaked cheese sticks may be frozen for up to 4 months. Bake as directed.

APPLE NUT BREAD

June Mullins, Livonia, Missouri

A friend brought a loaf of this bread to a ladies' church meeting at my house. It was still warm from the oven—what a mouth-watering aroma! My family likes the nutty texture and fresh apple flavor.

1/2 cup butter *or* margarine, softened
    1 cup plus 2 tablespoons sugar, *divided*
    2 eggs
    1 cup grated peeled apple
    2 cups all-purpose flour
    1 teaspoon baking soda
1/2 teaspoon salt
    2 tablespoons buttermilk
1/2 teaspoon vanilla extract
    1 cup chopped nuts
3/4 teaspoon ground cinnamon

In a mixing bowl, cream the butter and 1 cup sugar. Add eggs, one at a time, beating well after each addition. Stir in apple. Combine the flour, baking soda and salt; add to creamed mixture alternately with buttermilk. Stir in vanilla and nuts. Pour into a greased and floured 9-in. x 5-in. x 3-in. loaf pan. Combine cinnamon and remaining sugar; sprinkle over batter. Bake at 350° for 60-65 minutes or until a toothpick inserted near the center comes out clean. Cool for 10 minutes; remove from pan to a wire rack. **Yield:** 1 loaf.

SWEET CORN BREAD

Virginia Hanker, Essex Junction, Vermont

(Pictured above)

This slightly sweet corn bread goes well with just about any main dish, soup or salad. I always make it when we have a hot bowl of chili. The sour cream makes it nice and moist.

    1 cup all-purpose flour
    1 cup cornmeal
1/4 cup sugar
    2 teaspoons baking powder
1/2 teaspoon salt
    1 egg
    1 cup (8 ounces) sour cream
1/3 cup milk
1/4 cup butter *or* margarine, softened

In a bowl, combine the first five ingredients. In another bowl, combine the egg, sour cream, milk and butter; stir into dry ingredients just until moistened. Pour into a greased 8-in. square baking pan. Bake at 400° for 20-25 minutes or until a toothpick inserted near the center comes out clean. Serve warm. **Yield:** 9 servings.

THREE-FLOUR BRAID

(Pictured below)

Audrey Benson, Flagler, Colorado

Beautiful sliced or whole, this very pretty multicolored bread freezes well so you can enjoy it any time of year. And it tastes as great as it looks!

- 2 packages (1/4 ounce *each*) active dry yeast
- 2-1/4 cups warm water (110° to 115°)
- 1/4 cup vegetable oil
- 2 tablespoons sugar
- 1 teaspoon salt
- 3-1/4 cups all-purpose flour

RYE DOUGH:
- 2 tablespoons molasses
- 1 tablespoon baking cocoa
- 1 teaspoon caraway seed
- 1-1/4 cups rye flour

WHEAT DOUGH:
- 2 tablespoons molasses
- 1 cup whole wheat flour

WHITE DOUGH:
- 1-1/4 cups all-purpose flour
- 1 tablespoon butter *or* margarine, melted

In a large mixing bowl, dissolve yeast in water. Add oil, sugar, salt and 2-1/4 cups flour; beat for 2 minutes. Add remaining flour; beat for 2 minutes. Divide evenly into three mixing bowls. To the first bowl, add molasses, cocoa and caraway seed; mix well. Gradually add rye flour. Turn onto a floured surface; knead until smooth and elastic, about 6-8 minutes. Place in a greased bowl, turning once to grease top. Cover and set aside. To the second bowl, add molasses; mix well. Gradually add whole wheat flour. Turn onto a floured surface; knead until smooth and elastic, about 6-8 minutes. Place in a greased bowl, turning once to grease top. Cover and set aside. To the third bowl, gradually add all-purpose flour. Turn onto a floured surface; knead until smooth and elastic, about 6-8 minutes. Place in a greased bowl, turning once to grease top. Cover all three bowls and let rise in a warm place until doubled, about 1 hour. Punch doughs down; divide each in half. Shape each half into a 15-in. rope. Place a rope of each dough on a greased baking sheet and braid. Seal ends. Repeat with remaining ropes. Cover and let rise until nearly doubled, about 30 minutes. Bake at 350° for 25-30 minutes or until golden brown. Brush with butter. **Yield:** 2 loaves. **Editor's Note:** Use all-purpose flour on kneading surface for all three doughs.

TURN ANY DAY into a special occasion by treating family and friends to generous slices of cake, scrumptious cookies and sweet confections.

SWEET REWARDS. Clockwise from top left: Raspberry Truffles (p. 91), English Toffee Bars (p. 91), Buttery Almond Crunch (p. 91) and Maple Peanut Delights (p. 92).

Cakes, Cookies & Candies

ENGLISH TOFFEE BARS

Dianne Brooks, Augusta, Kansas

(Pictured at left)

My mother and I get together every year around Christmastime to make this delicious chocolate-coated toffee, using a recipe she got years ago in a cooking class. It's a tradition I plan to continue with my daughters and grandchildren.

1 tablespoon plus 1-3/4 cups butter
  (no substitutes), softened, *divided*
2 cups sugar
1 tablespoon light corn syrup
1 cup chopped pecans
1/4 teaspoon salt
1 pound milk chocolate candy coating

Butter a 15-in. x 10-in. x 1-in. baking pan with 1 tablespoon butter; set aside. In a heavy 3-qt. saucepan, melt the remaining butter. Add sugar and corn syrup; cook and stir over medium heat until a candy thermometer reads 295° (soft-crack stage). Remove from the heat; stir in pecans and salt. Quickly pour into prepared pan. Let stand for 5 minutes. Using a sharp knife, score into squares; cut along scored lines. Let stand at room temperature until cool. Separate into squares, using a sharp knife if necessary. In a microwave or heavy saucepan, melt candy coating, stirring often. Dip squares, one at a time, in coating. Place on waxed paper until set. **Yield:** 2-1/4 pounds. **Editor's Note:** We recommend that you test your candy thermometer before each use by bringing water to a boil; the thermometer should read 212°. Adjust your recipe temperature up or down based on your test.

BUTTERY ALMOND CRUNCH

Mildred Clothier, Oregon, Illinois

(Pictured at left)

This delectable candy is crisp but not as hard as peanut brittle. Some people say it reminds them of the toffee center of a well-known candy bar.

1 tablespoon plus 1/2 cup butter
  (no substitutes), softened, *divided*
1/2 cup sugar
1 tablespoon light corn syrup
1 cup sliced almonds

Line an 8-in. square pan with foil; butter the foil with 1/2 tablespoon butter. Set aside. Spread the sides of a heavy saucepan with 1/2 tablespoon butter. Add 1/2 cup of butter, sugar and corn syrup. Bring to a boil over medium-high heat, stirring constantly. Cook and stir until mixture is golden brown, about 3 minutes. Stir in almonds. Quickly pour into prepared pan. Refrigerate until firm. Invert pan and remove foil. Break candy into pieces. **Yield:** 10 ounces.

RASPBERRY TRUFFLES

Helen Vail, Glenside, Pennsylvania

(Pictured at left)

Christmas is my very favorite time of year. I make many cookies, cakes and candies—including this easy but elegant recipe—to give to relatives and friends. The aroma of the chocolate and raspberry is heavenly when you're making these truffles.

1 tablespoon butter (no substitutes)
2 tablespoons whipping cream
1-1/3 cups semisweet chocolate chips
7-1/2 teaspoons seedless raspberry jam
6 ounces white *or* dark chocolate candy
  coating
2 tablespoons shortening

In a heavy saucepan, combine butter, cream and chocolate chips. Cook over low heat for 4-5 minutes or until chocolate is melted. Remove from the heat; stir in jam until combined. Transfer to a small freezer container; cover and freeze for 20 minutes. Drop by teaspoonfuls onto a foil-lined baking sheet. Freeze for 15 minutes. Roll into balls; freeze until very firm. In a microwave or heavy saucepan, melt candy coating and shortening, stirring often. Cool slightly; spoon over balls. Place on a wire rack over waxed paper. Let stand for 15 minutes or until firm. Store in an airtight container in the refrigerator. **Yield:** 4 dozen.

Grandma's Candy Pleases Crowds

MAPLE PEANUT DELIGHTS are a flavorful favorite with all of Katie Stutzman's candy-loving Amish family.

"I never have to hunt for helpers when I'm making it," says this grandma from Goshen, Indiana. "Our 17 grandchildren stand in line when it's time for mixing, dipping and nibbling.

"This recipe can't be beat for holiday treats, get-togethers or gifts. Luckily, one batch is enough to please a crowd," conveys Katie.

"Now and then, I'll substitute some chopped pecans for the peanuts. Or, I'll spread the maple mixture into a pan, pour the coating and nuts on top and cut the candy into squares.

"Since the recipe is flexible, I've even adapted it into a sweet family tradition. Each of our five children received a 5-pound candy-coated maple egg as a wedding present."

MAPLE PEANUT DELIGHTS

(Pictured on page 90)

1 package (8 ounces) cream cheese, softened
1/2 cup butter (no substitutes), softened
6 cups confectioners' sugar
1 teaspoon maple flavoring
2 pounds dark chocolate candy coating
1 cup chopped peanuts

In a mixing bowl, beat cream cheese, butter, confectioners' sugar and flavoring until smooth. Cover and refrigerate for 1 hour. Shape into 1-in. balls. In a heavy saucepan (or microwave), melt candy coating, stirring often. Dip balls in coating; sprinkle with peanuts. Place on waxed paper-lined baking sheets. Refrigerate. **Yield:** about 8 dozen.

CHOCOLATE CUPCAKES

Margaret Hooper, Winchester, New Hampshire

If your family is a fan of chocolate, they're going to love these scrumptious cupcakes.

3 cups all-purpose flour
2 cups sugar
3/4 cup baking cocoa
2 teaspoons baking soda
1 teaspoon salt
2 cups water
2/3 cup vegetable oil
2 tablespoons vinegar
2 teaspoons vanilla extract
FROSTING:
1/2 cup butter *or* margarine, softened
1/2 cup shortening
1 teaspoon vanilla extract
4 cups confectioners' sugar
3 tablespoons milk

In a bowl, combine the first five ingredients. In another bowl, combine the water, oil, vinegar and vanilla; stir into dry ingredients just until combined. Pour into greased muffin cups. Bake at 350° for 20-25 minutes or until a toothpick inserted near the center comes out clean. Cool for 10 minutes; remove to wire racks. In a mixing bowl, cream butter, shortening and vanilla. Add confectioners' sugar alternately with milk. Frost cupcakes. **Yield:** 1-1/2 dozen.

APPLE PIE COOKIES

Sharon Smith, Neosho, Missouri

These sandwich cutouts with apple filling were taste-tested by my grandchildren, so they're certified kid-pleasers! To save time, you can use purchased pie filling for the centers. Or instead of "painting" the tops with food coloring, sprinkle them with cinnamon.

1/2 cup shortening
1 cup sugar
1 egg
1/2 cup milk
1 teaspoon vanilla extract
3-1/2 cups all-purpose flour
2 teaspoons cream of tartar
1 teaspoon baking soda
1 teaspoon salt
FILLING:
1/2 cup packed brown sugar
2 teaspoons all-purpose flour
1/2 teaspoon ground cinnamon
3 medium tart apples, peeled and grated (about 2 cups)

3/4 cup water
GLAZE:
    4 tablespoons water
Red and green liquid food coloring

In a mixing bowl, cream shortening and sugar. Beat in egg, milk and vanilla. Combine flour, cream of tartar, baking soda and salt; gradually add to creamed mixture. Divide in half. Refrigerate for 2-3 hours or until easy to handle (dough will be soft). Meanwhile, combine filling ingredients in a saucepan. Cook over medium heat until apples are softened and mixture is thickened; cool. On a lightly floured surface, roll out each portion of dough to 1/8-in. thickness. Cut with a 2-1/2-in. apple cookie cutter dipped in flour. Place 2 in. apart on ungreased baking sheets. Spread with 2 teaspoons of filling to within 1/4 in. of edge. Top with another cutout and seal edges. Bake at 375° for 10-12 minutes or until lightly browned. Cool on wire racks. In a small bowl, combine 3 tablespoons water and 18 drops red food coloring. In another bowl, combine remaining water and 6 drops green food coloring. Using a pastry brush, "paint" apples red with green leaves. **Yield:** 2 dozen.

BANANA PECAN TORTE

Linda Fryar, Stanton, Texas

(Pictured below right)

The state tree of Texas is the pecan tree, so this impressive-looking cake definitely represents my area. A friend shared the recipe with me. It's been in her family for years.

    1 cup butter *or* margarine, softened
2-1/2 cups sugar
    4 eggs
    2 cups mashed ripe bananas (about 4 medium)
    2 teaspoons vanilla extract
3-1/2 cups all-purpose flour
    2 teaspoons baking soda
    3/4 teaspoon salt
    1/2 cup buttermilk
    1 cup chopped pecans, toasted
FROSTING:
    1 package (8 ounces) cream cheese, softened
    1/2 cup butter *or* margarine, softened
3-1/2 cups confectioners' sugar
    1 teaspoon vanilla extract
Toasted chopped pecans

In a mixing bowl, cream butter and sugar. Add the eggs, one at a time, beating well after each addition. Beat in bananas and vanilla. Combine dry ingredients; add to creamed mixture alternately with buttermilk. Stir in pecans. Pour into three greased and floured 9-in. round cake pans. Bake at 350° for 30-35 minutes or until a toothpick inserted near the center comes out clean. Cool in pans 10 minutes; remove to wire racks to cool completely. For frosting, beat cream cheese, butter and sugar in a small mixing bowl. Add vanilla. Spread between layers and on top of cake. Sprinkle with pecans. **Yield:** 12-16 servings.

SWEDISH SPRITZ COOKIES

Irmgard Sinn, Sherwood Park, Alberta

Every Christmas, my daughter and I have a 1-day cookie-making spree. We roll out more than 60 dozen cookies, including these mouth-watering morsels.

    1 cup butter (no substitutes), softened
2/3 cup sugar
    1 egg
1/2 teaspoon almond extract
1/2 teaspoon vanilla extract
2-1/4 cups all-purpose flour
    1 teaspoon baking powder
Frosting

In a mixing bowl, cream butter and sugar until light and fluffy. Beat in egg and extracts. Combine the flour and baking powder; gradually add to the creamed mixture. Using a cookie press fitted with disk of your choice, press dough into desired shapes 1 in. apart on ungreased baking sheets. Bake at 400° for 7-9 minutes or until edges are firm and lightly browned. Remove to wire racks to cool. Frost as desired. **Yield:** 4-5 dozen.

▚▚▚▚▚▚▚▚▚▚▚▚▚
RAISIN PEANUT BUTTER BALLS

Lorna Gunter, Kemmerer, Wyoming

My daughter, who is a diabetic, can't get enough of this candy. But even folks without special diet needs gobble it up as well.

> ✓ **Uses less fat, sugar or salt. Includes Nutritional Analysis and Diabetic Exchanges.**

  1/2 cup flaked coconut
  1/2 cup raisins
Artificial sweetener equivalent to 4 teaspoons
  sugar
  2 tablespoons finely chopped walnuts
  1/3 cup reduced-fat creamy peanut butter
  1/4 teaspoon coconut extract

In a mixing bowl, combine the first four ingredients; beat well. Add peanut butter and extract. Refrigerate for 30 minutes or until easy to handle. Shape into 3/4-in. balls. **Yield:** 2 dozen. **Nutritional Analysis:** One piece equals 39 calories, 24 mg sodium, 0 cholesterol, 4 gm carbohydrate, 1 gm protein, 2 gm fat. **Diabetic Exchange:** 1 fat.

▚▚▚▚▚▚▚▚▚▚▚▚▚
WALNUT THUMBPRINTS

Sherrie Pickle, Kent, Washington

(Pictured above)

Out of all my cookie recipes, I get the most requests for this one. A friend gave the recipe to me years ago, and it's become our family's favorite.

  1/2 cup butter *or* margarine, softened
  1 cup packed brown sugar
  1 egg
  1 teaspoon vanilla extract
  1-3/4 cups all purpose-flour
  1/2 teaspoon baking soda
  1/4 teaspoon salt
FILLING:
  1 cup chopped walnuts
  1/2 cup packed brown sugar
  1/4 cup sour cream

In a mixing bowl, cream the butter and brown sugar. Beat in egg and vanilla. Combine flour, baking soda and salt; gradually add to the creamed mixture. Refrigerate for 30 minutes. Roll into 1-in. balls. Place 2 in. apart on greased baking sheets. Using the end of a wooden spoon handle, make an indentation in the center of each ball. Combine filling ingredients; spoon about 1 teaspoonful into each cookie. Bake at 350° for 11-13 minutes or until lightly browned. Cool for 5 minutes before removing to wire racks. **Yield:** about 3 dozen.

▚▚▚▚▚▚▚▚▚▚▚▚▚
ANGEL FOOD CAKE
WITH CARAMEL SAUCE

Carolyn Troyer, Sugarcreek, Ohio

I enjoy making desserts, and it's especially satisfying when goodies like this cake are devoured quickly. The caramel sauce makes a tasty topping.

  1 package (3 ounces) cream cheese,
    softened
  1/4 cup confectioners' sugar
  1 carton (8 ounces) frozen whipped
    topping, thawed
  1 prepared angel food cake (10 inches)
CARAMEL SAUCE:
  1 cup half-and-half cream, *divided*
  3/4 cup sugar
  1/2 cup light corn syrup
  1/4 cup butter (no substitutes)
Pinch salt
  1/2 teaspoon vanilla extract

In a mixing bowl, beat cream cheese and confectioners' sugar until smooth. Fold in whipped topping; set aside. Cut cake horizontally into two layers. Place the bottom layer on a serving plate; spread with cream cheese mixture. Replace top; refrigerate. In a saucepan, combine 3/4 cup of cream, sugar, corn syrup, butter and salt. Cook and stir until mixture reaches soft-ball stage (234°). Slowly add remaining cream. Cook and stir until mixture returns to soft-ball stage (234°). Remove from the heat; stir in vanilla. Cool. Drizzle over cake. Store in the refrigerator. **Yield:** 12 servings.

CHOCOLATE CHOCOLATE CHIP CAKE

Roni Goodell, Spanish Fork, Utah

This is a chocolate lover's dream! It will definitely satisfy any chocolate craving you may have. I often make this cake for birthdays or other special occasions.

>   1 cup shortening
>   2 cups sugar
>   4 squares (1 ounce *each*) unsweetened
>   chocolate, melted and cooled
>   2 teaspoons vanilla extract
>   5 eggs
> 2-1/4 cups cake flour
>   1 teaspoon baking soda
>   1 teaspoon salt
>   1 cup buttermilk
>   2 cups (12 ounces) semisweet chocolate
>   chips

FROSTING:
>   2/3 cup butter *or* margarine, softened
> 5-1/3 cups confectioners' sugar
>   1 cup baking cocoa
>   1 cup milk
>   2 teaspoons vanilla extract

In a mixing bowl, cream shortening and sugar. Add chocolate and vanilla; mix well. Add eggs, one at a time, beating well after each addition. Combine flour, baking soda and salt; add to creamed mixture alternately with buttermilk. Fold in the chocolate chips. Pour into three greased and floured 9-in. round cake pans. Bake at 350° for 30-35 minutes or until a toothpick inserted near the center comes out clean. Cool for 10 minutes; remove from pans to wire racks to cool completely. In a mixing bowl, cream butter. Combine sugar and cocoa; add to creamed mixture alternately with milk. Add vanilla; beat well. Frost between layers and top and sides of cake. **Yield:** 12 servings.

ORANGE APRICOT BALLS

Shelly Detwiler, Marysville, Ohio

I first tried this citrusy candy as a child at my grandmother's house. I enjoyed it so much, my dad has been making it every Christmas since.

✓ **Uses less fat, sugar or salt. Includes Nutritional Analysis and Diabetic Exchanges.**

>   1 pound dried apricots (3 cups)
> 1/2 medium unpeeled navel orange
>   1 cup sugar, *divided*

In a food processor or grinder, coarsely chop apricots and orange. Add 2/3 cup sugar; mix well. Shape into 3/4-in. balls; roll in remaining sugar. Store in refrigerator. **Yield:** 1-1/2 pounds (5

dozen). **Nutritional Analysis:** One piece equals 34 calories, trace sodium, 0 cholesterol, 8 gm carbohydrate, trace protein, trace fat. **Diabetic Exchange:** 1/2 fruit.0

PUMPKIN POUND CAKE

Virginia Loew, Leesburg, Florida

(Pictured below)

This cake is perfect for fall. As it bakes, the aroma fills the house with a spicy scent.

> 2-1/2 cups sugar
>   1 cup vegetable oil
>   3 eggs
>   3 cups all-purpose flour
>   2 teaspoons baking soda
>   1 teaspoon ground cinnamon
>   1 teaspoon ground nutmeg
> 1/2 teaspoon salt
> 1/4 teaspoon ground cloves
>   1 can (15 ounces) solid-pack pumpkin
> Confectioners' sugar

In a mixing bowl, blend sugar and oil. Add eggs, one at a time, beating well after each addition. Combine flour, baking soda, cinnamon, nutmeg, salt and cloves; add to egg mixture alternately with pumpkin. Transfer to a greased 12-cup fluted tube pan. Bake at 350° for 60-65 minutes or until a toothpick inserted near the center comes out clean. Cool for 10 minutes before inverting onto a wire rack. Remove pan and cool completely. Dust with confectioners' sugar. **Yield:** 12-16 servings.

Marbled Chocolate Cheesecake Bars

Elaine Hanson, Waite Park, Minnesota

(Pictured below)

I learned to bake and cook from my mother. I grew up in a family of 12, and we all had chores to do—mine was to help prepare the meals. The more I cooked, the more I enjoyed it. Now it's my favorite hobby.

- 3/4 cup water
- 1/2 cup butter (no substitutes)
- 1-1/2 squares (1-1/2 ounces) unsweetened chocolate
- 2 cups all-purpose flour
- 1-1/2 cups packed brown sugar
- 1 teaspoon baking soda
- 1/2 teaspoon salt
- 2 eggs
- 1/2 cup sour cream

CREAM CHEESE MIXTURE:
- 1 package (8 ounces) cream cheese, softened
- 1/3 cup sugar
- 1 egg, beaten
- 1 tablespoon vanilla extract
- 1 cup (6 ounces) semisweet chocolate chips

In a small saucepan, combine water, butter and chocolate; cook and stir over low heat until smooth. Cool. In a mixing bowl, combine flour, brown sugar, baking soda and salt. Add eggs and sour cream; beat on low just until combined. Stir in chocolate mixture until smooth. In another bowl, beat cream cheese, sugar, egg and vanilla; set aside. Spread chocolate batter into a greased 15-in. x 10-in. x 1-in. baking pan. Drop cream cheese mixture by tablespoonfuls over batter; cut through the batter with a knife to swirl. Sprinkle with chocolate chips. Bake at 375° for 20-25 minutes or until a toothpick inserted near the center comes out clean. Cool on a wire rack. **Yield:** about 6 dozen.

Plantation Gingerbread

Wanda Burchell, Lynnville, Tennessee

I like to make this recipe for Christmas. The wonderful aroma of the gingerbread fills the entire house while it's baking in the oven.

- 1 cup butter *or* margarine, softened
- 1 cup sugar
- 3 eggs
- 1 cup molasses
- 3/4 cup hot water
- 2-1/2 cups all-purpose flour
- 1-1/2 teaspoons ground ginger
- 1 teaspoon baking soda
- 1 teaspoon ground cinnamon
- 1/2 teaspoon ground nutmeg
- 1/2 teaspoon salt
- 1 cup whipping cream
- 1 to 2 tablespoons confectioners' sugar

Additional nutmeg, optional

In a mixing bowl, cream butter and sugar for 3 minutes. Add eggs; beat on low speed for 2 minutes. Gradually add the molasses and hot water. Combine flour, ginger, baking soda, cinnamon, nutmeg and salt; gradually add to creamed mixture. Beat on low for 1 minute. Pour into a greased 13-in. x 9-in. x 2-in. baking pan. Bake at 350° for 30-35 minutes or until a toothpick inserted near the center comes out clean. Cool. In a mixing bowl, beat cream and confectioners' sugar until soft peaks form. Serve with the gingerbread. Sprinkle with nutmeg if desired. **Yield:** 12-16 servings.

Walnut Apple Cake

Jacquelyn Remsberg, La Canada, California

I first tasted this delicious cake at a Halloween party and quickly asked for the recipe. It's not too sweet, and the butter sauce makes it a super dessert.

- 2 eggs
- 2 cups sugar
- 1/2 cup vegetable oil
- 2 teaspoons vanilla extract
- 2 cups all-purpose flour

2-1/2 teaspoons ground cinnamon
2 teaspoons baking soda
1 teaspoon salt
1/4 teaspoon ground nutmeg
4 cups chopped peeled tart apples
1 cup chopped walnuts
BUTTER SAUCE:
3/4 cup sugar
3 tablespoons all-purpose flour
1 cup milk
2 tablespoons butter (no substitutes)
1 teaspoon vanilla extract
Walnut halves, optional

In a mixing bowl, combine eggs, sugar, oil and vanilla; mix well. Combine dry ingredients; add to the egg mixture and mix well (batter will be stiff). Stir in apples and walnuts. Spread into a greased 13-in. x 9-in. x 2-in. baking pan. Bake at 350° for 45-50 minutes or until a toothpick inserted near the center comes out clean. Cool on a wire rack. For the sauce, combine sugar, flour, milk and butter in a saucepan. Bring to a boil over medium heat; boil and stir for 2 minutes. Remove from the heat; stir in vanilla. Cut cake into squares; top with warm sauce. Garnish with walnut halves if desired. **Yield:** 12-15 servings.

PINEAPPLE LAYER CAKE

Debbie Norling, Harris, Minnesota

(Pictured above right)

My mother had a large family to care for and not a lot of spare time for fixing fancy desserts. But somehow she regularly found a way to bake this cake for us. These days, I make it for my family.

1/2 cup shortening
1-2/3 cups sugar
3 egg yolks
1 egg
2-1/2 cups cake flour
4 teaspoons baking powder
1 teaspoon salt
1-1/4 cups buttermilk
1/2 teaspoon vanilla extract
FILLING:
1/2 cup sugar
3 tablespoons cornstarch
1/2 teaspoon salt
1 can (8 ounces) crushed pineapple
1 tablespoon butter *or* margarine
1 teaspoon lemon juice
SEVEN-MINUTE FROSTING:
1-1/2 cups sugar
2 egg whites
1/3 cup water

1/4 teaspoon cream of tartar
1 teaspoon vanilla extract

In a mixing bowl, cream shortening and sugar. Add egg yolks and egg, one at a time, beating well after each. Combine flour, baking powder and salt; add to the creamed mixture alternately with buttermilk. Beat in vanilla. Pour into two greased and floured 9-in. round cake pans. Bake at 350° for 30-35 minutes or until a toothpick inserted near the center comes out clean. Cool for 10 minutes; remove from pans to wire racks. In a saucepan, combine sugar, cornstarch and salt. Drain pineapple, reserving juice. Add pineapple to pan. Add water to juice to measure 3/4 cup; pour into pan and mix well. Bring to a boil over medium heat; cook and stir for 2 minutes. Add butter and lemon juice. Cool completely. For frosting, in a heavy saucepan or double boiler, combine sugar, egg whites, water and cream of tartar. With a portable mixer, beat mixture on low speed over low heat until frosting reaches 160°, about 8-10 minutes. Pour into a mixing bowl; add vanilla. Beat on high speed until frosting forms stiff peaks, about 7 minutes; set frosting aside. Set aside a third of the filling. Spread remaining filling between cake layers. Spread reserved filling in a 4-in. circle in the center of top layer. Frost the sides of cake and around the filling on top. **Yield:** 12 servings.

*A HOST of homemade candy presented on
pretty platters will sweeten the holidays.*

DANDY CANDY. Clockwise from top right: Fondant-Filled Candies (p. 100), Cashew Caramel Fudge (p. 100), Chocolate Pecan Caramels (p. 100), Holiday Pecan Logs (p. 101), Pulled Molasses Taffy (p. 102), Toasted Coconut Truffles (p. 105), Anise Hard Candy (p. 103) and Nutty Chocolate Marshmallow Puffs (p. 102).

FONDANT-FILLED CANDIES

Debbi Loney, Central City, Kentucky

(Pictured on page 99)

Here's an easy way to make two festive and unique candies from one basic recipe! Half of the creamy fondant is flavored with mint for the centers of peppermint patties. Then you mix a little maraschino cherry juice with the rest of the fondant and use it to "wrap" cherries before dipping them in chocolate.

     2/3 cup sweetened condensed milk
       1 tablespoon light corn syrup
 4-1/2 to 5 cups confectioners' sugar
       2 to 4 drops peppermint oil*
 2-1/2 pounds dark chocolate candy coating,
         divided
       1 jar (16 ounces) maraschino cherries

In a mixing bowl, combine milk and corn syrup. Gradually beat in confectioners' sugar (mixture will be stiff). Divide into two portions. For peppermint patties, add the peppermint oil to one portion. Shape 1/2 teaspoonfuls into balls and flatten. In a microwave or heavy saucepan, melt 1 pound of candy coating, stirring often. With a slotted spoon, dip peppermint disks in coating; place on waxed paper to harden. Refrigerate in an airtight container. For chocolate-covered cherries, drain cherries, reserving 3 tablespoons of juice; set cherries aside. Combine juice with remaining fondant. Add additional confectioners' sugar if necessary to form a stiff mixture. Roll into 1-in. balls; flatten into 2-in. circles. Wrap each circle around a cherry and carefully shape into a ball. Place on waxed paper-lined baking sheets. Cover loosely. Melt remaining candy coating; dip cherries in coating. Place on waxed paper to harden. Refrigerate in an airtight container for 1-2 weeks for candy to ripen and center to soften. **Yield:** 4-1/2 dozen. ***Editor's Note:** Peppermint oil can be found in some pharmacies or at kitchen and cake decorating supply stores.

CASHEW CARAMEL FUDGE

Cathy Grubelnik, Raton, New Mexico

(Pictured on page 99)

A pretty plate of this yummy confection makes a great present! Cashews and caramel are such a delicious combination. I especially enjoy making this fudge for a holiday treat. Our four children are always ready with their appetites and compliments.

       2 teaspoons plus 1/2 cup butter (no
         substitutes), softened, *divided*
       1 can (5 ounces) evaporated milk

 2-1/2 cups sugar
       2 cups (12 ounces) semisweet chocolate
         chips
       1 jar (7 ounces) marshmallow creme
      24 caramels, quartered
     3/4 cup salted cashew halves
       1 teaspoon vanilla extract

Line a 9-in. square baking pan with foil; butter the foil with 2 teaspoons butter. Set aside. In a large heavy saucepan, combine milk, sugar and remaining butter. Cook and stir over medium heat until sugar is dissolved. Bring to a rapid boil; boil for 5 minutes, stirring constantly. Remove from the heat; stir in chocolate chips and marshmallow creme until melted. Fold in caramels, cashews and vanilla; mix well. Pour into prepared pan. Cool. Remove from pan and cut into 1-in. squares. Store at room temperature. **Yield:** about 3 pounds.

CHOCOLATE PECAN CARAMELS

June Humphrey, Strongsville, Ohio

(Pictured on page 99)

I haven't missed a year making this candy for the holidays since a friend gave me the recipe in 1964! It is made like a pan of upside-down bars and tastes like my favorite caramel pecan candies.

       1 tablespoon plus 1 cup butter (no
         substitutes), softened, *divided*
 1-1/2 cups coarsely chopped pecans, toasted
       1 cup (6 ounces) semisweet chocolate
         chips
       2 cups packed brown sugar
       1 cup light corn syrup
     1/4 cup water
       1 can (14 ounces) sweetened condensed
         milk
       2 teaspoons vanilla extract

Line a 13-in. x 9-in. x 2-in. baking pan with foil; butter the foil with 1 tablespoon butter. Sprinkle with pecans and chocolate chips; set aside. In a heavy saucepan over medium heat, melt remaining butter. Add brown sugar, corn syrup and water. Cook and stir until mixture comes to a boil. Stir in milk. Cook, stirring constantly, until a candy thermometer reads 248° (firm-ball stage). Remove from the heat and stir in vanilla. Pour into prepared pan (do not scrape saucepan). Cool completely before cutting. **Yield:** about 2-1/2 pounds (about 6-3/4 dozen). **Editor's Note:** We recommend that you test your candy thermometer before each use by bringing water to a boil; the thermometer should read 212°. Adjust your recipe temperature up or down based on your test.

HOLIDAY PECAN LOGS

Maxine Ruhl, Fort Scott, Kansas

(Pictured on page 98)

For more than 50 years, I've turned to this beloved recipe to make candy to give away at Christmas. Of the many types I've tried, these pecan logs continue to be the most popular.

2 teaspoons plus 1/2 cup butter (no substitutes), softened, *divided*
3-3/4 cups confectioners' sugar
1/2 cup instant nonfat dry milk powder
1/2 cup sugar
1/2 cup light corn syrup
1 teaspoon vanilla extract
1 package (14 ounces) caramels
1 tablespoon milk *or* half-and-half cream
2 cups chopped pecans

Butter an 8-in. square pan with 2 teaspoons butter; set aside. Combine confectioners' sugar and milk powder; set aside. In a heavy saucepan, combine 1/2 cup butter, sugar and corn syrup; cook and stir until sugar is dissolved and mixture comes to a boil. Stir in confectioners' sugar mixture, about a third at a time, until blended. Remove from the heat; stir in vanilla. Continue stirring until the mixture mounds slightly when dropped from a spoon. Spread into prepared pan. Cool. Cut candy into four strips; cut each strip in half. Shape each into a log; wrap in waxed paper and twist ends. Freeze or refrigerate until firm. In a microwave or heavy saucepan, melt caramels with milk, stirring often. Roll logs in caramel mixture, then in pecans. Wrap in waxed paper. Store at room temperature in airtight containers. Cut into slices with a serrated knife. **Yield:** about 3-1/4 pounds.

Tiny Candy Cones Scoop Up Fun!

FOR NOTABLE TREATS to serve at birthday parties, summer get-togethers or during the holidays, Dianne Conway of London, Ontario happily cranks out cool confections in the form of miniature ice cream cones!

"Making them is a breeze," explains this busy wife and mother of two. "I simply whip up a sugary filling, roll it into small balls to resemble scoops of ice cream and perch them on top of Bugle corn snacks. Then I roll them in sprinkles or nuts.

"The crunchy morsels are always a hit at parties—and they make a great novelty gift for family and friends."

Interested in dishing up the candies for your own festive party? Simply follow Dianne's recipe here. In no time at all, the air will be ringing with sweet compliments at your house!

BUGLE CONES

2 tablespoons butter (no substitutes), softened
1-1/3 cups confectioners' sugar
1/4 teaspoon salt
1/4 teaspoon vanilla extract
2 tablespoons sweetened condensed milk
1 package (6 ounces) Bugles
1/2 cup semisweet chocolate chips, melted, optional
Assorted colored and chocolate sprinkles *and/or* ground nuts

In a small mixing bowl, cream butter and sugar. Beat in salt and vanilla. Add condensed milk (mixture will be stiff). Shape into 1/2-in. balls. Place one ball on top of each Bugle. Dip the tops of some or all in melted chocolate if desired. Decorate with sprinkles and/or nuts. **Yield:** 2-1/2 dozen.

toothpick inserted near the center comes out clean. Cool for 10 minutes. Turn cake onto a linen towel dusted with confectioners' sugar. Remove paper; roll up cake in towel, starting with a short side. Cool on a wire rack. For filling, in a mixing bowl, beat cream cheese, butter, sugar and vanilla until smooth. Unroll cake. Spread filling over cake to within 1 in. of edges. Gently roll up; place seam side down on a platter. Refrigerate until serving. **Yield:** 10 servings.

PUMPKIN CAKE ROLL

June Mullins, Livonia, Missouri

(Pictured above)

Roll out this well-rounded dessert and get set to harvest plenty of compliments. It earns me rave reviews whenever I serve it. My youngest daughter shared the recipe with me. It's a hit at her house, too.

    3 eggs
    1 cup sugar
  2/3 cup cooked *or* canned pumpkin
  3/4 cup biscuit/baking mix
    2 teaspoons ground cinnamon
    1 teaspoon pumpkin pie spice
  1/2 teaspoon ground nutmeg
    1 cup chopped nuts
Confectioners' sugar
FILLING:
    2 packages (3 ounces *each*) cream cheese, softened
  1/4 cup butter *or* margarine, softened
    1 cup confectioners' sugar
    1 teaspoon vanilla extract

In a mixing bowl, beat eggs. Gradually add sugar. Stir in pumpkin; mix well. Combine the biscuit mix, cinnamon, pie spice and nutmeg; add to egg mixture and mix well. Line a 15-in. x 10-in. x 1-in. pan with waxed paper; grease and flour the paper. Spread batter evenly in pan. Sprinkle with nuts. Bake at 375° for 13-15 minutes or until a

NUTTY CHOCOLATE MARSHMALLOW PUFFS

Pat Ball, Abilene, Texas

(Pictured on page 98)

We like to do things big here in Texas, so don't expect a dainty little barely-a-bite truffle from this surprising recipe. Folks are delighted to discover a big fluffy marshmallow inside the chocolate and nut coating.

    2 cups milk chocolate chips
    1 can (14 ounces) sweetened condensed milk
    1 jar (7 ounces) marshmallow creme
  40 large marshmallows
    4 cups coarsely chopped pecans (about 1 pound)

In a microwave or heavy saucepan, heat chocolate chips, milk and marshmallow creme just until melted; stir until smooth (mixture will be thick). With tongs, immediately dip marshmallows, one at a time, in chocolate mixture. Shake off excess chocolate; quickly roll in pecans. Place on waxed paper-lined baking sheets. (Reheat chocolate mixture if necessary for easier coating.) Refrigerate until firm. Store in the refrigerator in an airtight container. **Yield:** 40 candies.

PULLED MOLASSES TAFFY

Betty Woodman, Wolfe Island, Ontario

(Pictured on page 98)

French-Canadian children traditionally make this soft, chewy taffy on November 25, the feast day of St. Catherine. Often some of our children and grandchildren get in on the fun of pulling the taffy.

    5 teaspoons butter (no substitutes), softened, *divided*
  1/4 cup water
1-1/4 cups packed brown sugar
    2 tablespoons cider vinegar

1/4 teaspoon salt
1/3 cup molasses

Butter a 15-in. x 10-in. x 1-in. pan with 3 teaspoons butter; set aside. In a heavy saucepan, combine water, brown sugar, vinegar and salt. Bring to a boil over medium heat. Cook and stir until a candy thermometer reads 245° (firm-ball stage), stirring occasionally. Add molasses and remaining butter. Cook, uncovered, until a candy thermometer reads 260° (hard-ball stage), stirring occasionally. Remove from the heat; pour into prepared pan. Cool for 5 minutes or until cool enough to handle. With buttered fingers, quickly pull half of the candy until firm but pliable. Pull and shape into a 1/2-in. rope. Cut into 1-1/4-in. pieces. Repeat with remaining taffy. Wrap pieces individually in foil or waxed paper; twist ends. Store in airtight containers in the refrigerator. Remove from the refrigerator 30 minutes before serving. **Yield:** 14-1/2 dozen. **Editor's Note:** For easier candy making, enlist family members to help twist and pull the taffy with you. We recommend that you test your candy thermometer before each use by bringing water to a boil; the thermometer should read 212°. Adjust your recipe temperature up or down based on your test.

ANISE HARD CANDY

Jobyna Carpenter, Poulsbo, Washington

(Pictured on page 98)

Making this old-fashioned candy has become an annual Christmas project for me. I first prepared this recipe at the home of a friend who made candy for a shop. To vary the recipe a little, substitute peppermint extract for the anise, and green food coloring for red.

  1-1/2 teaspoons butter (no substitutes),
    softened
  3/4 cup water
  2/3 cup light corn syrup
  2 cups sugar
  1 teaspoon anise extract
Red food coloring
  2 to 3 tablespoons confectioners' sugar

Butter an 8-in. square baking pan with 1-1/2 teaspoons butter; set aside. In a large heavy saucepan, combine water, corn syrup and sugar. Bring to a boil over medium heat, stirring occasionally. Cover and cook for 3 minutes to dissolve any sugar crystals. Uncover; cook over medium-high heat, without stirring, until a candy thermometer reads 300° (hard-crack stage). Remove from the heat; stir in extract and food coloring (keep face away from mixture as odor is very strong). Pour in-

to prepared pan. Using a sharp knife, score into 3/4-in. squares. Cool. Separate into squares, using a sharp knife if necessary. Place confectioners' sugar in a baking pan; add candy and roll until coated. Brush off excess sugar with a pastry brush. Store at room temperature in an airtight container. **Yield:** about 1 pound (about 8 dozen). **Editor's Note:** We recommend that you test your candy thermometer before each use by bringing water to a boil; the thermometer should read 212°. Adjust your recipe temperature up or down based on your test.

SHORTBREAD SQUARES

Mrs. G.C. Mayhew, Grass Valley, California

(Pictured below)

Here's a traditional shortbread recipe that's perfect with a cup of hot tea or coffee. It's a favorite during the holidays.

  1 pound butter (no substitutes), softened
  1 cup sifted confectioners' sugar
3-1/2 cups all-purpose flour
  1/2 cup cornstarch

In a mixing bowl, cream butter and sugar. Combine flour and cornstarch; gradually add to creamed mixture. Pat into an ungreased 15-in. x 10-in. x 1-in. baking pan. Pierce several times with a fork. Bake at 325° for 40-45 minutes or until lightly browned. Cut while warm. **Yield:** about 6 dozen.

Food Editor's Fast Fudge

By Janaan Cunningham, Food Editor

MY FAVORITE holiday candy is fudge. When I was a little girl, my mom made fudge using a candy thermometer. It seemed to take forever for that rich chocolate mixture to reach the soft-ball stage…and longer yet for the fudge to cool. But the results were well worth my watchful wait!

When I became a teenager and showed an interest in cooking, my mom decided it was time to pass the candy thermometer down to a new generation.

But like a typical teen, I elected to try a quicker, easier fudge recipe—one that didn't require the dreaded candy thermometer. (Secretly, I think even my mom was tired of using it!)

At any rate, much to my amazement, my family liked my quicker version of that candy almost as much as Mom's old-fashioned fudge.

Over the years, I've stirred up so many batches I wore away the nonstick coating on my favorite fudge-making saucepan. To this day, it's still my job to bring fudge to our family gatherings.

You'll find my recipe at right.

JANAAN'S FUDGE

2-1/4 cups sugar
3/4 cup evaporated milk
16 large marshmallows
1/4 cup butter (no substitutes)
1/4 teaspoon salt
1 cup (6 ounces) semi-sweet chocolate chips
1 cup chopped walnuts
1 teaspoon vanilla extract

In a heavy saucepan, combine the first five ingredients. Cook and stir over medium heat until mixture comes to a boil. Boil and stir 5 minutes longer. Remove from the heat. Stir in the chocolate chips until melted. Stir in the nuts and vanilla. Spread in a buttered 8-in. square pan. Cool. Cut into squares. Store in the refrigerator. **Yield:** 2-1/2 dozen.

APPLE PEAR CAKE

Mary Ann Lees, Centreville, Alabama

When my sister Catherine made an apple cake for me, I asked her for the recipe. I made it a short time later and added some pears to the recipe, since we have pear trees on our acreage. The cake was very moist and tasted so good. Now every time I make it, people want my recipe.

2 cups shredded peeled apples
2 cups shredded peeled pears
2 cups sugar
1-1/4 cups vegetable oil
1 cup raisins
1 cup chopped pecans
2 eggs, beaten
1 teaspoon vanilla extract
3 cups all-purpose flour
2 teaspoons baking soda
2 teaspoons ground cinnamon
1/2 teaspoon ground nutmeg
1/2 teaspoon salt
CREAM CHEESE FROSTING:
1 package (3 ounces) cream cheese, softened
1/4 cup butter *or* margarine, softened
3 cups confectioners' sugar
2 tablespoons milk
1/2 teaspoon vanilla extract

In a large bowl, combine the first eight ingredients. Combine dry ingredients; stir into the fruit mixture. Pour into a greased 13-in. x 9-in. x 2-in. baking pan. Bake at 325° for 1 hour or until a toothpick inserted near the center comes out clean. Cool on a wire rack. For frosting, beat cream cheese and butter in a mixing bowl until fluffy. Add sugar, milk and vanilla; mix well. Spread over cooled cake. Store in the refrigerator. **Yield:** 12-15 servings.

TOASTED COCONUT TRUFFLES

Beth Nagel, West Lafayette, Indiana

(Pictured on page 98)

"Ooh" and "Mmmm" are common comments when folks taste these delectable bites. Toasted coconut in the coating makes the truffles especially tempting. I always include them in my Christmas packages and gift containers.

- 4 cups (24 ounces) semisweet chocolate chips
- 1 package (8 ounces) cream cheese, softened and cubed
- 3/4 cup sweetened condensed milk
- 3 teaspoons vanilla extract
- 2 teaspoons water
- 1 pound white candy coating
- 2 tablespoons flaked coconut, finely chopped and toasted

In a microwave or heavy saucepan, melt chocolate chips. Add the cream cheese, milk, vanilla and water; beat with a hand mixer until blended. Cover and refrigerate until easy to handle, about 1-1/2 hours. Shape into 1-in. balls and place on waxed paper-lined baking sheets. Loosely cover and refrigerate for 1-2 hours or until firm. In a microwave or heavy saucepan, melt candy coating, stirring often. Dip balls in coating; place on waxed paper-lined baking sheets. Sprinkle with coconut. Refrigerate until firm, about 15 minutes. Store in the refrigerator in an airtight container. **Yield:** about 5-1/2 dozen.

ITALIAN CHRISTMAS COOKIES

Doris Marshall, Strasburg, Pennsylvania

(Pictured at right)

A single batch of these mouth-watering cookies is never enough. I usually make one to give away and two more to keep at home. Adding ricotta cheese to the batter makes the morsels extra moist.

- 1 cup butter (no substitutes), softened
- 2 cups sugar
- 3 eggs
- 1 carton (15 ounces) ricotta cheese
- 2 teaspoons vanilla extract
- 4 cups all-purpose flour
- 1 teaspoon salt
- 1 teaspoon baking soda

FROSTING:
- 1/4 cup butter (no substitutes), softened
- 3 to 4 cups confectioners' sugar
- 1/2 teaspoon vanilla extract

- 3 to 4 tablespoons milk
- Colored sprinkles

In a mixing bowl, cream butter and sugar. Add the eggs, one at a time, beating well after each addition. Beat in ricotta and vanilla. Combine flour, salt and baking soda; gradually add to creamed mixture. Drop by rounded teaspoonfuls 2 in. apart onto greased baking sheets. Bake at 350° for 10-12 minutes or until lightly browned. Remove to wire racks to cool. In a mixing bowl, cream butter, sugar and vanilla. Add enough milk until frosting reaches spreading consistency. Frost cooled cookies and immediately decorate with sprinkles. Store in the refrigerator. **Yield:** 8-1/2 dozen.

DRIED FRUIT SQUARES

Martha Voss, Dickinson, North Dakota

Honey and orange juice add a tasty touch of sweetness to these fruity squares.

✓ **Uses less fat, sugar or salt. Includes Nutritional Analysis and Diabetic Exchanges.**

- 1 pound dates (3-1/2 cups)
- 1 pound dried figs (3 cups)
- 1 package (15 ounces) raisins (3 cups)
- 1 pound dried apricots (3 cups)
- 2 tablespoons honey
- 1 tablespoon orange juice

Line a 13-in. x 9-in. x 2-in. pan with foil; coat foil with nonstick cooking spray. Set aside. In a food processor or grinder, coarsely chop the fruit. Add honey and orange juice. Press into prepared pan. Let stand at room temperature for 5 hours. Cut into 1-1/2-in. pieces. **Yield:** 4 pounds (6-1/2 dozen). **Nutritional Analysis:** One piece equals 65 calories, 2 mg sodium, 0 cholesterol, 17 gm carbohydrate, 1 gm protein, trace fat. **Diabetic Exchange:** 1 fruit.

Chocolate Almond Sheet Cake

Mary Ann Kosmas, Minneapolis, Minnesota

(Pictured below)

This cake was one of my children's favorite desserts when they were growing up. They're all adults now, but I still make it for them when they come to visit.

- 3/4 cup butter *or* margarine
- 1 cup water
- 1/4 cup baking cocoa
- 2-1/2 cups all-purpose flour
- 2 cups sugar
- 1 teaspoon baking soda
- 1/2 teaspoon salt
- 2 eggs
- 1/2 cup buttermilk
- 1 teaspoon vanilla extract
- 1 teaspoon almond extract

FROSTING:
- 1/2 cup butter *or* margarine
- 1/4 cup milk
- 3 cups confectioners' sugar
- 1/4 cup baking cocoa
- 1 teaspoon vanilla extract

In a saucepan over medium heat, bring butter, water and cocoa to a boil. Remove from the heat and cool to room temperature. In a mixing bowl, combine the flour, sugar, baking soda and salt. Beat in cocoa mixture. Add eggs, buttermilk and extracts; mix well. Pour into a greased 15-in. x 10-in. x 1-in. baking pan. Bake at 375° for 20-22 minutes or until a toothpick inserted near the center comes out clean. Cool for 10 minutes. Meanwhile, for frosting, place butter and milk in a saucepan. Cook and stir over medium heat until butter is melted. Remove from the heat; add remaining ingredients and beat well. Carefully spread over warm cake. Cool. **Yield:** 16-20 servings.

Giant Snowball Cake

Betty Friesen, Lake Oswego, Oregon

Just like the frosty version would, this snowball is sure to disappear fast at warm-weather gatherings. Tangy citrus is the delightful surprise when you taste the coconut-topped confection. My family's enjoyed the refreshing dessert at Christmas for nearly 50 years, but it would be wonderful any time of year.

- 1 envelope unflavored gelatin
- 1/4 cup cold water
- 1/2 cup boiling water
- 1 cup sugar
- 1 cup orange juice
- 1/4 cup lemon *or* lime juice
- 2 cups whipping cream, *divided*
- 1 angel food cake (12 ounces), cut into cubes (10 cups)
- 1 cup flaked coconut

In a bowl, sprinkle gelatin over cold water; let stand for 1 minute. Add boiling water; stir until gelatin is dissolved. Add sugar and juices; stir until sugar is dissolved. Refrigerate until partially thickened, about 2 hours. Beat 1 cup cream until stiff peaks form; fold into gelatin mixture. Line a 4-qt. round bowl with plastic wrap. Spoon about 1 cup whipped cream mixture into bowl. Alternate layers of cake and whipped cream mixture until bowl is filled, ending with cream mixture. Refrigerate for at least 3 hours. Unmold onto a serving plate. Whip remaining cream; frost cake. Sprinkle with coconut. **Yield:** 16 servings.

Peanut Butter Cookie Pops

Martha Hoover, Coatesville, Pennsylvania

A miniature candy bar is the hidden treat inside fun-for-all-ages pops. My sons brought these cookies home from school after their teacher made a bunch for her class. The kids loved nibbling them on a stick. Of course, the taste also was an instant hit!

1/2 cup butter (no substitutes), softened
1/2 cup creamy peanut butter
1/2 cup packed brown sugar
1/2 cup sugar
1 egg
1 teaspoon vanilla extract
1-1/2 cups all-purpose flour
1/2 teaspoon baking powder
1/2 teaspoon baking soda
1/4 teaspoon salt
12 wooden craft sticks
12 miniature Snickers *or* Milky Way
   candy bars

In a mixing bowl, cream butter, peanut butter and sugars. Beat in egg and vanilla until light and fluffy. Combine flour, baking powder, baking soda and salt; gradually add to creamed mixture. Insert a wooden stick into the small end of each candy bar. Divide dough into 12 pieces; wrap one piece around each candy bar. Place 4 in. apart on ungreased baking sheets. Bake at 375° for 14-16 minutes or until golden brown. Cool for 10 minutes; remove from pan to a wire rack to cool completely. **Yield:** 1 dozen.

SOUR CREAM PEANUT FUDGE

Mrs. Edward Stacy, Lexington, Kentucky

With both peanuts and peanut butter, this fancy fudge will delight nut lovers and sweet tooths alike. Since my variety won't crumble and stays surprisingly soft, it's ideal for either get-togethers or gifts.

4 cups sugar
1 cup (8 ounces) sour cream
2/3 cup light corn syrup
1/4 cup butter (no substitutes)
1/2 teaspoon salt
1 tablespoon vanilla extract
1 cup chopped peanuts
2/3 cup peanut butter

In a large saucepan, combine the first five ingredients; bring to a boil. Cover and simmer for 5 minutes. Uncover; cook over medium-high heat until a candy thermometer reads 238° (soft-ball stage). Remove from the heat; stir in vanilla. Let stand, without stirring, for 15 minutes. Add peanuts and peanut butter. With a wooden spoon, beat until thick and creamy, about 10 minutes. Transfer to a buttered 13-in. x 9-in. x 2-in. pan. Cool; cut into squares. Store in the refrigerator. **Yield:** 3 pounds. **Editor's Note:** We recommend that you test your candy thermometer before each use by bringing water to a boil; the thermometer should read 212°. Adjust your recipe temperature up or down based on your test.

STAINED GLASS CUTOUT COOKIES

Margaret Milleker, Baltimore, Maryland
(Pictured above)

Light up your dessert tray at Christmas with these heavenly confections. They're twice the treat, since they feature hard candy in the middle of crisp sugar cookies. The candy creates the "stained glass" effect.

3/4 cup butter (no substitutes), softened
1 cup sugar
1 egg
1 tablespoon milk
1 teaspoon vanilla extract
2-1/4 cups all-purpose flour
1 teaspoon baking powder
1/8 teaspoon salt
Assorted colors of clear hard candy

In a mixing bowl, cream butter and sugar. Beat in egg, milk and vanilla; mix well. Combine flour, baking powder and salt; gradually add to the creamed mixture. Cover and refrigerate for 2 hours or until easy to handle. Meanwhile, coarsely crush each color of hard candy separately; set aside. On a lightly floured surface, roll out dough to 1/8-in. thickness. Cut with 4-in. cookie cutters dipped in flour. Cut out centers with 1-in. cookie cutters. Place cookies 1 in. apart on lightly greased foil-lined baking sheets. Fill centers with crushed candy. Bake at 375° for 8-10 minutes or until candy is melted and edges begin to brown. Cool completely on baking sheet. Carefully peel cookies off the foil. **Yield:** about 3 dozen.

Short and Sweet Treats

LOOKING FOR a candy recipe you can make in a flash? All of the speedy treats here can be stirred up in a mere 30 minutes! Plan ahead, though—they need to chill.

CHOCOLATE MINT CANDY

Kendra Pedersen, Battle Ground, Washington

(Pictured below)

I never made candy before until I tried this recipe. Now I make it every holiday.

> 2 cups (12 ounces) semisweet chocolate chips
> 1 can (14 ounces) sweetened condensed milk, *divided*
> 2 teaspoons vanilla extract
> 6 ounces white candy coating
> 2 to 3 teaspoons peppermint extract
> 3 drops green food coloring

In a heavy saucepan, melt chocolate chips with 1 cup milk. Remove from the heat; stir in vanilla. Spread half into a waxed paper-lined 8-in. square pan; chill for 10 minutes or until firm.

Meanwhile, in a heavy saucepan over low heat, cook and stir candy coating with remaining milk until coating is melted and mixture is smooth. Stir in peppermint extract and food coloring. Spread over bottom layer; chill for 10 minutes or until firm. Warm remaining chocolate mixture if necessary; spread over mint layer. Chill for 2 hours or until firm. Remove from pan; cut into 1-in. squares. **Yield:** about 2 pounds.

SHORTCUT FUDGE

Jean Knapik, Bremond, Texas

This recipe was given to me over 35 years ago. It's a wonderful addition to candy trays.

> 1 package (3.4 ounces) cook-and-serve chocolate pudding mix
> 1 cup sugar
> 1/2 cup evaporated milk
> 1 tablespoon butter (no substitutes), softened
> 1 cup chopped pecans

In a heavy saucepan, combine dry pudding mix, sugar, milk and butter. Bring to a boil; boil and stir

until a candy thermometer reads 224°, about 3 minutes. Remove from the heat and beat rapidly for 1 minute. Add pecans; continue beating until mixture thickens slightly. Drop by tablespoonfuls onto waxed paper-lined baking sheets. Refrigerate until firm, about 45 minutes. **Yield:** 3/4 pound (about 1-1/2 dozen). **Editor's Note:** We recommend that you test your candy thermometer before each use by bringing water to a boil; the thermometer should read 212°. Adjust your recipe temperature up or down based on your test.

CRANBERRY ALMOND BARK

Elizabeth Hodges, Regina Beach, Saskatchewan

The addition of dried cranberries makes this almond bark extra special. It looks impressive but is really quick and easy to make.

- 8 squares (1 ounce *each*) white baking chocolate
- 3 squares (1 ounce *each*) semisweet chocolate
- 3/4 cup whole blanched almonds, toasted
- 3/4 cup dried cranberries

In a microwave or heavy saucepan, melt white chocolate; set aside. Repeat with semisweet chocolate. Stir almonds and cranberries into white chocolate. Thinly spread onto a waxed paper-lined baking sheet. With a spoon, drizzle semisweet chocolate over the white chocolate. Cut through with a knife to swirl. Chill until firm. Break into pieces. Refrigerate in an airtight container. **Yield:** 1 pound.

BUTTERSCOTCH PEANUT CANDY

Callie Gregg, St. Lawrence, South Dakota

This easy-to-make candy is always a hit during the holidays. The sweet and salty combination is so irresistible, no one can ever eat just one piece.

- 1 package (11-1/2 ounces) milk chocolate chips
- 1 package (10 ounces) butterscotch chips
- 1 teaspoon butter-flavored shortening
- 3 cups salted peanuts

In a microwave, heat chips and shortening, uncovered, at 50% power for 3 minutes or until melted. Stir until smooth. Add peanuts. Drop by tablespoonfuls onto waxed paper-lined baking sheets. Refrigerate until firm, about 45 minutes.

Yield: 2-1/4 pounds (3-1/2 to 4 dozen). **Editor's Note:** This recipe was tested in an 850-watt microwave.

CHOCOLATE-DIPPED TREATS

Donna Hickok, Olds, Alberta

Kids of all ages love these chocolaty treats. They're easy to make and make great Christmas gifts.

- 1 cup (6 ounces) semisweet chocolate chips
- 1 tablespoon shortening
- 1/4 teaspoon ground cinnamon
- Large marshmallows, miniature pretzel twists *and/or* whole fresh strawberries

In a microwave or heavy saucepan, melt chocolate chips and shortening. Stir in cinnamon. Dip three-quarters of each marshmallow, pretzel and/or strawberry in chocolate. Place on a waxed paper-lined baking sheet. Refrigerate until set, about 30 minutes. **Yield:** about 4 dozen.

COCONUT DROPS

Diane Rathburn, Mt. Pleasant, Michigan

We enjoy giving friends a gift of the festive candy each holiday season. With such limited time, I can rely on this recipe, which is quick and easy.

- 1 package (14 ounces) flaked coconut
- 6 drops red food coloring
- 6 drops green food coloring
- 1 pound white candy coating

Divide coconut between two bowls. Add red food coloring to one bowl and green to the other; toss to coat. In a heavy saucepan over low heat, melt candy coating. Drop by tablespoonfuls onto waxed paper. While coating is still warm, sprinkle half of each drop with pink coconut and the other half with green; press down gently. Refrigerate until firm. **Yield:** 1-1/4 pounds.

KEEPING CANDY COATING

Candy coating keeps best in a cool dry place. If stored in the refrigerator, it can pick up flavors, odors and moisture that will affect its quality.

IF YOU'RE *sweet on desserts, don't pass up this tempting selection of crisps, cobblers, pies, cheesecakes and more.*

FRUITY FAVORITES. Clockwise from top left: Gingered Apriot-Apple Crumble (p. 112), Rhubarb Granola Crisp (p. 113), ABC Slump (p. 112) and Cherry Nut Crisp (p. 111).

Pies & Desserts

EASY APPLE BETTY

Sharon Knelsen, Coaldale, Alberta

I've been cooking since I was a young girl and am always on the lookout for easy yet delicious dishes. This recipe fits the bill.

> ✓ Uses less fat, sugar or salt. Includes Nutritional Analysis and Diabetic Exchanges.

  10 cups sliced peeled tart apples
     (about 3 pounds)
  1/4 cup unsweetened apple juice
1-3/4 cups crushed oatmeal cookies
     (about 18)
  1/4 cup margarine, melted
  1/2 teaspoon ground cinnamon

Toss the apples and apple juice; arrange half in a 13-in. x 9-in. x 2-in. baking dish coated with non-stick cooking spray. Combine the cookie crumbs, margarine and cinnamon; sprinkle half over the apples. Repeat layers. Bake at 375° for 40-45 minutes or until apples are tender and topping is golden brown. **Yield:** 12 servings. **Nutritional Analysis:** One serving equals 213 calories, 148 mg sodium, 0 cholesterol, 34 gm carbohydrate, 2 gm protein, 9 gm fat. **Diabetic Exchanges:** 2 fat, 1 starch, 1 fruit.

CHERRY NUT CRISP

Melissa Radulovich, Byers, Colorado

(Pictured at left)

I used my favorite cherry pie recipe to create this one after my fiance asked me to make a treat for his rugby team's meeting. Since I didn't have time to roll out a crust, I just used a simple crisp crust.

  2 cans (14-1/2 ounces *each*) pitted tart
    cherries
  1 cup sugar
  1/4 cup quick-cooking tapioca
  1 teaspoon almond extract
  1/8 teaspoon salt
  4 to 5 drops red food coloring, optional
CRUST:
  1 cup all-purpose flour
  1/3 cup sugar

  1/4 teaspoon salt
  1/8 teaspoon baking powder
  6 tablespoons butter *or* margarine, melted
TOPPING:
  1/2 cup all-purpose flour
  1/2 cup packed brown sugar
  1/2 cup chopped pecans
  1/3 cup quick-cooking oats
  6 tablespoons cold butter *or* margarine

Drain cherries, reserving 3/4 cup juice (discard remaining juice or save for another use). In a bowl, combine cherries, sugar, tapioca, extract, salt, food coloring if desired and reserved juice; set aside for 15 minutes, stirring occasionally. Meanwhile, combine crust ingredients. Press onto the bottom and 1 in. up the sides of a greased 9-in. square baking dish; set aside. In another bowl, combine first four topping ingredients; cut in butter until mixture resembles coarse crumbs. Stir cherry mixture; pour into crust. Sprinkle with topping. Bake at 400° for 10 minutes. Reduce heat to 375°; bake 30-35 minutes longer or until filling is bubbly and topping is golden. **Yield:** 9 servings.

FRESH BLUEBERRY PIE

Linda Kernan, Mason, Michigan

I've been making this dessert for more than 30 years. It represents our state well because Michigan is the leader in blueberry production.

  3/4 cup sugar
  3 tablespoons cornstarch
  1/8 teaspoon salt
  1/4 cup cold water
  5 cups fresh blueberries, *divided*
  1 tablespoon butter *or* margarine
  1 tablespoon lemon juice
  1 pastry shell (9 inches), baked

In a saucepan over medium heat, combine sugar, cornstarch, salt and water until smooth. Add 3 cups blueberries. Bring to a boil; cook and stir for 2 minutes or until thickened and bubbly. Remove from the heat. Add butter, lemon juice and remaining berries; stir until butter is melted. Cool. Pour into the pastry shell. Refrigerate until serving. **Yield:** 6-8 servings.

Crumble Captures High Praise

SYLVIA RICE came across the recipe for Gingered Apricot-Apple Crumble in a nutritional cooking class, and it became a family-favorite dessert. "It's so delicious no one believes it's also lower in fat," declares this Didsbury, Alberta resident.

High on family-pleasing flavor, Sylvia's eye-catching crumble is a regular at get-togethers with the Rices' seven grown children and 10 grandchildren. "My husband, Larry, especially likes the sweet and tangy blending of maple syrup, apples and citrus," Sylvia says.

So do friends and neighbors, who count on seeing the dessert on bake sale and potluck tables. "The topping's very moist," Sylvia comments, "and with cardamom and ginger, the fruit filling stays flavorful for days—if it lasts that long!

"Hot or cold, plain or topped with ice cream, this crumble is tasty. For variety, leave out the apricots and make a traditional apple crisp if you'd like."

Although she and Larry are empty nesters, that hasn't curbed Sylvia's bent for baking. "After making this crumble, I divide it into fruit dishes, wrap them in plastic and store them in the freezer," she details. "That way, Larry can warm up a serving any time he wants one."

Earn the admiration of your own family and friends by treating them to this exceptional crumble. But don't count on one crumb being left over!

GINGERED APRICOT-APPLE CRUMBLE

(Pictured on page 110)

- 1 cup orange juice *or* apricot nectar
- 3/4 cup finely chopped dried apricots
- 1/3 cup honey
- 1/4 cup maple syrup
- 2 tablespoons lemon juice
- 8 cups sliced peeled tart apples (about 8 large)
- 3 tablespoons all-purpose flour
- 1 teaspoon ground cinnamon
- 1/2 teaspoon ground ginger *or* 1 teaspoon minced fresh gingerroot
- 1/2 teaspoon ground cardamom

TOPPING:
- 3/4 cup all-purpose flour
- 1/2 cup quick-cooking oats
- 1/2 cup chopped pecans, optional
- 1/4 cup vegetable oil
- 1/4 cup maple syrup

In a bowl, combine orange juice, apricots, honey, maple syrup and lemon juice; set aside. Arrange apples in an ungreased 13-in. x 9-in. x 2-in. baking dish. Combine flour, cinnamon, ginger and cardamom; stir into the apricot mixture. Spoon over apples. Combine topping ingredients; sprinkle over fruit. Bake at 350° for 50-60 minutes or until topping is golden brown and fruit is tender. **Yield:** 12 servings.

ABC SLUMP

Becky Burch, Marceline, Missouri

(Pictured on page 110)

The "ABC" in this recipe's name comes from the apple, blueberries and cranberries it uses. The other part refers to the way the dumplings "slump" during cooking—presumably the sound made by the fruit as it bubbles on the stove. I've taken my slump to work, picnics and church carry-ins. No matter where, the result is the same...all that I ever bring home is the empty dish.

- 1 cup chopped peeled tart apple
- 1 cup fresh *or* frozen blueberries
- 3/4 cup fresh *or* frozen cranberries
- 1 cup water
- 2/3 cup sugar

DUMPLINGS:
- 3/4 cup all-purpose flour
- 1/4 cup sugar
- 1 teaspoon baking powder
- 1/4 teaspoon ground cinnamon
- 1/8 teaspoon ground nutmeg
- 3 tablespoons cold butter *or* margarine
- 1/3 cup milk

Half-and-half cream

In a 3-qt. saucepan, combine the fruit, water and sugar; bring to a boil. Reduce heat; cover and simmer for 5 minutes. Meanwhile, in a bowl, combine the flour, sugar, baking powder, cinnamon and nutmeg; cut in butter until mixture resembles coarse crumbs. Add milk; stir just until moistened. Drop into six mounds onto simmering fruit. Cover and simmer for about 10 minutes or until a toothpick inserted into a dumpling comes out clean (do not lift the cover while simmering). Serve warm with cream. **Yield:** 6 servings.

RHUBARB GRANOLA CRISP

Arlene Beitz, Cambridge, Ontario

(Pictured on page 110)

When my husband and I moved to our house in town, the rhubarb patch had to come along! This is a hit whether I serve it warm with ice cream or cold.

      4 cups chopped fresh *or* frozen rhubarb, thawed and drained
1-1/4 cups all-purpose flour, *divided*
   1/4 cup sugar
   1/2 cup strawberry jam
1-1/2 cups granola cereal
   1/2 cup packed brown sugar
   1/2 cup chopped pecans
   1/2 teaspoon ground cinnamon
   1/2 teaspoon ground ginger
   1/2 cup cold butter *or* margarine
Ice cream, optional

In a bowl, combine the rhubarb, 1/4 cup flour and sugar; stir in jam and set aside. In another bowl, combine the granola, brown sugar, pecans, cinnamon, ginger and remaining flour. Cut in butter until the mixture resembles coarse crumbs. Press 2 cups of the granola mixture into a greased 8-in. square baking dish; spread rhubarb mixture over the crust. Sprinkle with remaining granola mixture. Bake at 375° for 30-40 minutes or until filling is bubbly and topping is golden brown. Serve warm with ice cream if desired. **Yield:** 9 servings.

STRAWBERRY BANANA TRIFLE

Kim Waterhouse, Randolph, Maine

(Pictured at right)

No matter where I take this dessert, the bowl gets emptied in minutes. It's fun to make because everyone "oohs" and "aahs" over how pretty it is.

      1 cup sugar
   1/4 cup cornstarch
      3 tablespoons strawberry gelatin powder
      1 cup cold water
      1 pint fresh strawberries, sliced

1-3/4 cups cold milk
      1 package (3.4 ounces) instant vanilla pudding mix
      3 medium firm bananas, sliced
      1 tablespoon lemon juice
      6 cups cubed angel food cake
      2 cups whipping cream, whipped
Additional strawberries *or* banana slices, optional

In a saucepan, combine the sugar, cornstarch and gelatin; stir in water until smooth. Bring to a boil; cook and stir for 2 minutes or until thickened. Remove from the heat. Stir in strawberries; set aside. In a mixing bowl, combine milk and pudding mix. Beat on low speed for 2 minutes; set aside. Toss bananas with lemon juice; drain and set aside. Place half of the cake cubes in a trifle bowl or 3-qt. serving bowl. Layer with half of the pudding, bananas, strawberry sauce and whipped cream. Repeat layers. Cover and refrigerate for at least 2 hours. Garnish with additional fruit if desired. **Yield:** 14 servings.

en edges with water; fold dough over filling and press edges with a fork to seal. Prick tops with a fork 4-5 times. In an electric skillet, heat 1/2 in. of oil to 375°. Fry pies, a few at a time, for 1 minute on each side or until golden brown. Drain on paper towels. Dust with confectioners' sugar if desired. Store in refrigerator. **Yield:** 25 pies.
*Editor's Note: As a substitute for each cup of self-rising flour, place 1-1/2 teaspoons baking powder and 1/2 teaspoon salt in a measuring cup; add all-purpose flour to equal 1 cup. For 1/2 cup of self-rising flour, place 3/4 teaspoon baking powder and 1/4 teaspoon salt in a measuring cup; add all-purpose flour to equal 1/2 cup.

FRIED SWEET POTATO PIES

Marilyn Moseley, Toccoa, Georgia

(Pictured above)

My farmer dad used to grow sweet potatoes. They have graced our table for as long as I can recall. These, though, resulted from an experiment at a church bake sale when we had excess pastry.

  4-1/2 **cups self-rising flour***
     3 **tablespoons sugar**
  1/2 **cup shortening**
     2 **eggs**
     1 **cup milk**
FILLING:
     3 **cups mashed sweet potatoes**
     2 **cups sugar**
     3 **eggs, lightly beaten**
     1 **can (5 ounces) evaporated milk**
  1/4 **cup butter *or* margarine, melted**
     3 **tablespoons all-purpose flour**
     1 **teaspoon vanilla extract**
Oil for frying
Confectioners' sugar, optional

In a bowl, combine flour and sugar; cut in shortening until mixture resembles coarse crumbs. Combine eggs and milk; add to crumb mixture, tossing with a fork until a ball forms. Cover and chill several hours. In a large bowl, combine the seven filling ingredients; stir until smooth. Divide the dough into 25 portions. On a floured surface, roll each portion into a 5-in. circle. Spoon 2 tablespoons of filling on half of each circle. Moist-

ADAMEK'S BEST PEACH COBBLER

Janet Adamek, Yoakum, Texas

As peach growers, we eat these golden fruits in all kinds of different ways. I share this cobbler recipe with people visiting our orchard.

     8 **cups sliced fresh *or* frozen peaches**
  1/2 **cup butter (no substitutes), softened**
     1 **cup sugar**
     1 **cup all-purpose flour**
Cinnamon-sugar

Place the peaches in an ungreased 13-in. x 9-in. x 2-in. baking dish; set aside. In a mixing bowl, cream butter and sugar. Add flour and mix well. Sprinkle over the peaches. Sprinkle with cinnamon-sugar. Bake at 325° for 1 hour or until the topping is golden brown. Serve warm. **Yield:** 8-12 servings.

LUCK O' THE IRISH CHEESECAKE

Mary Berger, Bernville, Pennsylvania

The combination of chocolate and peppermint in this elegant cheesecake quickly becomes a favorite of everyone who tries it.

  20 **chocolate cream-filled sandwich cookies, crushed**
     3 **tablespoons butter *or* margarine, melted**
     3 **packages (8 ounces *each*) cream cheese, softened**
     1 **can (14 ounces) sweetened condensed milk**
     1 **teaspoon peppermint extract**
     6 **drops green food coloring**
     3 **eggs**
     1 **cup miniature chocolate chips, *divided***

Combine cookie crumbs and butter; press onto the bottom of a greased 9-in. springform pan. In

a mixing bowl, beat the cream cheese, milk, extract and food coloring until smooth. Add eggs, beating on low speed just until combined. Stir in 1/2 cup chocolate chips. Pour onto crust. Bake at 300° for 1 hour or until the center is almost set. Cool on a wire rack for 10 minutes; run a knife around pan to loosen. Cool 50 minutes longer. Refrigerate overnight. In a microwave, melt the remaining chips; drizzle over cheesecake. **Yield:** 8-10 servings.

CIDER APPLE BAKE

Shelly Schierman, Louisburg, Kansas

From Labor Day to Thanksgiving, it's crunch time at our apple cider mill. This simple fruity dessert features apples as well as cider.

- 6 large tart apples, peeled and sliced
- 2 cups apple cider
- 1/3 cup packed brown sugar
- 1/4 teaspoon ground cinnamon
- 1 cup half-and-half *or* whipping cream

Place apples in a greased 2-qt. baking dish. Combine cider and brown sugar; pour over apples. Bake, uncovered, at 350° for 50-60 minutes or until apples are tender, stirring once. Sprinkle with cinnamon. Cool slightly. Serve warm in bowls with cream. **Yield:** 6 servings.

PEACH DREAM COBBLER

Sue Eberly, Fayetteville, Pennsylvania

This light and luscious cobbler is wonderful warm from the oven or served cold. With such great flavor, no one will guess it's good for you!

> ✓ Uses less fat, sugar or salt. Includes Nutritional Analysis and Diabetic Exchanges.

- 2 cups fresh *or* frozen sliced peaches
- 3/4 cup sugar, *divided*
- Egg substitute equivalent to 1 egg
- 1 tablespoon margarine, softened
- 1 tablespoon skim milk
- 1/2 cup all-purpose flour
- 1 teaspoon baking powder
- 1/8 teaspoon salt

In a saucepan, combine peaches and 1/4 cup sugar; let stand for 5 minutes. Bring to a boil. Reduce heat; cook and stir for 1 minute or until the sugar is dissolved. Set aside. In a mixing bowl, beat egg substitute, margarine and remaining sugar until fluffy. Stir in milk. Combine flour, baking powder and salt; add to egg mixture just until combined. Pour into an 8-in. square baking pan coat-

ed with nonstick cooking spray. Top with peach mixture. Bake at 350° for 35-40 minutes or until lightly browned. Serve warm or cold. **Yield:** 9 servings. **Nutritional Analysis:** One serving equals 124 calories, 82 mg sodium, 0 cholesterol, 26 gm carbohydrate, 2 gm protein, 2 gm fat. **Diabetic Exchanges:** 1 fruit, 1/2 starch, 1/2 fat.

PEANUT BUTTER PIE

Gloria Pittman, Shelby, North Carolina

(Pictured below)

This pie is always a treat at our house. I haven't met anyone who doesn't like it.

- 1/3 cup creamy peanut butter
- 1 package (3 ounces) cream cheese, softened
- 2 tablespoons butter *or* margarine, softened
- 1 cup confectioners' sugar
- 1/4 cup milk
- 1 carton (8 ounces) frozen whipped topping, thawed
- 1 chocolate crumb crust (9 inches)
- 2 tablespoons chopped peanuts, optional
Chocolate curls, optional

In a mixing bowl, beat peanut butter, cream cheese and butter until smooth. Add sugar and milk; fold in whipped topping. Pour into the crust. Cover and freeze for at least 4 hours. Remove from the freezer just before serving. Garnish with peanuts and chocolate curls if desired. **Yield:** 6 servings.

APPLE MERINGUE PIE

Virginia Kraus, Pocahontas, Illinois

(Pictured below)

I received this recipe from my mother-in-law, and it's one of my husband's favorites. It's a nice variation on traditional apple pie.

    7 cups thinly sliced peeled tart apples
    2 tablespoons lemon juice
2/3 cup sugar
    2 tablespoons all-purpose flour
1/3 cup milk
    2 egg yolks, beaten
    1 teaspoon grated lemon peel
Pastry for single-crust pie (9 inches)
    1 tablespoon butter *or* margarine, cubed
MERINGUE:
    3 egg whites
1/4 teaspoon cream of tartar
    6 tablespoons sugar

In a large bowl, toss apples with lemon juice. In a small bowl, whisk sugar, flour, milk, egg yolks and lemon peel until smooth. Pour over apples and toss to coat. Line a 9-in. pie plate with pastry; trim to 1/2 in. beyond edge of pie plate and flute edges. Pour filling into crust; dot with butter. Cover edges loosely with foil. Bake at 400° for 20 minutes. Remove foil; bake 25-30 minutes longer or until apples are tender. Reduce heat to 350°. In a mixing bowl, beat the egg whites and cream of tartar on medium speed until foamy. Gradually beat in sugar, 1 tablespoon at a time, on high just until stiff peaks form and sugar is dissolved. Spread evenly over hot filling, sealing edges to crust. Bake for 15 minutes or until golden brown. Cool on a wire rack. Store in the refrigerator. **Yield:** 6-8 servings.

APRICOT COBBLER

Mrs. Curtis Jeffery, Burr Oak, Kansas

Even folks who watch their diets deserve to splurge on dessert. This fruity cobbler featuring apricots is simply delicious!

✓ **Uses less fat, sugar or salt. Includes Nutritional Analysis and Diabetic Exchanges.**

    1 can (29 ounces) light apricot halves
    1 package (.8 ounce) sugar-free cook-and-serve vanilla pudding mix
    1 cup all-purpose flour
1/4 teaspoon salt
1/3 cup cold margarine
1/4 cup water

Drain apricots, reserving juice. In a bowl, whisk the juice and pudding mix until smooth; stir in apricots. Pour into an 8-in. square baking dish coated with nonstick cooking spray; set aside. In a bowl, combine flour and salt; cut in margarine until crumbly. Gradually add water, tossing with a fork until dough forms a ball. On a floured surface, roll out dough to fit top of baking dish; place over filling. Trim and flute edges; cut slits in top. Bake at 450° for 15 minutes. Reduce heat to 350°; bake 40-45 minutes longer or until crust is golden brown and filling is bubbly. **Yield:** 9 servings. **Nutritional Analysis:** One serving equals 138 calories, 181 mg sodium, 0 cholesterol, 17 gm carbohydrate, 2 gm protein, 7 gm fat. **Diabetic Exchanges:** 1-1/2 fat, 1/2 starch, 1/2 fruit

RHUBARB PUDDING DESSERT

Marion Meyer, Eau Claire, Wisconsin

Of the many recipes I've tried with rhubarb as the main ingredient, this is the one my family thinks is best. We can't wait for spring to arrive and the rhubarb to sprout.

    1 cup graham cracker crumbs
    2 tablespoons sugar
1/4 cup butter *or* margarine, melted
FILLING:
    1 cup sugar
    3 tablespoons cornstarch
    4 cups chopped fresh *or* frozen rhubarb
1/2 cup water
    3 drops red food coloring, optional

1/2 cup whipping cream, whipped
1-1/2 cups miniature marshmallows
1 package (3.4 ounces) instant vanilla
 pudding mix

Combine the crumbs, sugar and butter; set aside 2 tablespoons. Press remaining crumbs into an ungreased 11-in. x 7-in. x 2-in. baking dish. Bake at 350° for 8-10 minutes; cool. For filling, combine sugar and cornstarch in a saucepan. Add rhubarb and water; bring to a boil. Cook and stir for 2 minutes or until thickened. Stir in food coloring if desired. Spread over the crust; chill. Combine whipped cream and marshmallows; spread over rhubarb layer. Prepare pudding mix according to package directions for pie filling; spread over marshmallow layer. Sprinkle with reserved crumbs. Cover and refrigerate for 4 hours or overnight. **Yield:** 9-12 servings.

SNAPPY PUMPKIN DESSERT

Nilah Fischer, Morton, Illinois

(Pictured at right)

Our town has a pumpkin-canning factory, so we're known as the "Pumpkin Capital of the World". New pumpkin recipes are always welcomed by our family, and this has become a favorite. The gingersnap crust goes great with the pumpkin.

2-1/2 cups finely crushed gingersnaps (about
 40 cookies)
1/2 cup butter *or* margarine, melted
1 package (8 ounces) cream cheese,
 softened
1/2 cup confectioners' sugar
2 tablespoons milk
TOPPING:
3 cups cold milk
2 packages (3.4 ounces *each*) instant
 vanilla pudding mix
1 can (15 ounces) solid-pack pumpkin
2-1/2 teaspoons pumpkin pie spice
2 cups whipped topping
Additional whipped topping, optional

Combine gingersnap crumbs and butter; press into an ungreased 13-in. x 9-in. x 2-in. baking pan. Bake at 325° for 10 minutes. Cool. In a mixing bowl, beat the cream cheese, confectioners' sugar and milk until fluffy. Spread over the crust. In another mixing bowl, beat milk and pudding mix for 1 minute. Add pumpkin and pie spice; beat until well blended. Fold in whipped topping. Spread over the cream cheese layer. Refrigerate for at least 3 hours. Cut into squares; garnish with whipped topping if desired. **Yield:** 12-15 servings.

GINGER PEAR PIE

Delilah Stauffer, Mt. Pleasant Mills, Pennsylvania

My mother, who collected many recipes over the years, made this delicious pie often. It's wonderful served warm with a scoop of ice cream on top.

3 tablespoons cornstarch
1/4 teaspoon ground ginger
1/2 cup water
1/2 cup dark corn syrup
1 teaspoon lemon juice
1/8 teaspoon grated lemon peel
4 large pears, peeled and thinly sliced
1 tablespoon butter *or* margarine
1 unbaked pastry shell (9 inches)
TOPPING:
1/2 cup all-purpose flour
1/4 cup packed brown sugar
1/8 teaspoon ground ginger
1/4 cup cold butter *or* margarine
1/4 cup chopped pecans

In a saucepan, combine the first six ingredients until blended. Gently stir in pears. Bring to a boil over medium heat, stirring occasionally; boil for 1 minute. Add butter. Pour into pastry shell. For topping, combine flour, brown sugar and ginger in a bowl. Cut in butter until mixture resembles coarse crumbs. Stir in pecans. Sprinkle over pears. Bake at 425° for 20-25 minutes or until topping is golden brown. **Yield:** 6-8 servings.

THESE CRISPS AND COBBLERS *offer plenty of great eating ripe for the picking. They use a wide variety of fruits, so you're certain to find a few new winners to add to your kitchen file.*

CRUMBLY CREATIONS. Clockwise from top left: Berry Apple Crumble (p. 123), Macaroon Apple Cobbler (p. 122), Magic Pumpkin Buckle (p. 120), Date Pudding Cobbler (p. 120), Applescotch Crisp (p. 121), Pear Crisp (p. 121), Almond Plum Kuchen (p. 121) and Caramel Apricot Grunt (p. 122).

DATE PUDDING COBBLER

Carolyn Miller, Guys Mills, Pennsylvania

(Pictured on page 119)

There were eight children in my family when I was a girl, and all of us enjoyed this cobbler. I now serve it for everyday and special occasions alike.

    1 cup all-purpose flour
1-1/2 cups packed brown sugar, *divided*
    2 teaspoons baking powder
    1 tablespoon cold butter *or* margarine
1/2 cup milk
3/4 cup chopped dates
3/4 cup chopped walnuts
    1 cup water
Whipped cream and ground cinnamon, optional

In a bowl, combine flour, 1/2 cup brown sugar and baking powder. Cut in butter until crumbly. Gradually add milk, dates and walnuts. In a saucepan, combine water and remaining brown sugar; bring to a boil. Remove from the heat; add the date mixture and mix well. Transfer to a greased 8-in. square baking pan. Bake at 350° for 30 minutes or until golden brown. If desired, top each serving with a dollop of whipped cream and sprinkling of cinnamon. **Yield:** 9 servings.

MAPLE PECAN PIE

Mildred Wescom, Belvidere, Vermont

(Pictured below)

Our Vermont maple syrup can't be beat. This is one of my favorite pies featuring that sweet treat. It's also quick and easy to make.

    3 eggs
1/2 cup sugar
    1 cup maple syrup
    3 tablespoons butter *or* margarine, melted
1/2 teaspoon vanilla extract
1/4 teaspoon salt
    1 cup pecan halves
    1 unbaked pastry shell (9 inches)

In a bowl, whisk eggs and sugar until smooth. Add syrup, butter, vanilla, salt and pecans. Pour into pie shell. Bake at 375° for 40-45 minutes or until a knife inserted near the center comes out clean. **Yield:** 8 servings.

MAGIC PUMPKIN BUCKLE

Darlene Markel, Stayton, Oregon

(Pictured on page 119)

Probably my family's favorite pumpkin dessert, this is something I've been making for years. The crust mixture, which is actually poured in first, rises to the top during baking to form a rich topping.

1/2 cup butter *or* margarine, melted
    1 cup all-purpose flour
    1 cup sugar
    4 teaspoons baking powder
1/2 teaspoon salt
    1 cup milk
    1 teaspoon vanilla extract
FILLING:
    3 cups cooked *or* canned pumpkin
    1 cup evaporated milk
    2 eggs
    1 cup sugar
1/2 cup packed brown sugar
    1 tablespoon all-purpose flour
    1 teaspoon ground cinnamon
1/2 teaspoon salt
1/4 teaspoon *each* ground ginger, cloves and nutmeg
TOPPING:
    1 tablespoon butter *or* margarine
    2 tablespoons sugar

Pour butter into a 13-in. x 9-in. x 2-in. baking dish; set aside. In a bowl, combine the flour, sugar, baking powder and salt. Stir in milk and vanilla until smooth. Pour into the prepared pan. In a mixing bowl, beat the pumpkin, milk and eggs. Combine the remaining filling ingredients; add to pumpkin mixture. Pour over crust mixture (do not stir). Dot with butter and sprinkle with sugar. Bake at 350° for 55-60 minutes or until a knife inserted near the center comes out clean and the top is golden brown. **Yield:** 12 servings.

PEAR CRISP

Joanne Korevaar, Burgessville, Ontario

(Pictured on page 118)

Since he's a livestock truck driver, my husband often starts work around 2 or 3 a.m. A piece of this crisp will keep him going 'til breakfast. And our two boys love to have it for dessert and in their school lunches.

> 8 medium ripe pears, peeled and thinly
>   sliced
> 1/4 cup orange juice
> 1/2 cup sugar
>   1 teaspoon ground cinnamon
> 1/4 teaspoon ground allspice
> 1/4 teaspoon ground ginger
> TOPPING:
>   1 cup all-purpose flour
>   1 cup old-fashioned oats
> 1/2 cup packed brown sugar
> 1/2 teaspoon baking powder
> 1/2 cup cold butter *or* margarine
> Fresh mint and additional pear slices, optional

Toss pears with orange juice; place in a greased 13-in. x 9-in. x 2-in. baking dish. Combine the sugar, cinnamon, allspice and ginger; sprinkle over the pears. In a bowl, combine flour, oats, brown sugar and baking powder; cut in butter until crumbly. Sprinkle over pears. Bake at 350° for 35-40 minutes or until topping is golden brown and fruit is tender. Serve warm. Garnish with mint and additional pears if desired. **Yield:** 12 servings.

ALMOND PLUM KUCHEN

Norma Enders, Edmonton, Alberta

(Pictured on page 118)

You'll find this dessert both easy and very tasty. Everyone who tries it comments on how the orange and plum flavors complement each other. We like it best when it is served warm with ice cream.

> 1-1/2 cups all-purpose flour
> 3/4 cup packed brown sugar
> 1/2 cup ground almonds
>   1 tablespoon grated orange peel
> 3/4 cup cold butter *or* margarine
> FILLING:
>   3 eggs
> 3/4 cup sugar
> 1/2 cup all-purpose flour
> 1/2 cup ground almonds
>   1 tablespoon grated orange peel

> 1/2 teaspoon baking powder
>   7 to 8 cups quartered fresh plums
> TOPPING:
> 1/4 cup sugar
> 1/4 cup all-purpose flour
> 1/4 cup butter *or* margarine, softened
> 1/2 cup sliced almonds

In a bowl, combine the first four ingredients; cut in butter until the mixture resembles coarse crumbs. Press into a greased 13-in. x 9-in. x 2-in. baking dish. Bake at 375° for 15 minutes. Meanwhile, in a mixing bowl, beat eggs and sugar until thick and lemon-colored, about 5 minutes. Stir in flour, almonds, orange peel and baking powder. Arrange plums over crust; pour egg mixture over plums. Combine the first three topping ingredients; sprinkle over filling. Top with almonds. Bake for 40-45 minutes or until golden brown. **Yield:** 12 servings.

APPLESCOTCH CRISP

Elaine Nicholl, Nottingham, Pennsylvania

(Pictured on page 118)

Just as soon as the first crop of apples is off the trees, I fix this crisp. Thanks to the butterscotch pudding, it's moist and sweet. It's popular at potlucks, and it's a nice snack. In fact, I'm reluctant to make it in the evening—I'm afraid someone will sneak down to the refrigerator at midnight and claim it!

> 4 cups sliced peeled tart apples
> 1/2 cup packed brown sugar
> 2/3 cup plus 1 tablespoon all-purpose flour,
>   *divided*
> 1/2 cup water
> 1/4 cup milk
> 1/2 cup quick-cooking oats
>   1 package (3-1/2 ounces) cook-and-serve
>   butterscotch pudding mix
> 1/4 cup sugar
>   1 teaspoon ground cinnamon
> 1/2 teaspoon salt
> 1/2 cup cold butter *or* margarine
> Ice cream, optional

Place the apples in an ungreased 11-in. x 7-in. x 2-in. baking dish. In a bowl, whisk brown sugar, 1 tablespoon flour, water and milk. Pour over apples. In another bowl, combine oats, pudding mix, sugar, cinnamon, salt and the remaining flour. Cut in butter until mixture resembles coarse crumbs. Sprinkle over apples. Bake at 350° for 45-50 minutes or until topping is golden brown and fruit is tender. Serve with ice cream if desired. **Yield:** 8 servings.

4 cups thinly sliced peeled tart apples
1/3 cup sugar
1/2 teaspoon ground cinnamon
1/2 cup flaked coconut
1/4 cup chopped pecans
TOPPING:
1/2 cup butter *or* margarine, softened
1/2 cup sugar
1 egg
1/2 teaspoon vanilla extract
3/4 cup all-purpose flour
1/4 teaspoon baking powder

Place the apples in an ungreased 9-in. pie plate. Combine sugar and cinnamon; sprinkle over apples. Top with coconut and pecans; set aside. In a mixing bowl, cream butter and sugar. Add egg and vanilla; mix well. Combine flour and baking powder; add to the creamed mixture until blended. Carefully spread over apples. Bake at 350° for 25-30 minutes or until top is golden brown and fruit is tender. Serve warm. **Yield:** 6-8 servings.

CHOCOLATE PRALINE ICE CREAM TOPPING

Angie Zalewski, Dripping Springs, Texas

(Pictured above)

Friends tell me they look forward to ice cream socials just to have this topping.

1 cup whipping cream
2/3 cup packed brown sugar
2/3 cup butter *or* margarine
1 cup (6 ounces) semisweet chocolate chips
1 cup chopped pecans
Ice cream

In a saucepan over medium heat, bring cream, brown sugar and butter to a boil, stirring constantly. Reduce heat; simmer for 2 minutes, stirring occasionally. Remove from the heat; stir in the chocolate chips until melted and smooth. Stir in pecans. Serve warm over ice cream. Store in the refrigerator. **Yield:** 3 cups.

MACAROON APPLE COBBLER

Phyllis Hinck, Lake City, Minnesota

(Pictured on page 119)

Especially when I'm just serving a dessert, I like to prepare this. I'll usually make it with fresh apples—but I've also sometimes used home-canned ones.

CARAMEL APRICOT GRUNT

Shari Dore, Brantford, Ontario

(Pictured on page 118)

The "guinea pig" for my cooking is my husband. But this recipe is one we enjoyed at my grandmother's house. It's perfect for dessert or church socials.

2 cans (15-1/4 ounces *each*) apricot halves, undrained
2 teaspoons quick-cooking tapioca
1/3 cup packed brown sugar
1 tablespoon butter *or* margarine
1 tablespoon lemon juice
DUMPLINGS:
1-1/2 cups all-purpose flour
1/2 cup sugar
2 teaspoons baking powder
2 tablespoons cold butter *or* margarine
1/2 cup milk
TOPPING:
1/4 cup packed brown sugar
2 tablespoons water
Half-and-half cream, optional

In a saucepan, combine apricots and tapioca; let stand for 15 minutes. Add brown sugar, butter and lemon juice. Cook and stir until mixture comes to a full boil. Reduce heat to low; keep warm. For dumplings, combine flour, sugar and baking powder in a bowl; cut in butter until crumbly. Add milk; mix just until combined. Pour warm fruit mixture into an ungreased 2-qt. baking dish (mixture will be very thick). Drop the batter into six mounds onto fruit mixture. Cover and bake at

425° for 15 minutes or until a toothpick inserted into a dumpling comes out clean (do not lift the cover while baking). In a saucepan, bring brown sugar and water to a boil; cook until sugar is dissolved. Spoon over dumplings; bake, uncovered, 5 minutes longer. Serve with cream if desired. **Yield:** 6 servings.

BERRY APPLE CRUMBLE

Ginger Isham, Williston, Vermont

(Pictured on page 118)

You can serve this crumble as a snack, and it's also great for a breakfast gathering or church supper. It is good hot...and good on the second day as well.

- 8 to 10 tart apples, peeled and sliced
- 2 tablespoons cornstarch
- 1 can (12 ounces) frozen apple juice concentrate, thawed
- 2 tablespoons butter *or* margarine
- 1 teaspoon ground cinnamon
- 1 teaspoon lemon juice
- 1 cup fresh *or* frozen blackberries
- 1 cup fresh *or* frozen raspberries

TOPPING:
- 2 cups quick-cooking oats
- 1/2 cup all-purpose flour
- 1/2 cup chopped walnuts
- 1/3 cup vegetable oil
- 1/3 cup maple syrup

Place the apples in a greased 13-in. x 9-in. x 2-in. baking dish; set aside. In a saucepan, combine cornstarch and apple juice. Bring to a boil; cook and stir for 2 minutes or until thickened. Add butter, cinnamon and lemon juice. Pour over the apples. Sprinkle with berries. In a bowl, combine the oats, flour and walnuts; add oil and syrup. Sprinkle over berries. Bake at 350° for 40-45 minutes or until filling is bubbly and topping is golden brown. **Yield:** 10-12 servings.

CHOCOLATE BANANA CREAM PIE

Jaquelin McTee, Eatonville, Washington

(Pictured at right)

My husband loves banana cream pie, and I like chocolate, so I combined the two. It's our favorite dessert, which means I get a lot of practice making it!

- 1/2 cup sugar
- 1/4 cup cornstarch
- 1/4 teaspoon salt
- 1-1/2 cups milk

- 1 cup whipping cream
- 3 egg yolks, lightly beaten
- 1 tablespoon butter *or* margarine
- 2 teaspoons vanilla extract
- 1 pastry shell (9 inches), baked
- 4 squares (1 ounce *each*) semisweet chocolate, melted
- 2 medium firm bananas, sliced

Whipped cream and chocolate shavings, optional

In a saucepan, combine sugar, cornstarch and salt. Gradually add milk and cream until smooth. Cook and stir over medium-high heat until thickened and bubbly, about 2 minutes. Add a small amount to egg yolks; mix well. Return all to the pan. Bring to a gentle boil; cook for 2 minutes, stirring constantly. Remove from the heat; stir in butter and vanilla. Pour half into the pastry shell; cover and refrigerate. Add chocolate to remaining custard; mix well. Cover and refrigerate for 1 hour. Do not stir. Arrange bananas over filling. Carefully spoon chocolate custard over all. Refrigerate for at least 2 hours. Garnish with whipped cream and chocolate shavings if desired. **Yield:** 6-8 servings.

SUMMER BERRY CHEESE PIE

Mrs. C. Florkewicz, Caldwell, New Jersey

(Pictured below and on the front cover)

I love to make this pie with fresh blueberries and strawberries from area farms. It's an easy summer treat that my family just gobbles up.

- 1 pint fresh strawberries, sliced, *divided*
- 1 tablespoon lemon juice
- 2/3 cup sugar, *divided*
- 1 package (8 ounces) cream cheese, softened
- 1 teaspoon grated lemon peel
- 1 graham cracker crust (9 inches)
- 2 tablespoons cornstarch
- 3 to 4 drops red food coloring, optional
- 1 pint fresh blueberries

In a bowl, combine half of the strawberries and lemon juice; mash berries. Add 1/3 cup plus 2 tablespoons sugar; set aside. In a mixing bowl, combine cream cheese, lemon peel and remaining sugar. Spread into the crust. In a saucepan, combine cornstarch and reserved strawberry mixture until blended. Bring to a boil; boil and stir for 2 minutes. Stir in food coloring if desired. Cool slightly. Fold in blueberries and remaining strawberries. Spread over cream cheese mixture. Cover and refrigerate for at least 3 hours. **Yield:** 6-8 servings.

PISTACHIO PUFFS

This old-fashioned pastry from the Reiman Publications kitchen staff mixes up quickly before baking.

Then a smooth green filling of whipped cream and pistachio pudding fills the round shells easily—thanks to a simple instant mix.

- 1 cup water
- 1/2 cup butter *or* margarine
- 1 teaspoon sugar
- 1/4 teaspoon salt
- 1 cup all-purpose flour
- 4 eggs
- 1 package (3.4 ounces) instant pistachio pudding mix
- 1-3/4 cups whipped topping

In a large saucepan, bring water, butter, sugar and salt to a boil. Add flour all at once; stir until a smooth ball forms. Remove from the heat; let stand for 5 minutes. Add eggs one at a time, beating well after each addition. Beat until mixture is smooth and shiny. Drop by rounded teaspoonfuls 2 in. apart onto ungreased baking sheets. Bake at 400° for 15-20 minutes or until golden brown. Remove to wire racks. Immediately cut a slit in each puff to allow steam to escape; cool. Split puffs; remove soft dough from inside with a fork. Prepare pudding according to package directions for pie; fold in whipped topping. Spoon into cream puffs. **Yield:** about 2 dozen.

GRAPEFRUIT MERINGUE PIE

Barbara Soliday, Winter Haven, Florida

There's a grapefruit tree in our backyard, so I like to use fresh grapefruit juice when I make this pie. I just love the unique citrus flavor of this dessert.

- 1-1/3 cups sugar
- 1/3 cup cornstarch
- 2 cups pink grapefruit juice
- 3/4 cup water
- 3 egg yolks, lightly beaten
- 2 tablespoons butter *or* margarine
- 1/2 teaspoon lemon extract
- 1 pastry shell (9 inches), baked

MERINGUE:

- 3 egg whites
- 1/4 teaspoon cream of tartar
- 6 tablespoons sugar

In a saucepan, combine sugar and cornstarch. Gradually add grapefruit juice and water. Cook and stir over medium-high heat until thickened and bubbly, about 2 minutes. Reduce heat; cook and stir 2 minutes longer. Gradually stir 1/2 cup into egg yolks; return all to the pan. Bring to a gentle boil; cook and stir for 2 minutes. Remove from the heat; stir in butter and extract. Pour hot filling into pastry shell. In a mixing bowl, beat the egg whites and cream of tartar on medium speed until foamy. Gradually beat in sugar, 1 tablespoon at a time, on high just until stiff peaks form and sugar is dissolved. Spread meringue evenly over hot filling, sealing edges to crust. Bake at 350° for 12-15 minutes or until the meringue is golden brown. Cool on a wire rack for 1 hour. Refrigerate for at least 3 hours before serving. Store in the refrigerator. **Yield:** 6-8 servings.

RHUBARB ELDERBERRY CRISP

Carolyn Scouten, Wyalusing, Pennsylvania

Rhubarb and elderberries are quite abundant around these parts, so I combined the two in this wonderful crisp. It's been well received by our friends.

     1 cup all-purpose flour
   3/4 cup quick-cooking oats
 1-1/2 cups sugar, *divided*
     1 teaspoon ground cinnamon
   1/2 cup cold butter *or* margarine
     3 cups diced rhubarb
     2 cups elderberries *or* blackberries
     2 tablespoons cornstarch
     1 cup water
     1 teaspoon vanilla extract

In a bowl, combine the flour, oats, 1/2 cup sugar and cinnamon; cut in butter until mixture resembles coarse crumbs. Set aside half for topping. Press remaining crumb mixture into an ungreased 11-in. x 7-in. x 2-in. baking dish. Top with rhubarb and berries. In a small saucepan, combine cornstarch and remaining sugar. Gradually stir in water; bring to a boil. Reduce heat; cook and stir for 1-2 minutes or until thickened. Remove from the heat; stir in vanilla. Pour over the fruit. Sprinkle with the reserved crumb mixture. Bake at 350° for 50-55 minutes or until golden brown. Serve warm or cold. **Yield:** 10 servings.

CHOCOLATE-COVERED WHITE CHEESECAKE

Carol Staniger, Springdale, Arkansas

(Pictured above right)

The inside scoop on this tasty treat is the white chocolate center, which makes for an especially rich dessert. I serve it when company calls and at holiday meals.

 1-1/2 cups chocolate wafer crumbs
     3 tablespoons butter *or* margarine, melted
FILLING:
     1 package (12 ounces) vanilla baking
       chips, *divided*

     3 packages (8 ounces *each*) cream cheese,
       softened
   1/2 cup sugar
     1 teaspoon vanilla extract
     3 eggs
GLAZE:
     1 package (12 ounces) semisweet
       chocolate chips
     1 cup whipping cream
     2 tablespoons butter *or* margarine
     2 tablespoons sugar
**White and milk chocolate striped Hershey's
   kisses, optional**
Raspberries *or* cranberries, optional

Combine crumbs and butter; press into the bottom of an ungreased 9-in. springform pan. Bake at 350° for 10 minutes. Cool. For filling, melt 1-1/2 cups vanilla chips; set aside to cool. In a mixing bowl, beat cream cheese, sugar and vanilla until well blended. Add eggs; mix well. Blend in melted vanilla chips. Pour into crust. Bake at 350° for 40 minutes. Turn oven off. Let cheesecake stand in oven for 2 hours (do not open oven door). Cool completely on a wire rack. Chill 4 hours. For glaze, place chocolate chips in a medium bowl; set aside. Heat cream, butter and sugar in a heavy saucepan over medium-high heat; bring to a boil, stirring constantly. Pour over chocolate chips. Cool 3 minutes. Stir until smooth and cool. Remove rim of pan. Spread glaze over the top and sides of the cheesecake. Chill for 2 hours. Melt remaining vanilla chips; drizzle over cheesecake. Garnish with kisses and raspberries if desired. **Yield:** 16 servings.

Quick Crisps & Cobblers

THE BEST of both worlds combine in the recipes on this page. The cobblers and crisps here offer lots of old-fashioned goodness...but are extra fast at the same time, thanks to canned fruits and other handy convenience items.

▪▪▪▪▪▪▪▪▪▪▪▪▪▪

QUICK STRAWBERRY COBBLER

Sue Poe, Hayden, Alabama

(Pictured below)

Blueberry or cherry pie filling also works great with this easy cobbler. A good friend shared this recipe with me.

> 2 cans (21 ounces *each*) strawberry pie filling *or* fruit filling of your choice

1/2 cup butter *or* margarine, softened
1 package (3 ounces) cream cheese, softened
2 teaspoons vanilla extract
2 packages (9 ounces *each*) yellow cake mix

Pour pie filling into a greased 13-in. x 9-in. x 2-in. baking dish. Bake at 350° for 5-7 minutes or until heated through. Meanwhile, in a mixing bowl, cream butter, cream cheese and vanilla. Place cake mixes in another bowl; cut in cream cheese mixture until crumbly. Sprinkle over hot filling. Bake 25-30 minutes longer or until topping is golden brown. **Yield:** 12 servings.

▪▪▪▪▪▪▪▪▪▪▪▪▪▪

CHERRY PINEAPPLE CRISP

Annabell Jordan, Broken Arrow, Oklahoma

I made this crisp often when our children were growing up. Now our grandchildren love it as well. It's terrific topped with ice cream. Cherries and pineapple are a tasty combination.

> 2 cans (16 ounces *each*) pitted tart cherries
> 1 can (20 ounces) crushed pineapple, undrained
> 1 cup sugar
> 1/3 cup quick-cooking tapioca
> 2 cups all-purpose flour
> 1 cup packed brown sugar
> 3/4 cup quick-cooking oats
> 1 teaspoon baking powder
> 1/2 teaspoon salt
> 1-1/2 teaspoons vanilla extract
> 3/4 cup cold butter *or* margarine

Ice cream, optional

Drain cherries, reserving 1/3 cup juice. Place cherries and juice in a saucepan; add pineapple, sugar and tapioca. Let stand for 5 minutes. Meanwhile, in a bowl, combine flour, brown sugar, oats, baking powder and salt. Add vanilla; toss. Cut in butter until crumbly; press half into a greased 13-in. x 9-in. x 2-in. baking dish. Bring cherry mixture to a boil, stirring occasionally; cook and stir for 1 minute or until thick and bubbly. Pour over crust. Sprinkle with remaining oat mixture. Bake at 375° for 25-30 minutes or until filling is bub-

bly and topping is golden brown. Serve warm with ice cream if desired. **Yield:** 12 servings.

CRAN-APPLE COOKIE COBBLER

Renee Ryno, Spokane, Washington

For a nice change of pace from traditional cobbler, give this recipe a try. Folks enjoy the sugar cookie topping, and I love the convenience!

- 4 medium tart apples, peeled and sliced 1/4 inch thick
- 1 can (16 ounces) whole-berry cranberry sauce
- 1/3 cup packed brown sugar
- 3 tablespoons all-purpose flour
- 1 teaspoon ground cinnamon
- 1 tube (18 ounces) refrigerated sugar cookie dough

Ice cream, optional

Place apples in a greased 9-in. square baking dish. Combine cranberry sauce, brown sugar, flour and cinnamon; pour over apples. Cut cookie dough in half widthwise (refrigerate half of the dough for another use). Cut remaining dough into 1/4-in. slices. Place over apple mixture. Bake at 400° for 25-30 minutes or until topping is golden brown and apples are tender. Serve with ice cream if desired. **Yield:** 9 servings.

CRANBERRY CRUMBLE

Karen Riordan, Louisville, Kentucky

My family likes this crumble so much I make it year-round. But I especially like to serve it warm on cool winter evenings.

- 1-1/2 cups quick-cooking oats
- 1 cup packed brown sugar
- 1/2 cup all-purpose flour
- 1/3 cup cold butter *or* margarine
- 1 can (16 ounces) whole-berry cranberry sauce

Whipped cream *or* ice cream, optional

In a bowl, combine oats, brown sugar and flour. Cut in butter until crumbly. Press half into a greased 8-in. square baking dish. Spread the cranberry sauce evenly over crust. Sprinkle with remaining oat mixture. Bake at 350° for 35-40 minutes or until golden brown and filling is hot. Serve warm with whipped cream or ice cream if desired. **Yield:** 9 servings.

CRISPY RHUBARB COBBLER

Martha Freeman, Villisca, Iowa

I worked in a school cafeteria for 15 years. I'm retired now but still love to cook. This rhubarb cobbler is one of my favorites.

- 1 cup sugar
- 1/3 cup pancake mix
- 4 cups diced fresh *or* frozen rhubarb, thawed and drained

TOPPING:
- 1 egg, beaten
- 1/4 cup vegetable oil
- 2/3 cup sugar
- 1/2 cup pancake mix

In a bowl, combine sugar and pancake mix. Add the rhubarb and toss to coat. Transfer to a greased 8-in. square baking dish. Combine topping ingredients; spread over rhubarb mixture. Bake at 350° for 45 minutes or until filling is bubbly and top is golden brown. **Yield:** 6 servings.

BLUEBERRY RASPBERRY CRUNCH

Harriett Catlin, Nanticoke, Maryland

This quick-to-fix dessert comes in handy when I need to make something sweet in a hurry. I often have the ingredients in my pantry.

- 1 can (21 ounces) blueberry pie filling
- 1 can (21 ounces) raspberry pie filling
- 1 package (18-1/4 ounces) white cake mix
- 1/2 cup chopped walnuts
- 1/2 cup butter *or* margarine, melted

Combine pie fillings in a greased 13-in. x 9-in. x 2-in. baking dish. In a bowl, combine cake mix, walnuts and butter until crumbly; sprinkle over filling. Bake at 375° for 25-30 minutes or until filling is bubbly and topping is golden brown. Serve warm. **Yield:** 12 servings.

TIPS ON CRISPS

A shortcut in preparing apple filling for a crisp is to add the sugar and spices to your sliced apples, then freeze in heavy-duty plastic bags. When needed, just pour the slices into a baking dish, add a crumb topping and bake.

Speedy Dishes Fit into a Busy Schedule

AN ACTIVE FAMILY of four growing children, an on-the-road truck-driver husband and her own part-time job as a seamstress can cause a challenge at mealtime for Nova MacIsaac of Souris, Prince Edward Island.

At least once a month, though, she solves the scheduling problem with the tried-and-true tasty menu featured here. Like all the complete meals in this chapter, it can be prepared in half an hour or under.

"The main dish," Nova says, "is a nice change of pace from traditional sweet-and-sour meatballs. It's much quicker to make, too. For variety, I like to substitute a different kind of sausage, like spicy Italian.

"Because my broccoli salad won't wilt like lettuce salads, you can make it ahead for added convenience.

"To enhance the salad," she notes, "I will sometimes add walnuts, green grapes, mushrooms and a touch of onion. You can also mix in cauliflower florets with the broccoli, then squeeze on a hint of lemon juice.

"A plain purchased pound cake's at the heart of the elegant-looking dessert," Nova shares.

"I've used angel food cake, cupcakes, doughnuts and even a stack of cookies as the base in place of the pound cake. Top it off with a fun selection of sundae makings—nuts, orange rinds, cherries, etc."

SWEET-AND-SOUR SAUSAGE

1 package (12 ounces) uncooked sausage links, cut into bite-size pieces
1 cup sugar
3 tablespoons cornstarch
1 cup water
1/2 cup vinegar
1/2 cup ketchup
1 can (8 ounces) crushed pineapple, drained
Hot cooked rice

In a skillet, cook sausage until no longer pink; drain and set aside. Combine sugar, cornstarch, water, vinegar and ketchup; add to skillet. Bring to a boil. Reduce heat; cook for 2 minutes or until thickened. Add pineapple and sausage; heat through. Serve over rice. **Yield:** 4 servings.

SIMPLE BROCCOLI SALAD

2 cups broccoli florets
4 bacon strips, cooked and crumbled
1/4 cup chopped sweet red pepper
1/2 cup mayonnaise
2 tablespoons sugar
1 tablespoon vinegar

In a bowl, combine broccoli, bacon and red pepper. In another bowl, stir the mayonnaise, sugar and vinegar until smooth. Pour over broccoli mixture and toss to coat. **Yield:** 4 servings.

CARAMEL TOP HATS

1 cup packed brown sugar
1/4 cup evaporated milk
2 tablespoons butter *or* margarine
2 tablespoons corn syrup
4 slices pound cake
Butter pecan ice cream

In a saucepan, combine the brown sugar, evaporated milk, butter and corn syrup; mix well. Cook and stir over medium-low heat until heated through (do not boil). Top each slice of pound cake with a scoop of ice cream; drizzle with warm caramel sauce. Serve immediately. Refrigerate any leftover sauce. **Yield:** 4 servings.

Kid-Pleasing Fare Cooks Up Quickly

THE MORE the merrier makes meals that take 30 minutes or less "musts" for LaVerna Mjones of Moorhead, Minnesota.

"My husband, Arnold, and I have four grown children and 10 grandchildren," she explains, "and all of us live in the same town. We always welcome drop-in visits. With a number of 'meals in minutes' in my recipe file, I can easily ask, 'Will you join us for dinner?' "

The one she shares here is a favorite with her grandkids.

"Several of them attend junior high school a few blocks from our home," LaVerna notes. "Often, they will bring friends over for this fun-to-eat meal before they go back to school for evening sports practices.

"For me, my menu is as much of a treat to fix as it is to eat. Each recipe calls for basic ingredients that I generally have on hand. There are also nice and easy steps even young children can help with—like crushing tortilla chips or stirring up the pudding.

"In place of the ground beef and mozzarella cheese," suggests LaVerna, "consider topping the zesty pie with lean ground sausage and cheddar cheese. It tastes just as good."

The salad, she adds, can easily be varied by using whatever greens you wish. For the dressing, either oil and vinegar or a sweet-and-sour mix is a good choice.

As for the dessert, "You can substitute other kinds of candy bars to suit your preference," she says. "The pudding flavor can be changed as well—perhaps to vanilla or butterscotch."

NACHO PIE

4 cups nacho cheese tortilla chips, coarsely crushed
1 pound ground beef
1/2 cup chopped onion
Salt and pepper to taste
1 can (15-1/2 ounces) chili beans
1 can (8 ounces) tomato sauce
1 cup (4 ounces) shredded mozzarella cheese

Place chips in a lightly greased 9-in. pie plate and set aside. In a skillet over medium heat, cook beef and onion until meat is no longer pink; drain. Season with salt and pepper. Spoon over chips. Top with beans, tomato sauce and mozzarella. Bake, uncovered, at 375° for 15-17 minutes or until heated through. **Yield:** 4-6 servings.

CRUNCHY TOSSED SALAD

6 cups torn salad greens
2 green onions, chopped
1 cup chow mein noodles
1/2 cup chopped cashews
2 tablespoons crumbled cooked bacon
2 tablespoons sesame seeds
Salad dressing of your choice

In a large salad bowl, combine the salad greens, onions, chow mein noodles, cashews, bacon and sesame seeds. Toss with dressing or serve on the side. **Yield:** 4-6 servings.

BANANA BUTTERFINGER PUDDING

1 cup cold milk
1 package (3.4 ounces) instant banana pudding mix
3 Butterfinger candy bars (2.1 ounces *each*), crushed
1 carton (8 ounces) frozen whipped topping, thawed
3 medium firm bananas, sliced

In a mixing bowl, combine milk and pudding mix until thickened and smooth. Set aside 1/3 cup crushed candy bars for topping. Fold whipped topping, bananas and remaining candy bars into pudding. Spoon into serving dishes; refrigerate until ready to serve. Sprinkle with the reserved candy bars. **Yield:** 4-6 servings.

PEANUTTY PUDDING

Does your family prefer peanut butter cups? This pudding's just as easy to make!

Add 1 teaspoon of peanut butter to individual servings of prepared instant chocolate pudding. Microwave on high for 30 seconds or until warm; stir gently. Sprinkle with chopped up peanut butter cups.

Sub Supper Saves Time in The Kitchen

WHEN summer beams 20 hours of sun on Alaska per day, Heidi Doudna of Fairbanks doesn't want to spend many of them cooking meals for her family in the kitchen.

"My husband, David, and I love to go hiking, biking, camping and canoeing with our four youngsters," she remarks. "Plus, we have fun growing Alaska-size vegetables in our backyard garden."

So, especially in the warmer months, this teacher relies on quick-to-fix dishes that she can get ready in 30 minutes or less. The complete meal on this page is one she serves often for lunch or dinner.

"People like the melding of melted cheese, juicy meat and crunchy bread in the main dish," Heidi shares. She suggests varying the taste of her sandwiches by occasionally substituting a different cheese—for example, cheddar—for the mozzarella and adding pepperoni for more zest.

"The vegetables in the green bean side dish make a colorful presentation that's a nice alternative to lettuce," she says. "To dress up the beans, use small tomato wedges. For a touch of crunch, sprinkle some buttered and browned bread crumbs on top."

The dessert's peach and pineapple complement the sandwiches. "I like to liven up individual servings with almond slices," Heidi notes.

"In summer," she reports, "I'll accompany this meal with my homemade sweet, dill or watermelon pickles. During winter, I'll start it off with bowls of hot soup. The temperatures up here can get all the way down to -50°!"

Hot 'n' Hearty Ham Subs

1/4 cup butter *or* margarine, melted
1 teaspoon garlic powder
1 teaspoon dried oregano
6 submarine *or* hot dog buns, split
1/2 cup mayonnaise
2 teaspoons Dijon mustard
1 teaspoon Worcestershire sauce
2 cups cubed fully cooked ham
1 cup (4 ounces) shredded mozzarella cheese
1 tablespoon minced fresh parsley

Combine the butter, garlic powder and oregano; brush on cut sides of buns. Place on a baking sheet; broil 4 in. from the heat until golden brown, about 2 minutes. In a bowl, combine mayonnaise, mustard and Worcestershire sauce; stir in the ham. Spoon about 1/3 cup onto each bun bottom; sprinkle with cheese and parsley. Broil 3-4 minutes longer or until cheese is melted. Replace bun tops. **Yield:** 6 servings.

Confetti Green Beans

1 package (10 ounces) frozen cut green beans, thawed and drained
1 can (7 ounces) whole kernel corn, drained
1/4 cup butter *or* margarine
1/4 cup sliced ripe olives
1/2 teaspoon dried basil
1/2 teaspoon dried oregano
1/4 teaspoon garlic powder

In a saucepan, combine the green beans, corn, butter and olives. Season with basil, oregano and garlic powder. Cover and cook over medium heat for 8-10 minutes or until beans are crisp-tender. **Yield:** 6 servings.

Peach Chiffon Cups

1 can (21 ounces) peach *or* cherry pie filling
1 can (20 ounces) pineapple tidbits, drained
1 carton (8 ounces) vanilla yogurt
1 cup miniature marshmallows
1 carton (8 ounces) frozen whipped topping, thawed
Fresh mint, optional

In a bowl, gently stir pie filling, pineapple, yogurt, marshmallows and whipped topping. Spoon into serving dishes. Garnish with mint if desired. Refrigerate leftovers. **Yield:** 12 servings.

Cooking Caution

Be careful not to overcook fresh beans—they should be crisp-tender when done. Overcooked beans will lose some of their bright green color as well as their fresh flavor.

Fast Foods Fit For On-the-Go Families

FAMILY ACTIVITIES often exceed the speed limit at Kim Dunbar's home in Willow Springs, Illinois. That's why quick recipes get a green light from this busy wife and mother.

"My husband, Jeff, works odd hours in road construction, and our son, Michael, just got his driver's license," she says. "And with Morgan on the go with Girl Scouts and little Madison already running, I move fast to fit meals into our schedules."

The family-tested menu featured here is one the Dunbar clan will happily sit still for. Not only is it fast—ready in under 30 minutes—but it's filling as well.

"The savory sub is ideal for brunch, lunch or dinner," Kim informs. "It's like eating an omelet sandwich." For variety, she suggests using a different cheese—such as provolone—on the egg sandwich, and French or Italian bread.

The salad has a creamy dressing and garden-fresh taste. "To trim calories in the salad, try light sour cream," Kim advises. "You can also substitute white or green onions and cherry or plum tomatoes."

Ice cream has long been a hassle-free dessert that complements any meal. Top it off with a yummy oat mixture, and you've got an instant success.

"My kids like to mix the no-bake granola topping themselves and sprinkle it over the ice cream of their choice," she shares.

Minutes saved in her kitchen are minutes earned for Kim's pastimes. "My latest project was editing a cookbook for Morgan's school," she reports. "This time-saving meal was my contribution."

SCRAMBLED EGG SANDWICH

1 loaf (16 ounces) frozen garlic bread
  (pre-sliced in half lengthwise)
1/2 cup finely chopped onion
1/2 cup finely chopped green pepper
  3 tablespoons butter *or* margarine
10 eggs
1/4 cup milk

Salt and pepper to taste
  6 to 8 mozzarella cheese slices

Bake garlic bread according to package directions. Meanwhile, saute onion and green pepper in butter until crisp-tender. In a bowl, beat eggs, milk, salt and pepper; pour into the skillet. Cook over medium heat; as eggs begin to set, gently move spatula across the bottom and sides of pan. When eggs are completely set, remove from the heat and keep warm. Arrange cheese slices on bottom half of bread; spoon eggs over cheese. Replace bread top. Slice and serve immediately. **Yield:** 6 servings.

CREAMY TOMATO SALAD

1 large cucumber, peeled and cut into
  1/4-inch slices
1 large tomato, chopped
1 small red onion, thinly sliced
1 cup (8 ounces) sour cream
1 tablespoon sugar
1 tablespoon vinegar
Salt and pepper to taste
Leaf lettuce, optional

In a bowl, combine cucumber, tomato and onion. In another bowl, combine the sour cream, sugar, vinegar, salt and pepper; mix well. Pour over vegetables and toss to coat. Refrigerate until serving. Serve over lettuce if desired. **Yield:** 6 servings.

GRANOLA SUNDAES

1 cup quick-cooking oats
1/2 cup packed brown sugar
1/4 cup peanut butter
1/4 cup butter *or* margarine, softened
Ice cream

In a bowl, combine oats and brown sugar. Stir in peanut butter and butter until mixture forms coarse crumbs. Sprinkle over ice cream. **Yield:** 2 cups topping.

GOOD USES FOR GRANOLA

The versatile granola mix can top off other foods besides ice cream...try it on yogurt, fresh fruit or pie filling. Or roll it into a ball for a sweet snack.

Home-Cooked Meal Made In a Hurry

"HOUSEWORK" is building around Darlene Markel's acreage near Mt. Hood, Oregon. Luckily, rapid recipes are also part of this constructive woman's plan.

"Now that our two daughters are grown, my husband, Duane, and I are busy building our dream house," she relates. "Quick dishes made in our temporary trailer home are lifesavers."

The snappy menu featured here has fast become a favorite of the Markels.

"The crispy and fruity chicken salad is refreshing served for lunch, dinner or a potluck supper—either warm or cold," Darlene affirms. For an easy change of pace, she suggests using a bottled salad dressing.

"Dipped in melted butter, the biscuit sticks are a special melt-in-your-mouth substitute for regular bread. I often dress them up by giving them a garlic or cheese flavor," she says.

"The fruit cobbler offers the fresh-picked flavor of pie without the fuss of making crusts."

Darlene sometimes pairs strawberries with raspberries, blackberries or blueberries for a two-toned cobbler.

"When we're ready for a housewarming, these three speedy courses will help us extend a tasty welcome."

MANDARIN CHICKEN SALAD

1 pound boneless skinless chicken breasts, cut into 1/2-inch cubes
1/2 cup water
1/3 cup vinegar
3 tablespoons brown sugar
3 tablespoons vegetable oil, *divided*
1 tablespoon soy sauce
2 chicken bouillon cubes
1/3 to 1/2 cup mayonnaise
2 tablespoons honey
2 tablespoons lemon juice
2 teaspoons minced parsley
2 teaspoons ground mustard
1/4 teaspoon dried minced onion
1 package (10 ounces) ready-to-serve salad *or* 4 cups torn lettuce
1 can (11 ounces) mandarin oranges, drained
1 cup chow mein noodles
1 green onion, thinly sliced
2 tablespoons sliced almonds

In a skillet, combine chicken, water, vinegar, brown sugar, 1 tablespoon oil, soy sauce and bouillon. Cook and stir over medium heat for 15-20 minutes or until chicken is tender and liquid has evaporated. Meanwhile, for dressing, whisk mayonnaise, honey, lemon juice, parsley, mustard, onion and remaining oil until blended. Arrange salad greens on a platter. Top with oranges, chicken mixture and chow mein noodles. Sprinkle with green onion and almonds. Serve with dressing. **Yield:** 4 servings.

BISCUIT STICKS

1/4 cup butter (no substitutes)
1-1/4 cups all-purpose flour
2 teaspoons baking powder
2 teaspoons sugar
1 teaspoon salt
1/2 to 2/3 cup milk

Place butter in a 9-in. square baking pan; place in a 425° oven for 4 minutes or until melted. Remove from the oven; set aside. Combine dry ingredients in a bowl; gradually add enough milk to form a soft dough. On a floured surface, knead 4-5 times. Roll out into an 8-in. square; cut in half with a sharp knife. Cut each half into eight strips. Dip each strip into melted butter in pan, carefully turning to coat; arrange in rows in pan. Bake at 425° for 18-20 minutes or until golden brown. **Yield:** 16 breadsticks.

STRAWBERRY COBBLER

1/2 cup sugar
1/4 cup cornstarch
2 packages (10 ounces *each*) frozen sweetened sliced strawberries, thawed
2 tablespoons butter *or* margarine, cubed
1 package (7 ounces) strawberry *or* raspberry muffin mix
1/4 cup milk

In a bowl, combine sugar, cornstarch and berries. Transfer to a greased 11-in. x 7-in. x 2-in. baking dish. Dot with butter. In another bowl, combine muffin mix and milk just until blended; drop by tablespoonfuls onto strawberry mixture. Bake at 425° for 18-22 minutes or until golden brown and bubbly. **Yield:** 4-6 servings.

Festive Meal Is Fast And Flavorful

TWO busy schedules keep life lively for Cheryl Norwood and husband Mike in Canton, Georgia. That's why this active couple doesn't think twice about trying double-quick recipes.

"Balancing full-time jobs with hobbies, church projects and remodeling our house keeps Mike and me on the go," Cheryl notes. "I'm always on the lookout for no-fuss nutritious meals."

The meaty menu here is one of the Norwoods' favorites. It's a hot and hearty meal that can be made in under half an hour.

"The tangy meat loaf 'muffins' are fun for dinner, supper or a take-along lunch," Cheryl suggests. "They're just as flavorful after freezing. Plus, they're the perfect size for sandwich slices. Mike is happy to eat *these* leftovers...if there are any left over, that is.

"The oniony potato cups are a nice switch from the usual side dishes. I sometimes add cheese to the cups for a tasty twist," she advises. "Either way, they're savory and satisfying. I use green onions when I want a bit more color.

"I downsized the fruit salad from a dessert trifle recipe. Everybody loves its luscious colors," she relates.

In-season fresh fruit can easily stand in for the canned fruit cocktail and pie filling. For a trifle-like salad, Cheryl substitutes instant pudding as a topping.

The hurry at her house has a merry air around the holidays, Cheryl cheerfully shares. "I'm the special projects coordinator for our church. In December, I work on our annual Hanging of the Greens—when we place fresh tree boughs around our church and community."

Since Christmas is also the season for potlucks and other gatherings, Cheryl adds, "It's simple to increase the quantities of all three of these recipes to satisfy a crowd quickly and easily."

MINI MEAT LOAVES

1/2 cup finely chopped onion
1/2 cup finely chopped green pepper
1/2 cup dry bread crumbs
1/4 cup barbecue sauce
1 egg
1-1/2 pounds lean ground beef
Ketchup

In a large bowl, combine the onion, green pepper, bread crumbs, barbecue sauce and egg. Add the beef and mix well. Press 1/3 cupfuls into six ungreased muffin cups. Top with ketchup. Bake at 375° for 18-20 minutes or until meat is no longer pink. **Yield:** 6 servings.

POTATO-STUFFED ONIONS

1 large sweet onion
1-1/2 cups frozen shredded hash brown
    potatoes, thawed
4 teaspoons beef bouillon granules
2 tablespoons butter *or* margarine
Pepper to taste
Minced fresh parsley, optional

Cut onion in half widthwise; remove ends and outside skin. Separate onion into layers; select six to fit lightly greased muffin cups. Finely dice remaining onion; place in a bowl. Add hash browns and bouillon. Spoon into onion cups; dot with butter. Bake at 375° for 18-20 minutes or until tender. Sprinkle with pepper and parsley if desired. **Yield:** 6 servings.

DESSERT FRUIT CUP

1 can (15 ounces) fruit cocktail, drained
1 to 2 medium firm bananas, sliced
1 can (8 ounces) pineapple tidbits, drained
1 can (21 ounces) cherry pie filling
Whipped topping, toasted flaked coconut and
    slivered almonds

Spoon fruit cocktail into individual bowls. Top with bananas, pineapple tidbits and pie filling. Garnish with whipped topping, coconut and almonds. **Yield:** 6 servings.

MEAT LOAF MAKEOVER

Replace the bread crumbs with crushed cheese crackers to coat the meat loaves. Adding mozzarella cheese and topping with tomato paste will yield Italian-style meat loaves...and salsa instead of barbecue sauce will add Southwestern zest.

Our Most Memorable Meals

Nothing will bring back the good old days like these simple yet satisfying dishes that graced family tables across the country.

Dishes Prove To Be Real Crowd-Pleasers

FOLKS will stand in line to sample this crowd-pleasing spread on your buffet table.

"A neighbor shared the recipe for Tangy Pork Barbecue with me in the late '50s," confides Carmine Walters of San Jose, California. "She found it in a Marine Officers' Wives cookbook. It's been a hit with my family ever since."

M.J. Zimmerman of Altoona, Pennsylvania tossed together Apple Iceberg Salad when her children were small and fussed about eating fruits and vegetables. "They loved the slightly sweet dressing," she says.

Whenever Orlando, Florida cook Reginald Davis serves Crabby Deviled Eggs, his guests are puzzled by the unique taste. "It's not the traditional taste of deviled eggs," Reginald shares. "The surprise ingredient is crab, which makes for a delightful change."

Jill McCon's mother copied the recipe for Date Bar Dessert from a Quaker Oats box in the 1950s. "It remains one of our favorite treats today," declares this Montrose, Michigan resident. "I serve the date-filled squares as a snack or for dessert topped with a dollop of whipped cream."

TANGY PORK BARBECUE

✓ Uses less fat, sugar or salt. Includes Nutritional Analysis and Diabetic Exchanges.

- 2 tablespoons butter *or* margarine
- 3 tablespoons all-purpose flour
- 1 bottle (28 ounces) ketchup
- 2 cups boiling water
- 1/4 cup vinegar
- 1/4 cup Worcestershire sauce
- 1 medium onion, chopped
- 1 garlic clove, minced
- 2 teaspoons chili powder
- 1 teaspoon salt, optional
- 1 teaspoon ground mustard
- 1/8 teaspoon cayenne pepper
- 1 boneless pork loin roast (3-1/2 to 4 pounds)
- 12 sandwich buns, split

In a Dutch oven over medium heat, melt butter. Stir in flour until smooth. Add the next 10 ingredients; bring to a boil. Add roast. Reduce heat; cover and simmer for 3 hours or until meat is very tender. Remove meat; shred with two forks or a pastry blender. Skim fat from cooking juices; return meat to juices and heat through. Serve with a slotted spoon on buns. **Yield:** 12 servings. **Nutritional Analysis:** One 3/4-cup serving (prepared with margarine and no-salt-added ketchup and without salt; calculated without bun) equals 245 calories, 141 mg sodium, 80 mg cholesterol, 5 gm carbohydrate, 29 gm protein, 5 gm fat. **Diabetic Exchanges:** 4 lean meat, 1 vegetable.

APPLE ICEBERG SALAD

- 1 cup mayonnaise
- 1/4 cup sugar
- 2 tablespoons cider vinegar
- 2 tablespoons evaporated milk
- 2 large red apples, diced
- 1 medium head iceberg lettuce, torn

In a bowl, combine the mayonnaise, sugar, vinegar and milk; mix well. Add apples. Cover and refrigerate for 1 hour. Just before serving, toss with lettuce. **Yield:** 8-10 servings.

CRABBY DEVILED EGGS

- 12 hard-cooked eggs
- 1 can (6 ounces) crabmeat, drained, flaked and cartilage removed
- 1/4 cup mayonnaise *or* salad dressing
- 2 tablespoons sweet pickle relish

1 tablespoon prepared mustard
2 teaspoons seafood seasoning
1/4 teaspoon pepper

Slice eggs in half lengthwise. Remove yolks and set the whites aside. In a bowl, mash yolks with a fork. Add crab, mayonnaise, relish, mustard, seafood seasoning and pepper; mix well. Stuff into egg whites. Refrigerate until serving. **Yield:** 1 dozen.

DATE BAR DESSERT

1-3/4 cups old-fashioned oats
1-1/2 cups all-purpose flour
  1 cup packed brown sugar
  1 teaspoon baking soda

1/2 teaspoon salt
  1 cup cold butter *or* margarine
2-1/2 cups chopped dates
  3/4 cup sugar
  3/4 cup water
  1/2 cup chopped walnuts
Whipped topping

In a large bowl, combine oats, flour, brown sugar, baking soda and salt. Cut in butter until mixture resembles coarse crumbs. Press into a greased 13-in. x 9-in. x 2-in. baking pan. In a saucepan, combine dates, sugar and water. Cook for 10 minutes or until thickened, stirring frequently. Stir in walnuts. Spread over crust. Bake at 350° for 30 minutes. Cool on a wire rack. Cut into squares; top with whipped topping. **Yield:** 18 servings.

Country Cooks Fall Back on Family Favorites

ONE TASTE and your family will request these tried-and-true favorites again and again.

Recalls Vivienne Abraham of Detroit, Michigan, "Pasties were a must years ago when men worked the mines in northern Michigan. Everyone said Mother's Pasties were the best in the world!"

Special Creamed Corn has a permanent place on Deb Hauptmann's holiday table. "My whole family loves it," declares this Mohnton, Pennsylvania mom, "but my son, especially, would be disappointed if it wasn't part of our meal."

Cathee Bethel of Philomath, Oregon relies on Bacon-Swiss Tossed Salad when she needs a side dish in a hurry. "This pretty salad can be put together a couple hours before serving," she shares. "When it's time, a simple toss and it's ready."

Credits Jo Peapples from Brooksville, Florida, "My mother made Raisin-Filled Torte many times when I was growing up, and it was always my favorite. The layers are different flavors, and combined they're deliciously unique."

MOTHER'S PASTIES

     3 cups diced peeled potatoes
     1 cup diced carrots
     1 medium onion, chopped
   3/4 teaspoon salt
   1/4 teaspoon pepper
   1/2 pound ground beef
   1/4 pound ground pork
     1 tablespoon butter *or* margarine, melted
PASTRY:
     4 cups all-purpose flour
 1-1/4 teaspoons salt
     1 cup shortening
   3/4 cup cold water

In a bowl, combine the first five ingredients. Add beef and pork; mix well. Add butter and toss; set aside. For pastry, combine flour and salt in a bowl. Cut in shortening until the mixture resembles coarse crumbs. Gradually add water, tossing with a fork until a ball forms. Divide into five portions; roll each into a 10-in. circle. Place 1 cup of filling in the center of each circle. Fold pastry over filling and seal edges tightly with a fork; cut slits in the top of each. Place on a greased baking sheet. Bake at 375° for 50-60 minutes or until golden brown. **Yield:** 5 servings.

SPECIAL CREAMED CORN

   1/3 cup butter *or* margarine
   1/3 cup all-purpose flour
     1 cup whipping cream
     1 cup milk
   1/4 cup sugar
     1 teaspoon salt
Dash white pepper
     5 cups frozen corn, thawed
   1/4 cup grated Parmesan cheese

In a saucepan, melt butter over medium heat. Stir in flour until smooth. Gradually add cream, milk, sugar, salt and pepper. Bring to a boil; boil and stir for 2 minutes. Add corn; heat through. Transfer to an ungreased 1-1/2-qt. broiler-proof dish. Sprinkle with Parmesan cheese. Broil 5 in. from the heat for 3-5 minutes or until lightly browned and bubbly. **Yield:** 6-8 servings.

BACON-SWISS TOSSED SALAD

   1/2 cup mayonnaise
     1 tablespoon sugar
   1/4 teaspoon salt
   1/4 teaspoon pepper
     6 cups mixed salad greens
     1 medium red onion, sliced
     1 package (10 ounces) frozen peas, thawed
     8 ounces sliced Swiss cheese, julienned
     1 pound bacon, cooked and crumbled

In a small bowl, combine mayonnaise, sugar, salt and pepper. In a large salad bowl, layer a third of the greens and a third of the mayonnaise mixture, onion, peas and cheese. Repeat the layers twice. Cover and refrigerate for at least 2 hours. Just before serving, add the bacon and toss. **Yield:** 6-8 servings.

RAISIN-FILLED TORTE

   1/2 cup shortening
 1-1/4 cups sugar
     2 eggs
     2 cups cake flour
     2 teaspoons baking powder
   3/4 teaspoon salt
   3/4 cup milk

1 teaspoon vanilla extract
1-1/2 teaspoons maple syrup
1/4 teaspoon ground cinnamon
1/8 teaspoon ground cloves
1/8 teaspoon ground nutmeg
FILLING:
1/3 cup sugar
1 tablespoon cornstarch
2/3 cup water
1-1/2 cups raisins
1 teaspoon lemon juice
1 teaspoon butter *or* margarine
1/4 teaspoon grated lemon peel
ICING:
1 cup confectioners' sugar
1 tablespoon butter *or* margarine, melted
1/4 teaspoon grated lemon peel
5 to 6 teaspoons milk

In a mixing bowl, cream shortening and sugar. Add eggs, one at a time, beating well after each. Combine flour, baking powder and salt; add to creamed mixture alternately with milk. Pour half of the batter into another bowl. Add vanilla to one bowl; add syrup, cinnamon, cloves and nutmeg to the second bowl. Pour each batter into a greased and floured 9-in. round cake pan. Bake at 375° for 20-25 minutes or until cakes test done. Cool for 10 minutes; remove from pans to wire racks to cool. Combine sugar and cornstarch in a saucepan; stir in water until smooth. Add raisins. Bring to a boil; boil and stir for 2 minutes. Remove from the heat; stir in lemon juice, butter and peel. Cool. In a small bowl, whisk sugar, butter and lemon peel. Add milk until icing reaches desired consistency. Place the spice cake layer on a serving platter; spread with filling. Top with vanilla cake layer and icing. **Yield:** 12 servings.

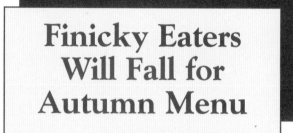

Finicky Eaters Will Fall for Autumn Menu

EVEN the palates of picky eaters will be pleased with this mouth-watering meal.

"People who don't normally care for turnips find they enjoy their distinctive flavor in Autumn Vegetable Beef Stew," says Martha Tonnies of Ft. Mitchell, Kentucky. "The recipe was given to me by a dear friend many years ago."

Making Lemony Marinated Vegetables was a good way to ensure that Helen Vail's daughters and other picky eaters would eat—and enjoy—their vegetables. Proclaims this Glenside, Pennsylvania cook, "The salad is so colorful and tasty."

Charles Steers of Anaheim, California makes his meals memorable with oven-fresh Crusty Rolls. "I told my sister-in-law I missed the crispy rolls I used to buy from the bakery, so she tracked down the recipe for me!" he shares.

The recipe for Country Plum Crumble was passed down to Shari Dore of Brantford, Ontario by her grandmother over 30 years ago. "Now history has repeated itself," says Shari. "I've given the recipe to many friends."

AUTUMN VEGETABLE BEEF STEW

   1 teaspoon salt
1/4 teaspoon pepper
1/4 teaspoon paprika
   1 pound round steak, cut into 1-inch cubes
   1 tablespoon vegetable oil
   1 tablespoon all-purpose flour
1-1/2 cups water
   1 medium onion, chopped
1/2 cup tomato sauce
   2 beef bouillon cubes
1/2 teaspoon caraway seeds
   1 bay leaf
   2 medium potatoes, peeled and cut into 1-inch cubes
   2 medium turnips, peeled and cut into 1-inch cubes
   2 medium carrots, cut into 1-inch slices

Combine salt, pepper and paprika; toss with beef. In a large saucepan over medium heat, brown beef in oil. Sprinkle with flour; stir well. Add water, onion, tomato sauce, bouillon, caraway seeds and bay leaf. Cover and simmer for 1 hour. Add potatoes, turnips and carrots; cover and simmer 45 minutes longer or until meat and vegetables are tender. Discard bay leaf. **Yield:** 4-6 servings.

LEMONY MARINATED VEGETABLES

✓ Uses less fat, sugar or salt. Includes Nutritional Analysis and Diabetic Exchanges.

   1 cup fresh brussels sprouts
1/2 pound carrots, cut into 1/2-inch slices
   3 cups cauliflowerets
1-1/2 cups broccoli florets
   3 tablespoons lemon juice
   2 teaspoons vegetable oil
   2 teaspoons minced fresh parsley
   1 garlic clove, minced
   1 lemon peel strip, 2-1/2 inches x 1/2 inch
1/2 teaspoon dried oregano
1/2 teaspoon dried basil
1/2 teaspoon salt, optional
1/8 teaspoon pepper
   2 cups cherry tomatoes

Place brussels sprouts and carrots in a large saucepan; add 1 in. of water. Bring to a boil; cook for 3 minutes. Add cauliflower and broccoli; return to a boil. Cook for 5 minutes or until vegetables are crisp-tender. Rinse in cold water; drain. In a large bowl, combine lemon juice, oil, parsley, garlic, lemon peel, oregano, basil, salt if desired and pepper. Add cooked vegetables and the tomatoes; toss to coat. Cover and refrigerate for at least 8 hours. Discard lemon peel. **Yield:** 6-8 servings. **Nutritional Analysis:** One 1-cup serving (prepared without salt) equals 50 calories, 39 mg sodium, 0 cholesterol, 9 gm carbohydrate, 2 gm protein, 1 gm fat. **Diabetic Exchange:** 2 vegetable.

CRUSTY ROLLS

✓ Uses less fat, sugar or salt. Includes Nutritional Analysis and Diabetic Exchanges.

   1 package (1/4 ounce) active dry yeast
   1 cup warm water (110° to 115°)
   2 tablespoons shortening
   1 tablespoon sugar
   1 teaspoon salt
3-1/2 to 4 cups all-purpose flour
   2 egg whites
Cornmeal

In a mixing bowl, dissolve yeast in water. Add shortening, sugar, salt and 1 cup flour; beat until smooth. Add egg whites; mix well. Add enough remaining flour to form a soft dough. Turn onto a floured surface; knead until smooth and elastic, about 6-8 minutes (dough will be stiff). Place in a greased bowl, turning once to grease top. Cover and let rise in a warm place until doubled, about 1-1/2 hours. Punch dough down; divide into 24 pieces and shape into balls. Sprinkle greased baking sheets with cornmeal. Place rolls 2 in. apart on baking sheets. Cover and let rise until doubled, about 30 minutes. Place a large shallow pan filled with boiling water on lowest rack in oven. Bake rolls on middle rack at 425° for 10-11 minutes or until golden brown. **Yield:** 2 dozen. **Nutritional Analysis:** One roll equals 90 calories, 102 mg sodium, 0 cholesterol, 17 gm carbohydrate, 3 gm protein, 1 gm fat. **Diabetic Exchange:** 1 starch.

COUNTRY PLUM CRUMBLE

   1 cup canned plums, drained
1/4 cup all-purpose flour
1/4 cup sugar
1/8 teaspoon salt
1/8 teaspoon ground nutmeg
1/4 cup cold butter *or* margarine
1/2 cup crushed cornflakes
Half-and-half cream, optional

Cut the plums in half; discard pits. Divide equally between four well-greased 6-oz. custard cups. In a bowl, combine the flour, sugar, salt and nutmeg; cut in butter until mixture is crumbly. Stir in cornflakes; sprinkle over plums. Bake at 350° for 40 minutes or until the topping is golden brown. Serve warm with cream if desired. **Yield:** 4 servings.

Light and Refreshing Supper Says "Spring"

CELEBRATE the arrival of spring with this comforting supper that fits the season.

"My mom was known as the best cook in the county," boasts Dorothy Smith of El Dorado, Arkansas. "Mustard-Glazed Ham was in her collection of handwritten recipes. I laminated the ones I use most often, and this favorite was included. It's easy to prepare, and everyone seems to like ham made this way."

Joyce Allison from Millsap, Texas always serves Creamy Asparagus Casserole on special holidays, particularly Easter. "My husband says he hates asparagus, but he loves this casserole. He doesn't know he's eating his 'enemy vegetable'!" Joyce laughs. "My sister created the family-pleasing recipe and shared it with me."

Karla Retzer of Grantsburg, Wisconsin frequently chooses easy and elegant Spring Fruit Salad when planning a menu. "The flavors blend nicely as it refrigerates," says Karla. "Also, it's nice to have the salad ready ahead of time when you're busy with the last-minute details of serving an entire meal."

"I can't think of a better time to shape homemade Potato Rolls into cloverleaf shapes than for the celebration of St. Patrick's Day," declares Beatrice McGrath of Norridgewock, Maine. "They are the lightest and tastiest dinner rolls I make and are always well received at potluck suppers throughout the year."

MUSTARD-GLAZED HAM

    1 fully cooked boneless ham
      (4 to 5 pounds)
3/4 to 1 cup water
1/4 cup orange marmalade
1/4 cup prepared mustard
1/4 teaspoon ground ginger

Place ham in a shallow roasting pan; add water to pan. Bake, uncovered, at 325° for 1 hour. In a bowl, combine marmalade, mustard and ginger; mix well. Brush some over the ham. Bake 1 hour longer or until a meat thermometer reads 140°, brushing occasionally with glaze. **Yield:** 12-15 servings.

CREAMY ASPARAGUS CASSEROLE

    2 pounds fresh asparagus, cut into 1-inch
      pieces
1/4 cup butter *or* margarine
1/4 cup all-purpose flour
    2 cups milk *or* half-and-half cream
1/2 teaspoon salt
1/4 teaspoon pepper
    6 hard-cooked eggs, sliced
    1 cup (4 ounces) shredded cheddar cheese
    1 cup crushed potato chips

Place the asparagus in a large saucepan with enough water to cover; cook until crisp-tender. Drain well; set aside. In a saucepan over medium heat, melt butter. Stir in flour until smooth. Gradually add milk. Bring to a boil over medium heat; cook and stir for 2 minutes. Add salt and pepper. Layer half of the asparagus in an ungreased 11-in. x 7-in. x 2-in. baking dish. Cover with half of the eggs, cheese and sauce. Repeat layers. Sprinkle with potato chips. Bake, uncovered, at 350° for 30 minutes or until heated through. **Yield:** 6-8 servings.

SPRING FRUIT SALAD

    1 can (11 ounces) mandarin oranges,
      drained
    1 cup flaked coconut, toasted
    1 cup miniature marshmallows
    1 can (8 ounces) pineapple tidbits, drained
    1 cup (8 ounces) sour cream
    2 tablespoons chopped walnuts
    1 tablespoon brown sugar
Fresh mint, optional

In a bowl, combine the mandarin oranges, coconut, marshmallows, pineapple tidbits and sour cream; mix well. Cover and refrigerate overnight. Just before serving, sprinkle with walnuts and brown sugar. Garnish with fresh mint if desired. **Yield:** 6 servings.

POTATO ROLLS

☑ **Uses less fat, sugar or salt. Includes Nutritional Analysis and Diabetic Exchanges.**

    1 package (1/4 ounce) active dry yeast
1/4 cup warm water (110° to 115°)
    1 cup warm milk (110° to 115°)
1/4 cup shortening
1/2 cup warm mashed potatoes
    1 egg

1/4 cup sugar
1-1/4 teaspoons salt
4 cups all-purpose flour

In a mixing bowl, dissolve yeast in water. Add milk, shortening, potatoes, egg, sugar, salt and 2 cups flour; beat until smooth. Add enough remaining flour to form a soft dough. Turn onto a floured surface; knead until smooth and elastic, about 6-8 minutes. Place in a greased bowl, turning once to grease top. Cover and let rise in a warm place until doubled, about 1 hour. Punch dough down and divide in half. Divide each half into 36 pieces; shape into balls. Place three balls each into greased muffin cups. Cover and let rise in a warm place until doubled, about 30 minutes. Bake at 400° for 12-15 minutes or until golden. Remove to wire racks. Serve warm. **Yield:** 2 dozen. **Nutritional Analysis:** One roll (prepared with skim milk) equals 115 calories, 142 mg sodium, 9 mg cholesterol, 19 gm carbohydrate, 3 gm protein, 3 gm fat. **Diabetic Exchanges:** 1 starch, 1 fat.

Great-Tasting Foods Are Good for You

WATCHING what you eat doesn't get any better than this down-home dinner that's full of flavor.

Freemont, Nebraska cook Nancy Wit created Slow-Cooked Orange Chicken in an effort to prepare a dish lower in calories and fat. "Everyone likes the taste, including my grandchildren," Nancy notes. "A hint of orange gives the chicken a delicious flavor."

As Oatmeal Yeast Bread bakes in the oven, it reminds Gloria Murtha from West Mifflin, Pennsylvania of childhood. "The light sweet flavor and crispy crust of this bread made for a special treat when Mom baked it for us," Gloria recalls.

"I've been a vegetarian for over 20 years," states Louiza Kemyan of Palm Springs, California, "and often experiment with flavors compatible to the many vegetables I prepare. Zesty Broccoli is not only delicious, it's nutritious, too."

When Elsie Wilson of Freeman, Missouri found out she has diabetes, her daughter introduced her to several recipes lower in sugar. "Pineapple Coconut Pie was one of them," says Elsie, "and it's become one of my favorite desserts."

SLOW-COOKED ORANGE CHICKEN

✓ Uses less fat, sugar or salt. Includes Nutritional Analysis and Diabetic Exchanges.

      1 broiler-fryer chicken (3 pounds), cut up
        and skin removed
      3 cups orange juice
      1 cup chopped celery
      1 cup chopped green pepper
      1 can (4 ounces) mushroom stems and
        pieces, drained
      4 teaspoons dried minced onion
      1 tablespoon minced fresh parsley *or* 1
        teaspoon dried parsley flakes
    1/2 teaspoon salt, optional
    1/4 teaspoon pepper
      3 tablespoons cornstarch
      3 tablespoons cold water
Hot cooked rice, optional

Combine the first nine ingredients in a slow cooker. Cover and cook on low for 4 hours or until meat

juices run clear. Combine cornstarch and water until smooth; stir into cooking juices. Cover and cook on high for 30-45 minutes or until thickened. Serve over rice if desired. **Yield:** 4 servings. **Nutritional Analysis:** One serving (prepared without salt; calculated without rice) equals 306 calories, 189 mg sodium, 70 mg cholesterol, 31 gm carbohydrate, 23 gm protein, 10 gm fat. **Diabetic Exchanges:** 3 lean meat, 1 fruit, 1 starch.

OATMEAL YEAST BREAD

      1 can (12 ounces) evaporated milk
    1/2 cup water
      2 tablespoons shortening
      2 cups plus 2 teaspoons old-fashioned oats,
        divided
    1/3 cup packed brown sugar
  1-1/2 teaspoons salt
      1 package (1/4 ounce) active dry yeast
      1 cup warm water (110° to 115°)
      5 to 5-1/2 cups all-purpose flour
      1 egg, beaten

In a saucepan over medium heat, bring the milk, water and shortening to a boil. Meanwhile, combine 2 cups oats, brown sugar and salt in a mixing bowl. Add the milk mixture; let stand until mixture reaches 110°-115°. In a small bowl, dissolve yeast in warm water; add to oat mixture. Add 3 cups flour; beat until smooth. Add enough remaining flour to form a soft dough. Turn onto a floured surface; knead until smooth and elastic, about 6-8 minutes. Place in a greased bowl, turning once to grease top. Cover and let rise in a warm place until doubled, about 1 hour. Punch dough down; divide in half. Shape into two loaves; transfer to greased 8-in. x 4-in. x 2-in. loaf pans. Cover and let rise until doubled, about 40 minutes. Brush with egg; sprinkle with remaining oats. Bake at 350° for 35-40 minutes or until golden. Remove from pans and cool on wire racks. **Yield:** 2 loaves.

ZESTY BROCCOLI

✓ Uses less fat, sugar or salt. Includes Nutritional Analysis and Diabetic Exchanges.

      4 cups broccoli florets
    1/4 cup water
      2 teaspoons olive *or* vegetable oil
      1 to 2 garlic cloves, minced
    1/2 teaspoon salt, optional
Dash crushed red pepper flakes

In a saucepan, combine the first five ingredients;

bring to a boil. Reduce heat; cover and simmer until broccoli is crisp-tender, about 5 minutes. Drain; add red pepper flakes and toss. **Yield:** 4 servings. **Nutritional Analysis:** One 1/2-cup serving (without salt) equals 44 calories, 22 mg sodium, 0 cholesterol, 4 gm carbohydrate, 3 gm protein, 3 gm fat. **Diabetic Exchanges:** 1 vegetable, 1/2 fat.

<hr />

PINEAPPLE COCONUT PIE

✓ Uses less fat, sugar or salt. Includes Nutritional Analysis and Diabetic Exchanges.

1 cup cold milk
1 package (3.4 ounces) instant vanilla pudding mix

1/2 cup flaked coconut
1 can (8 ounces) crushed unsweetened pineapple, drained
1 pastry shell (9 inches), baked
Whipped topping, optional

In a mixing bowl, beat the milk and pudding mix until thickened. Stir in the coconut and crushed pineapple. Pour into the pastry shell. Chill in the refrigerator for at least 2 hours. Garnish individual slices with whipped topping if desired. **Yield:** 8 servings. **Nutritional Analysis:** One serving (prepared with skim milk and sugar-free pudding and without whipped topping) equals 198 calories, 647 mg sodium, 1 mg cholesterol, 26 gm carbohydrate, 3 gm protein, 9 gm fat. **Diabetic Exchanges:** 2 fat, 1 starch, 1/2 fruit.

Make Someone's Holiday Merry with Festive Meal

ENJOY the flavors of the holidays by serving this festive feast to family and friends.

"Creamed Turkey Over Rice is one of our favorite ways to have leftover turkey," states Kathi Parker of Hendersonville, North Carolina. "When I buy a turkey, I choose the largest one I can find so we're sure to have plenty of leftovers to make this creamy dish."

The addition of carrots and green peppers makes Special Scalloped Corn a colorful side dish. Mrs. J. Brown of Fort Dodge, Iowa thinks it's great when she needs to prepare a dish ahead of time. "All you need to do is bake it before serving," she instructs.

A friend shared the recipe for Fruity Lime Salad Mold with Jean Kirkland over 30 years ago, and it has appeared on her Newport, Oregon table often ever since. Says Jean, "It's rich tasting, plus the touch of red maraschino cherries makes it a real treat for the holidays."

The mouth-watering aroma of homemade Gingerbread with Brown Sugar Sauce is what Toni Hamm of Vandergrift, Pennsylvania remembers most about her grandmother's kitchen. "That was over 50 years ago," says Toni, "but whenever I catch a whiff of ginger and cinnamon, I'm back in time with Grandma."

CREAMED TURKEY OVER RICE

1 medium onion, chopped
1/2 cup chopped celery
1/4 cup butter *or* margarine
1/4 cup all-purpose flour
1-1/2 cups chicken broth
2 cups cubed cooked turkey
1 cup milk
1/2 cup cubed Swiss cheese
1 tablespoon diced pimientos
1/2 teaspoon salt
1/4 teaspoon pepper
1/4 teaspoon ground nutmeg
Hot long grain and wild rice

In a skillet, saute onion and celery in butter until tender. Stir in flour until blended. Gradually stir in broth. Bring to a boil; boil and stir for 2 minutes. Reduce heat; stir in turkey, milk, cheese, pimientos, salt, pepper and nutmeg. Cook until cheese is melted and mixture is heated through. Serve over rice. **Yield:** 4 servings.

SPECIAL SCALLOPED CORN

1 can (14-3/4 ounces) cream-style corn
2 eggs
1/2 cup crushed saltines (about 15 crackers)
1/4 cup butter *or* margarine, melted
1/4 cup evaporated milk
1/4 cup shredded carrot
1/4 cup chopped green pepper
1 tablespoon chopped celery
1 teaspoon chopped onion
1/2 teaspoon sugar
1/2 teaspoon salt
1/2 cup shredded cheddar cheese

In a bowl, combine the first 11 ingredients; mix well. Transfer to a greased 1-qt. baking dish. Sprinkle with cheese. Bake, uncovered, at 350° for 30-35 minutes or until a knife inserted near the center comes out clean. **Yield:** 4 servings.

FRUITY LIME SALAD MOLD

1 package (3 ounces) lime gelatin
1 cup boiling water
1 package (3 ounces) cream cheese, softened
1 can (8 ounces) crushed pineapple, undrained
1 cup whipping cream, whipped
1/4 cup chopped pecans
1/4 cup chopped maraschino cherries

In a large bowl, dissolve gelatin in boiling water; chill until syrupy. In a small bowl, combine cream cheese and pineapple; stir into cooled gelatin. Fold in whipped cream, pecans and cherries. Pour into a 4-cup mold coated with nonstick cooking spray. Refrigerate for 3 hours or overnight. **Yield:** 6-8 servings.

GINGERBREAD WITH BROWN SUGAR SAUCE

6 tablespoons shortening
1/2 cup packed brown sugar
1/3 cup molasses
1 egg

1-1/2 cups all-purpose flour
  1/2 teaspoon baking soda
  1/2 teaspoon ground cinnamon
  1/2 teaspoon ground ginger
  1/8 teaspoon salt
  1/2 cup buttermilk
BROWN SUGAR SAUCE:
    1 cup packed brown sugar
4-1/2 teaspoons cornstarch
  1/2 cup cold water
1-1/2 teaspoons vinegar
    1 tablespoon butter *or* margarine
1-1/2 teaspoons vanilla extract

In a mixing bowl, cream shortening, brown sugar, molasses and egg; mix well. Combine flour, baking soda, cinnamon, ginger and salt; add to the molasses mixture alternately with buttermilk. Pour into a greased 9-in. round baking pan. Bake at 350° for 25-30 minutes or until a toothpick inserted near the center comes out clean. Cool for 10 minutes before removing from pan to a wire rack. For sauce, combine brown sugar, cornstarch, water and vinegar in a saucepan; stir until smooth. Add butter. Bring to a boil; boil and stir for 2 minutes. Remove from the heat and stir in vanilla. Serve over the gingerbread. **Yield:** 6-8 servings.

Cooking for Two

**When you're setting the table for two,
turn to these recipes especially tailored for couples.**

SOURDOUGH CHICKEN SANDWICHES

Joe Urban, West Chicago, Illinois

My family loves chicken, so I came up with this easy sandwich recipe. The chicken stays moist and tasty prepared this way. With potatoes or fries and a salad, it's a complete meal.

    2 boneless skinless chicken breast halves
    1 egg, beaten
    1/2 cup seasoned bread crumbs
    2 tablespoons butter *or* margarine
    4 slices sourdough bread
    2 to 3 teaspoons mayonnaise, optional
    2 lettuce leaves
    2 Swiss cheese slices
    2 tomato slices
    2 bacon strips, cooked

Pound chicken to 1/4-in. thickness. Dip chicken in egg, then coat with crumbs. In a skillet over medium-high heat, cook chicken in butter on both sides until juices run clear, about 8 minutes. Spread bread with mayonnaise if desired. Top two slices with lettuce, cheese, tomato, bacon and chicken. Top with the remaining bread. **Yield:** 2 servings.

SWEET-SOUR BEAN SALAD

Judi Brinegar, Liberty, North Carolina

This dish is a great substitute for a green salad and a little more filling. We especially enjoy it with grilled steaks. When I serve this colorful salad to guests, they always ask for the recipe.

    1 can (15 ounces) white kidney *or* cannellini
       beans, rinsed and drained
    1/4 cup chopped green pepper
    2 green onions, thinly sliced
    3 tablespoons vegetable oil
    2 tablespoons vinegar
    1 teaspoon sugar
    1/4 teaspoon salt
Dash pepper

In a bowl, combine beans, green peppers and onions. In a small bowl, combine oil, vinegar, sug-

ar, salt and pepper. Pour over bean mixture and toss to coat. Cover and refrigerate for at least 1 hour. Serve with a slotted spoon. **Yield:** 2 servings.

FROSTY STRAWBERRY DESSERT

Barb Griffith, Helena, Montana

I'm a "morning cook" and like to do most of the evening meal's preparation after breakfast. I can make this dessert early, pop it in the freezer and enjoy its refreshing, creamy taste after supper.

    1 package (10 ounces) frozen sweetened
       strawberries, thawed
    1 cup ice cubes
    1 can (5 ounces) evaporated milk
    1/4 cup sugar
    1 teaspoon lemon juice

Place all ingredients in a blender or food processor; cover and process until smooth. Pour into a freezer container; freeze until firm. Remove from the freezer 5-10 minutes before serving. **Yield:** 2 servings.

SKILLET RED POTATOES

Lois Collier, Vineland, New Jersey

When I'm in a hurry to prepare potatoes, I resort to this recipe that I created myself. The mix of seasonings is just right and makes a delicious, attractive side dish. It's been a family favorite for a long time and fits with most any meal.

    2 tablespoons vegetable oil
    2 medium red potatoes, cooked and cut
       into 1/2-inch chunks
    1/2 teaspoon dried parsley flakes
    1/4 to 1/2 teaspoon garlic powder
    1/4 to 1/2 teaspoon onion powder
    1/4 to 1/2 teaspoon paprika

In a skillet, heat oil over medium heat. Add potatoes; cook for 10 minutes, stirring occasionally. Stir in remaining ingredients; cook and stir 5 minutes longer or until potatoes are browned and tender. **Yield:** 2 servings.

BEEF CHOW MEIN

Margery Bryan, Royal City, Washington

This is my basic recipe for stir-fry. I've tried others over the years but always come back to this one. I have substituted chicken and chicken broth for the beef and beef broth and found it just as good. The recipe is also easily doubled for when you're cooking for a crowd, rather than just for the two of you.

- 4 teaspoons cornstarch
- 1 teaspoon sugar
- 4 teaspoons soy sauce
- 1 garlic clove, minced
- 1/2 pound beef tenderloin, cut into thin strips
- 1 tablespoon vegetable oil
- 2 cups uncooked vegetables—carrots, green pepper, broccoli, celery, cauliflower *and/or* green onions
- 1/3 cup beef broth
- Chow mein noodles *or* hot cooked rice

In a bowl, combine the cornstarch, sugar, soy sauce and garlic. Add the beef and toss to coat. In a large skillet or wok, stir-fry the beef in oil until no longer pink; remove and keep warm. Reduce heat to medium. Add the vegetables and broth; stir-fry for 4 minutes. Return beef to the pan; cook and stir for 2 minutes or until heated through. Serve over chow mein noodles or rice. **Yield:** 2 servings.

BISCUITS FOR TWO

Bessie Hulett, Shively, Kentucky

I created this scrumptious biscuit recipe in a larger quantity to enter in the Kentucky State Fair a number of years ago. I was so pleased it won first place! Since biscuits are best hot and fresh out of the oven, I sized my recipe down to yield four—the perfect amount for two people. I make them whenever biscuits fit into the menu.

- 1/2 cup all-purpose flour
- 1 teaspoon baking powder
- 1/8 teaspoon salt
- 2 tablespoons shortening
- 3 tablespoons milk
- 2 tablespoons butter *or* margarine, melted, *divided*

In a small bowl, combine flour, baking powder and salt. Cut in shortening until mixture resembles coarse crumbs. Add milk, tossing with a fork until a ball forms. Turn onto a lightly floured surface; knead 5-6 times. Roll or pat to 1/2-in. thickness; cut with a 2-1/2-in. biscuit cutter. Place on a greased baking sheet. Brush tops with 1 table-spoon butter. Bake at 450° for 9-11 minutes or until golden brown. Brush with remaining butter. Serve warm. **Yield:** 4 biscuits.

OLD-FASHIONED RICE PUDDING

Laura German, North Brookfield, Massachusetts

I was fortunate to grow up around fabulous cooks. My mother and grandmother taught me to experiment with recipes, and we tried a lot of variations on this one. No matter how we chose to embellish it, it was always tasty. When I make this, it brings fond memories to mind.

- 1 cup cooked long grain rice
- 1 cup milk
- 5 teaspoons sugar
- Dash salt
- 1/2 teaspoon vanilla extract
- Whipped cream, optional

In a saucepan, combine rice, milk, sugar and salt. Cook, uncovered, over medium heat for 20 minutes or until thickened, stirring often. Remove from the heat; stir in vanilla. Spoon into serving dishes. Serve warm; top with whipped cream if desired. **Yield:** 2 servings.

CARROT CHEESE SOUP

Terese Snyder, Marquette, Michigan

I thought this sounded like a compatible mix of ingredients when I read the recipe for the first time, and I was right—the soup is absolutely delicious. It's a pretty color and makes a hearty soup to serve during the cooler winter months. But it also tastes great the rest of the year, too!

- 2 to 3 tablespoons butter *or* margarine
- 2 tablespoons all-purpose flour
- 1 medium carrot, diced
- 2 green onions, sliced
- 2 tablespoons diced fully cooked ham
- 2 cups hot chicken broth
- 1/3 cup shredded cheddar cheese
- 1 tablespoon minced fresh parsley
- 1/8 teaspoon pepper
- Dash hot pepper sauce

In a saucepan, melt the butter; stir in flour until smooth. Cook and stir over medium heat for 2 minutes. Add carrot, onions and ham; cook and stir for 1 minute. Gradually add broth. Bring to a boil; boil and stir for 2 minutes. Add cheese, parsley, pepper and hot pepper sauce; heat until the cheese is melted and the vegetables are tender. **Yield:** 2 servings.

STUFFED HADDOCK

Jeannette Wojtowicz, Buffalo, New York

After I served this at a dinner party for eight, I decided to reduce the recipe to serve two. It turned out just as delicious.

    1 tablespoon chopped onion
    1 tablespoon butter *or* margarine
    5 butter-flavored crackers, crushed
    1 haddock, sole *or* cod fillet (1 pound)
    1/3 cup condensed cream of celery soup,
        undiluted
    1 tablespoon sour cream
Paprika

In a skillet, saute onion in butter until tender. Stir in crackers and enough water to hold mixture together. Cut a pocket into side of fillet; stuff with cracker mixture. Place in a greased baking dish. Combine soup and sour cream; spread over fish. Sprinkle with paprika. Bake, uncovered, at 350° for 25-30 minutes or until fish flakes easily with a fork. **Yield:** 2 servings.

SWEETHEART BROWNIE SUNDAE

Dottie Miller, Jonesborough, Tennessee

I like to make these brownies in a heart shape for Valentine's Day and garnish them with berries. But I also treat my family with them the rest of the year, too.

    1/4 cup butter (no substitutes)
    2 squares (1 ounce *each*) semisweet
        chocolate
    1 egg
    1/2 cup packed brown sugar
    1 teaspoon vanilla extract
    1/4 teaspoon salt
    1/4 cup all-purpose flour
    1 cup vanilla ice cream, softened
CHOCOLATE SAUCE:
    1 cup water
    1/2 cup baking cocoa
    1/4 cup sugar
    2 tablespoons butter (no substitutes)
Confectioners' sugar

In a microwave, melt butter and chocolate; cool for 10 minutes. In a mixing bowl, beat egg, brown sugar, vanilla and salt. Stir in chocolate mixture. Add flour; mix well. Line an 8-in. square baking pan with foil; grease foil. Spread batter into pan (batter will be thin). Bake at 350° for 15 minutes or until a toothpick inserted near the center comes out clean. Cool on a wire rack. Cover and refrigerate until firm. Using a 3-1/2-in. heart pattern or cookie cutter, mark four hearts on surface of brownies; cut with a knife. Spread ice cream on two hearts; top each with a second heart. Wrap in plastic wrap; freeze in a single layer overnight. For chocolate sauce, combine water, cocoa and sugar in a saucepan; bring to a boil over medium heat, stirring constantly. Reduce heat; simmer for 2-3 minutes or until thickened. Remove from the heat; stir in butter. To serve, dust brownies with confectioners' sugar and drizzle with sauce. Refrigerate any leftover sauce. **Yield:** 2 servings.

LEMONY SPROUTS SALAD

Ruth Hastings, Louisville, Illinois

This salad makes an attractive dish for a potluck. People always comment on the lemony dressing, which makes it different and distinctive.

    1/2 pound brussels sprouts, halved
    2 medium carrots, thinly sliced
    2 teaspoons vegetable oil
    1 tablespoon lemon juice
    1/4 teaspoon salt
Dash pepper
    2 cups chopped lettuce
    1 tablespoon chopped sweet red pepper

Place brussels sprouts and 1 in. of water in a saucepan; bring to a boil. Reduce heat; cover and simmer until crisp-tender, about 10 minutes. Rinse with cold water; drain. In a small skillet, saute carrots in oil until tender. Toss sprouts with lemon juice, salt and pepper. Place lettuce in a bowl; top with sprouts, carrots and red pepper. Refrigerate for 1 hour. **Yield:** 2 servings.

POTATO NESTS WITH PEAS

Margery Bryan, Royal City, Washington

I serve potatoes with just about every meal. Besides using this recipe as a side dish, I discovered I could serve it as a main dish for a lighter meal.

    1 cup hot mashed potatoes
    1 egg yolk, beaten
    1/4 cup shredded cheddar cheese
Dash dill weed
    2 teaspoons butter *or* margarine
    1 can (8-1/2 ounces) peas, drained

In a bowl, combine potatoes and egg yolk; stir in the cheese. Spoon two mounds onto a greased baking sheet. With the back of a spoon, shape each mound into a 4-in. nest. Top with dill and butter. Bake at 350° for 30-35 minutes or until golden. Fill nests with peas. Bake 10 minutes longer or until heated through. **Yield:** 2 servings.

WAFFLES FROM SCRATCH

Florence Dean, Towson, Maryland

Every Saturday afternoon while I was growing up, my mom and I always went shopping. But before we left, she always made my favorite lunch—homemade waffles. They were about 8 inches around and prepared in a grill set on top of the stove. Those waffles were delicious topped with fruit or maple syrup!

1-1/2 cups all-purpose flour
   1 teaspoon baking powder
1/2 teaspoon salt
   2 eggs, *separated*
   1 cup milk
1/4 cup butter *or* margarine, melted
Confectioners' sugar and fresh fruit *or* maple
  syrup

In a bowl, combine flour, baking powder and salt. Combine egg yolks, milk and butter; stir into dry ingredients just until moistened. In a small mixing bowl, beat egg whites until soft peaks form; gently fold into batter. Bake in a preheated waffle iron according to manufacturer's directions until golden brown. Top with confectioners' sugar and fruit or serve with syrup. **Yield:** 4 waffles (about 6 inches).

SAUSAGE-STUFFED PEACHES

Marcia Albury, Boca Raton, Florida

I made up this recipe while living in Spain. I wasn't used to the cuts of meat available there, but the sausage was always tasty. This colorful dish featuring that savory meat and sweet peaches never fails. The unusual combination of flavors is well received by guests, and I often get requests for the recipe. It's great for breakfast or brunch.

   1 can (15 ounces) peach halves
3/4 cup soft bread crumbs
   1 tablespoon chopped onion
   1 egg
1/2 teaspoon salt
1/8 teaspoon pepper
   6 ounces bulk pork sausage

Drain peaches, reserving 4 peach halves and 1/4 cup syrup (refrigerate remaining peaches and syrup for another use). In a bowl, combine bread crumbs, onion, egg, salt and pepper. Add sausage; mix well. Shape about 1/4 cupfuls of sausage mixture into balls; place each ball in the indentation of a peach half. Place peaches in a small greased baking dish. Bake, uncovered, at 350° for 30 minutes; drain. Pour reserved syrup over sausage; bake 5-10 minutes longer or until meat is

no longer pink and syrup is heated through. **Yield:** 2 servings.

CHEDDAR SOUFFLE

Dollypearle Martin, Douglastown, New Brunswick

My mother-in-law gave me this recipe many years ago, and I served it to my husband every year on our anniversary. Also on the menu were English muffins with honey, juice and coffee. Now our sons make this souffle, and their children love it for brunch.

1/2 cup milk
   5 teaspoons quick-cooking tapioca
1/4 teaspoon salt
1/3 cup shredded cheddar cheese
   2 eggs, *separated*

In a saucepan, combine milk, tapioca and salt; bring to a boil over medium heat, stirring constantly. Remove from the heat; stir in cheese until melted. In a small bowl, beat egg yolks; add to tapioca mixture. In another bowl, beat egg whites until stiff peaks form; fold into tapioca mixture. Pour into a greased 1-qt. baking dish. Place the dish in a larger pan of hot water. Bake, uncovered, at 350° for 25-30 minutes or until a knife inserted near the center comes out clean. **Yield:** 2 servings.

PINEAPPLE RAISIN CRISP

Lorraine Mix, Remer, Minnesota

(Not pictured)

Years ago, I found this basic recipe on the label of a can of pineapple. I adjusted it to suit our taste. This dessert is a refreshing change from the usual apple or berry fruit crisps. It's also easy to fix for two and can be served warm or cold.

   1 can (8-3/4 ounces) pineapple tidbits,
     drained
1/4 cup raisins
   2 tablespoons brown sugar
   2 tablespoons flaked coconut
   2 tablespoons quick-cooking oats
   1 tablespoon all-purpose flour
Dash ground cinnamon
Dash ground nutmeg
   1 tablespoon cold butter *or* margarine

Combine pineapple and raisins in a small ungreased baking dish. In a small bowl, combine brown sugar, coconut, oats, flour, cinnamon and nutmeg; cut in butter until crumbly. Sprinkle over fruit. Bake, uncovered, at 350° for 25 minutes or until topping is crisp. **Yield:** 2 servings.

STEAKS WITH SQUASH MEDLEY

Jim Tusing, Oklahoma City, Oklahoma

This recipe dates back to the 1960s, yet it's still a favorite. At that time, we operated a small inn, and every week after most of the guests had departed, my wife and I would enjoy a quiet, leisurely dinner.

 2 rib eye steaks (10 ounces *each*)
 3 tablespoons olive *or* vegetable oil, **divided**
1/2 cup chopped onion
1/2 cup chopped yellow summer squash
1/2 cup chopped zucchini
1/2 cup sliced okra, optional
 1 garlic clove, minced
1/4 cup tomato sauce
 3 tablespoons vinegar
1/2 teaspoon dried rosemary, crushed
1/2 teaspoon dried thyme
1/8 teaspoon pepper

In a skillet over medium heat, brown steaks on both sides in 2 tablespoons oil. Cook 8 minutes longer or until the meat reaches desired doneness (for rare, a meat thermometer should read 140°; medium, 160°; well-done, 170°). Remove and keep warm. Drain skillet. Saute onion, squash, zucchini, okra if desired and garlic in remaining oil for 6 minutes or until tender. Stir in the tomato sauce, vinegar, rosemary, thyme and pepper. Cook 3-4 minutes longer or until heated through. Serve over steaks. **Yield:** 2 servings.

PEACH COBBLER FOR TWO

Betty Clark, Mt. Vernon, Missouri

Everyone notices the special taste of orange peel in this cobbler. It enhances the color and gives this traditional dessert a delicious distinction. It's convenient to have a recipe that makes just enough for two.

 3 tablespoons brown sugar
 2 teaspoons cornstarch
1/4 cup water
1-1/2 cups sliced fresh *or* frozen peaches
 1 tablespoon butter *or* margarine
 1 teaspoon lemon juice
TOPPING:
1/3 cup all-purpose flour
 2 tablespoons sugar
1/2 teaspoon baking powder
Pinch salt
 2 tablespoons milk
4-1/2 teaspoons butter *or* margarine, melted
1/4 teaspoon grated orange peel

In a small saucepan, combine brown sugar, cornstarch and water until smooth. Add peaches;

bring to a boil. Cook and stir for 2 minutes. Reduce heat to low; stir in butter and lemon juice. For topping, combine flour, sugar, baking powder and salt in a bowl. Stir in milk, butter and orange peel. Transfer hot peach mixture to an ungreased 1-qt. baking dish. Spoon topping over peaches. Bake, uncovered, at 400° for 25 minutes or until golden brown. **Yield:** 2 servings.

CASHEW RICE

Pat Habiger, Spearville, Kansas

Because it is so versatile, this quick side dish is one of my standbys. The vegetables add a nice touch of color, while the cashews give this economical dish a "gourmet touch".

1/2 cup beef *or* chicken broth
 2 tablespoons shredded carrot
 2 tablespoons finely chopped celery
 1 tablespoon sliced green onion
 1 teaspoon butter *or* margarine
Dash pepper
1/2 cup uncooked instant rice
Chopped cashews

In a small saucepan, combine broth, carrot, celery, onion, butter and pepper. Bring to a boil; remove from the heat. Stir in rice; cover and let stand for 5 minutes or until the liquid is absorbed. Sprinkle with cashews. **Yield:** 2 servings.

MUSHROOM SPINACH SALAD

Patty Kile, Greentown, Pennsylvania

I've made this salad for my husband and me for years. I don't like cooked spinach, so I was looking for an alternative way to prepare this nutritious vegetable. It's especially delicious made with fresh spinach from the garden.

 3 cups torn fresh spinach
1/2 cup sliced fresh mushrooms
1/2 cup seasoned croutons
 2 tablespoons vegetable oil
 1 tablespoon cider *or* white wine vinegar
1-1/2 teaspoons sugar
 1 teaspoon lemon juice
1/8 teaspoon salt
1/8 teaspoon pepper
 1 tablespoon crumbled cooked bacon

In a bowl, combine the spinach, mushrooms and croutons. In a jar with a tight-fitting lid, combine oil, vinegar, sugar, lemon juice, salt and pepper; shake well. Drizzle over salad and toss to coat. Sprinkle with bacon. **Yield:** 2 servings.

CHEDDAR CHEESE TOASTIES

Helen Davis, Waterbury, Vermont

We were dairy farmers for years, so we all enjoyed a hearty breakfast after milking. Having a bit of cheese satisfies the appetite and helps hold you over until the next meal. Since I always had a lot of cheddar cheese on hand, I used it in many of my recipes, including these scrumptious sandwiches, which are a nice change from regular grilled cheese sandwiches.

1/2 cup shredded cheddar cheese
1 tablespoon mayonnaise
1 teaspoon finely chopped onion
1 teaspoon whipping cream *or* milk
1/4 teaspoon ground mustard
Dash *each* garlic powder, paprika and
   Worcestershire sauce
2 slices white bread, toasted
2 slices bacon, cooked and crumbled

In a bowl, combine the cheese, mayonnaise, onion, cream and seasonings; mix well. Spread over toast. Place on a lightly greased baking sheet. Sprinkle with bacon. Bake at 350° for 5-6 minutes or until the cheese is melted. **Yield:** 2 servings.

FLAVORFUL TOMATO SOUP

Jean Sullivan, Denver, Colorado

A cookbook recipe called for ingredients I didn't have on hand, so I improvised and came up with this savory version. I call it "razzmatazz" tomato soup. I often make a double batch and take it to church suppers, and I've given the recipe to many friends.

✓ **Uses less fat, sugar or salt. Includes Nutritional Analysis and Diabetic Exchanges.**

1/4 cup finely chopped onion
1 tablespoon butter *or* margarine
1/4 teaspoon dried basil
1/4 teaspoon paprika
1/8 teaspoon garlic powder
1 can (10-3/4 ounces) condensed tomato
   soup, undiluted
1 cup milk

In a saucepan, saute onion in butter until tender. Add basil, paprika and garlic powder. Stir in soup and milk until well blended. Cook over medium heat for 6 minutes or until heated through. **Yield:** 2 servings. **Nutritional Analysis:** One 1-cup serving (prepared with margarine, low-fat soup and skim milk) equals 214 calories, 696 mg sodium, 2 mg cholesterol, 30 gm carbohydrate, 6 gm protein, 8 gm fat. **Diabetic Exchanges:** 2 starch, 1-1/2 fat.

CREAMY GREEN BEAN SALAD

Lorraine Mix, Remer, Minnesota

In our early years of marriage, my husband asked me if I could try to make him bean salad just like his mother's. I've tried many versions since then, but this is the one our whole family agrees is the best of the bunch. In the past, I'd can about 50 quarts of fresh green beans from our garden every year, but now my husband suggests I can only enough to keep making this salad for him.

2 tablespoons sour cream
1 tablespoon prepared Italian salad
   dressing
1 can (8 ounces) cut green beans, drained
1 medium tomato, chopped and drained
2 tablespoons finely chopped onion
Lettuce leaves

In a bowl, combine sour cream and salad dressing; mix well. Stir in beans, tomato and onion. Cover and refrigerate for 1 hour. Serve on lettuce. **Yield:** 2 servings.

PECAN PIE FOR TWO

Noreen Johnson, Leesburg, Florida

Pecan pie was always requested by my family for special occasions. When we became empty nesters, it was hard to give up some of our family favorites when we found that leftovers were too much for the two of us. Smaller recipes were hard to come by, so I was delighted to find this one. Now we can have pecan pie—fresh—for just the two of us.

1/3 cup all-purpose flour
1/8 teaspoon salt
1 tablespoon shortening
1 tablespoon cold butter *or* margarine
1 teaspoon cold water
FILLING:
1/4 cup chopped pecans
2 tablespoons brown sugar
1 tablespoon all-purpose flour
1 egg, beaten
1/4 cup corn syrup
1/4 teaspoon vanilla extract

In a bowl, combine flour and salt. Cut in shortening and butter until crumbly. Add water, tossing with a fork until a ball forms. Roll out pastry to fit an 18-oz. baking dish. Press onto the bottom and up the sides of the dish. Combine filling ingredients; mix well. Pour into pastry shell. Bake at 375° for 35-40 minutes or until a knife inserted near the center comes out clean. **Yield:** 2 servings.

STUFFED CORNISH GAME HENS

Nancy Aubrey, Ruidoso, New Mexico

This entree makes an ordinary day special. I bake the extra stuffing separately so we have enough.

1/2 cup chopped celery
1/4 cup chopped onion
1/2 cup butter *or* margarine, *divided*
3 cups crumbled corn bread
3 cups soft bread crumbs
1 jar (2 ounces) diced pimientos, drained
1 cup chicken broth
1 egg
1/2 teaspoon poultry seasoning
1 teaspoon salt, *divided*
1/2 teaspoon pepper, *divided*
2 Cornish game hens (20 ounces *each*)
1 garlic clove, minced
1 teaspoon grated lemon peel
3/4 teaspoon chopped fresh mint *or* 1/4 teaspoon dried mint flakes

In a large skillet or saucepan, saute celery and onion in 2 tablespoons butter until tender. Remove from the heat. Stir in corn bread, bread crumbs, pimientos, broth, egg, poultry seasoning, 1/2 teaspoon salt and 1/4 teaspoon pepper; mix well. Stuff each hen with 3/4 cup stuffing. Place extra stuffing in a greased 1-qt. baking dish; refrigerate. Place hens breast side up on a rack in a greased 13-in. x 9-in. x 2-in. baking dish. Cover loosely with foil; bake at 375° for 45 minutes. Meanwhile, in a saucepan, melt the remaining butter; add garlic, lemon peel, mint and remaining salt and pepper. Brush over hens. Bake 15-30 minutes longer or until a meat thermometer reads 180° for hens and 165° for stuffing. Bake the extra stuffing, covered, for 30 minutes. **Yield:** 2 servings.

SPECIAL SWEET POTATOES

Ruby Williams, Bogalusa, Louisiana

Orange juice and cinnamon are wonderful for enhancing the flavor of sweet potatoes.

2 small sweet potatoes, peeled and cut into 1/2-inch cubes
2 tablespoons brown sugar
1/4 teaspoon ground cinnamon
1/8 teaspoon salt
1/4 cup orange juice
2 tablespoons butter *or* margarine
1/2 cup miniature marshmallows

In a saucepan, cook sweet potatoes in boiling salted water for 10 minutes or until tender; drain.

Transfer to a greased 1-qt. baking dish. Sprinkle with brown sugar, cinnamon and salt. Drizzle with orange juice and dot with butter. Bake, uncovered, at 450° for 15 minutes. Top with marshmallows. Bake 2 minutes longer or until marshmallows are puffed and golden. **Yield:** 2 servings.

MAPLE-NUT BAKED APPLES

Theresa Stewart, New Oxford, Pennsylvania

Now that our children have all married, baked apples are a perfect dessert for the two of us. Using the microwave makes them easy to prepare.

2 medium tart apples
2 tablespoons chopped walnuts
2 tablespoons raisins
1/8 teaspoon ground cinnamon
1/4 cup maple syrup, *divided*
2 teaspoons butter *or* margarine

Core apples and peel the top two-thirds. Place in a 1-qt. microwave-safe dish. Combine walnuts, raisins and cinnamon; press into the center of each apple. Drizzle each with 1 teaspoon maple syrup. Cover and microwave on high for 4-6 minutes or until tender, rotating a half turn twice. In a small microwave-safe dish, combine the butter and remaining syrup. Heat, uncovered, on high for 20-30 seconds or until butter is melted. Pour over apples; serve immediately. **Yield:** 2 servings. **Editor's Note:** This recipe was tested in an 850-watt microwave. The apples may also be baked in a conventional oven in a greased 1-1/2-qt. baking dish. Bake, uncovered, at 350° for 30-35 minutes or until tender.

TANGY FLORET SALAD

Sally Frizzell, New London, Ohio

One of my favorite and most-used recipes, this salad is easy to prepare for two or 20!

1 cup broccoli florets
1 cup cauliflowerets
1 cup frozen peas
1/2 cup mayonnaise
1 tablespoon sugar
1 tablespoon vinegar
1/2 teaspoon salt
1/8 teaspoon pepper

In a bowl, combine the first three ingredients. In a small bowl, combine mayonnaise, sugar, vinegar, salt and pepper; mix well. Add to vegetables and toss to coat. **Yield:** 2-3 servings.

BAVARIAN MEATBALLS

Gusty Crum, Dover, Ohio

Gingersnap cookies and mushrooms give these tender meatballs a special old-world flavor. The recipe was handed down from my husband's family several years ago. I love to cook and found that this was an easy recipe to double and share with friends. The meatballs also can be frozen for a convenient meal at a later time.

- 2 tablespoons chopped onion
- 1 teaspoon butter *or* margarine
- 3/4 cup soft bread crumbs
- 1 tablespoon milk
- 1/2 teaspoon prepared mustard
- 1/2 teaspoon salt
- Dash pepper
- 1/2 pound ground beef
- 1 can (4 ounces) mushroom stems and pieces, undrained
- 2 gingersnaps, coarsely crushed
- 2 tablespoons water
- 1 tablespoon brown sugar
- 1/2 teaspoon beef bouillon granules

In a skillet, saute onion in butter until tender. Transfer to a bowl; add bread crumbs, milk, mustard, salt and pepper. Add beef and mix well. Shape into six meatballs; place in a greased 1-qt. baking dish. In a small saucepan, combine mushrooms, gingersnap crumbs, water, brown sugar and bouillon. Cook and stir over low heat for 2-3 minutes or until thickened. Pour over meatballs. Cover and bake at 350° for 25 minutes or until the meat is no longer pink. **Yield:** 2 servings.

AU GRATIN CABBAGE

Katherine Stallwood, Kennewick, Washington

My heritage is Russian, and I have loved cabbage for as long as I can remember. My husband didn't like the taste of it at all—until I prepared it this way for him. Now he requests it often! Since we're diet-conscious these days, I scaled down the cheese a bit and use low-fat milk, but it's still delicious.

- 2 cups shredded cabbage
- 1/2 cup grated carrot
- 1/4 cup chopped green onions
- 1 egg
- 1/2 cup milk
- 3 tablespoons shredded Swiss cheese
- 1/4 teaspoon seasoned salt
- 1 tablespoon minced fresh parsley
- 1 tablespoon shredded Parmesan cheese

In a skillet coated with nonstick cooking spray, saute the cabbage, carrot and onions until crisp-tender. Transfer to a greased shallow 1-qt. baking dish. In a bowl, combine the egg, milk, Swiss cheese and seasoned salt. Pour over the vegetables. Sprinkle with parsley and Parmesan cheese. Bake, uncovered, at 350° for 30-35 minutes or until a knife inserted near the center comes out clean. **Yield:** 2-3 servings.

APPLE PAN BETTY

Shirley Leister, West Chester, Pennsylvania

I found this recipe soon after I was married almost 50 years ago. It uses few ingredients, which are usually on hand, and takes little time to put together. It's a favorite of ours during fall and winter, when apples are at their best.

- 1 medium apple, peeled and cubed
- 3 tablespoons butter *or* margarine
- 1 cup bread cubes
- 3 tablespoons sugar
- 1/4 teaspoon ground cinnamon

In a skillet over medium heat, saute apple in butter until tender, about 2-3 minutes. Add bread cubes. Sprinkle with sugar and cinnamon; mix well. Saute until bread is warmed. Serve immediately. **Yield:** 2 servings.

CREAMY POTATO CASSEROLE

Margaret Draughon, Clinton, North Carolina

(Not pictured)

Even though my family is grown and no longer living at home, I still like to make mashed potatoes. I came up with this variation a long time ago, thinking that it would be a nice change of pace. It became number one on my family's request list. It's also simple to make in larger quantities if needed.

- 1-1/2 cups hot mashed potatoes (prepared with milk and butter)
- 1/2 cup sour cream
- 1 to 2 tablespoons milk
- 1/8 teaspoon garlic powder
- 3/4 cup french-fried onions
- 1/2 cup shredded cheddar cheese

In a bowl, combine potatoes, sour cream, milk and garlic powder; mix well. Spoon half into a greased 1-qt. baking dish. Layer with half of the onions and cheese. Repeat layers. Bake, uncovered, at 350° for 30-35 minutes or until the cheese is melted. **Yield:** 2 servings.

TACO-TOPPED POTATO

Linda Brausen, Janesville, Wisconsin

This quick-and-easy recipe fits in well with a busy schedule. Along with a garden salad, it makes a nice light meal for two, but when we want something more filling, I'll serve this potato with a small steak.

     1 large baking potato
   1/4 pound ground beef
     1 tablespoon chopped onion
   1/4 cup salsa
   1/4 teaspoon Worcestershire sauce
     2 tablespoons shredded cheddar cheese
Sour cream

Scrub and pierce potato; place on a microwave-safe plate. Microwave, uncovered, on high for 4-5 minutes or until tender, turning once. Let stand while preparing topping. Crumble meat into a shallow microwave-safe bowl; add onion. Cover and microwave on high for 2 to 2-1/2 minutes or until meat is no longer pink, stirring once; drain. Stir in salsa and Worcestershire sauce. Cut potato in half lengthwise; fluff pulp with fork. Top each half with meat mixture, cheese and sour cream. **Yield:** 2 servings. **Editor's Note:** This recipe was tested in an 850-watt microwave. To prepare in a conventional oven, bake potato at 400° for 40 minutes or until tender. Cook beef and onion in a skillet until meat is no longer pink; drain. Stir in salsa and Worcestershire sauce. Assemble as directed.

TOMATOES WITH BASIL-GARLIC DRESSING

Ruby Williams, Bogalusa, Louisiana

In summer when it's peak time for fresh ripe tomatoes, this is the salad to serve! Meaty tomatoes topped with a touch of this dressing will bring on rave reviews. This tasty salad is also cool and colorful.

     2 medium tomatoes, sliced
Pepper to taste
     2 tablespoons chopped green onions
     2 tablespoons plain yogurt
     1 tablespoon cider vinegar
     1 teaspoon minced fresh basil *or*
   1/2 teaspoon dried basil
     1 garlic clove, minced

Arrange tomatoes on salad plates; sprinkle with pepper. In a small bowl, combine remaining ingredients; mix well. Spoon over tomatoes. **Yield:** 2 servings.

GUACAMOLE DIP

Virginia Burwell, Dayton, Texas

Since guacamole is a favorite in this area, with its emphasis on Mexican food, I decided to create my own recipe. I serve it as a dip for chips, with baked chicken or to top off a bed of lettuce.

     1 large ripe avocado, peeled
   1/4 cup plain yogurt
     2 tablespoons picante sauce *or* salsa
     1 tablespoon finely chopped onion
   1/8 teaspoon salt
     2 to 3 drops hot pepper sauce, optional
Tortilla chips

In a small bowl, mash avocado until smooth. Stir in yogurt, picante sauce, onion, salt and hot pepper sauce if desired. Cover and refrigerate until serving. Serve with tortilla chips. **Yield:** 2 servings (3/4 cup).

BLUEBERRY LOAF CAKE

Nancy Anderson, Broomall, Pennsylvania

(Not pictured)

My family loves fresh blueberries just about any way, but this loaf cake is a favorite at breakfast, as a delicious snack or quick dessert. We always look forward to summer, when fresh blueberries appear in the market.

   1/2 cup butter *or* margarine, softened
     1 cup sugar
     2 eggs
   1/2 cup milk
     1 teaspoon vanilla extract
 1-3/4 cups all-purpose flour
     1 teaspoon baking powder
     1 cup fresh *or* frozen blueberries
TOPPING:
     2 teaspoons sugar
     1 teaspoon ground cinnamon

In a mixing bowl, cream butter and sugar. Beat in eggs, milk and vanilla. Combine flour and baking powder; add to creamed mixture just until combined. Gently fold in blueberries. Pour into a greased 9-in. x 5-in. x 3-in. loaf pan. Combine sugar and cinnamon; sprinkle over top. Bake at 350° for 50-55 minutes or until a toothpick inserted near the center comes out clean. Cool for 10 minutes before removing from pan to a wire rack to cool completely. **Yield:** 1 loaf. **Editor's Note:** Individual slices can be wrapped and frozen, then thawed for a quick dessert.

GROUND BEEF STROGANOFF

Marjorie Kriegh, Nampa, Idaho

My mother-in-law gave me this recipe over 25 years ago. It's been a staple in my meal planning ever since because it's easy and takes little time to prepare. I usually serve it with green beans and a salad.

1/2 pound lean ground beef
1/4 cup chopped onion
   1 tablespoon butter *or* margarine
1/4 cup sliced fresh mushrooms
   1 tablespoon all-purpose flour
   1 garlic clove, minced
1/4 teaspoon salt
1/8 teaspoon pepper
   2 tablespoons chili sauce
1/4 teaspoon Worcestershire sauce
1/3 cup sour cream
Hot cooked noodles

In a skillet, cook beef and onion in butter until meat is no longer pink. Stir in mushrooms, flour, garlic, salt and pepper. Cook and stir for 5 minutes. Add chili sauce and Worcestershire sauce. Reduce heat; cook, uncovered, for 10 minutes. Stir in sour cream just before serving; heat through (do not boil). Serve over noodles. **Yield:** 2 servings.

SALAD WITH HOT ITALIAN DRESSING

Bessie Hulett, Shively, Kentucky

I created this recipe for a special dinner for our wedding anniversary, which is April 11. That's the perfect time to make this salad, when leaf lettuce is fresh and green onions and radishes come right out of the garden.

   2 cups torn leaf lettuce
   4 green onions, sliced
   2 radishes, sliced
   1 medium tomato, cut into wedges
   3 bacon strips, diced
   1 teaspoon all-purpose flour
1/4 cup vinegar
   2 tablespoons water
   2 tablespoons sugar
3/4 teaspoon Italian salad dressing mix

Arrange the lettuce, onions, radishes and tomato in salad bowls or plates; set aside. In a small skillet, cook bacon until crisp. Remove bacon to paper towels to drain; reserve 1 tablespoon drippings. Add flour to drippings; stir until smooth. Cook over low heat for 3 minutes. Combine vinegar, water, sugar and salad dressing mix; add to skillet. Bring to a boil over medium heat; cook and stir for 2 minutes. Pour over salads. Top with bacon. Serve immediately. Refrigerate leftover dressing for up to 2 weeks. **Yield:** 2 servings.

CARAWAY RYE MUFFINS

Jean Tyner, Darlington, South Carolina

My family enjoys the distinctive taste of caraway, and it abounds in these muffins, which use rye flour for a change of pace. I like to serve them for brunch, lunch or dinner.

   1 cup rye flour
3/4 cup all-purpose flour
1/4 cup sugar
2-1/2 teaspoons baking powder
1/2 teaspoon salt
1/2 teaspoon caraway seeds
3/4 cup shredded cheddar cheese
   1 egg, beaten
3/4 cup milk
1/3 cup vegetable oil

In a large bowl, combine the first six ingredients. Stir in cheese. In another bowl, combine the egg, milk and oil; stir into the dry ingredients just until moistened. Fill greased or paper-lined muffin cups two-thirds full. Bake at 400° for 20-23 minutes or until golden brown. Serve warm. **Yield:** 10 muffins.

PEACH MELBA DESSERT

Edna Christiansen, Edmore, Michigan

This pretty dessert is an impressive end to any meal. Refreshing and light, it's just the right touch for every sweet tooth.

   1 can (15-1/4 ounces) peach halves in syrup
   2 individual round sponge cakes
   2 scoops vanilla ice cream
   1 tablespoon raspberry *or* strawberry jam
   2 teaspoons chopped nuts, optional

Drain peaches, reserving syrup. Set aside two peaches and 1 tablespoon syrup (refrigerate remaining peaches and syrup for another use). Place each sponge cake on a plate; drizzle with reserved syrup. Top with ice cream and a peach half. In a small saucepan, heat jam until melted; drizzle over peaches. Top with nuts if desired. Serve immediately. **Yield:** 2 servings.

Lasagna Roll-Ups

Virginia Foley, Manchester, New Hampshire

Since our children left the nest, lasagna has been relegated to company fare because most recipes make enough for a crowd. But then I saw a recipe that rolled lasagna noodles into individual servings, and I adapted my original recipe to this efficient way of preparing it. Now my husband and I enjoy this entree often.

- 1/4 to 1/3 pound ground beef
- 2 tablespoons chopped onion
- 1 garlic clove, minced
- 1 can (16 ounces) crushed tomatoes
- 1/2 teaspoon salt
- 1/2 teaspoon dried oregano

Dash cayenne pepper

- 1-1/4 cups small-curd cottage cheese, drained
- 1/4 cup grated Parmesan cheese
- 1 egg, lightly beaten
- 1 tablespoon minced fresh parsley *or*
- 1 teaspoon dried parsley flakes
- 1/4 teaspoon onion powder
- 6 lasagna noodles, cooked and drained
- 1/2 cup shredded mozzarella cheese

In a skillet, cook beef, onion and garlic until meat is no longer pink; drain. Add tomatoes, salt, oregano and cayenne; simmer for 10 minutes. Spoon half of the meat sauce into a greased 9-in. square baking dish. Combine cottage cheese, Parmesan cheese, egg, parsley and onion powder; spread 1/4 cupful on each noodle. Carefully roll up and place seam side down over meat sauce. Top with remaining meat sauce. Sprinkle with mozzarella cheese. Cover and bake at 375° for 30-35 minutes or until heated through. Let stand 10 minutes before serving. **Yield:** 2 servings.

Garlic Crescent Rolls

Pat Habiger, Spearville, Kansas

Delicious rolls can embellish a dinner, and it only takes a minute using convenient refrigerator rolls. With a little imagination, you can create several flavor combinations to complement your menu.

- 1 package (4 ounces) refrigerated crescent rolls
- 2 teaspoons grated Parmesan cheese
- 1/4 to 1/2 teaspoon garlic powder
- 1 egg, beaten
- 1/2 teaspoon sesame *and/or* poppy seeds

Separate crescent dough into four triangles. Sprinkle with Parmesan cheese and garlic powder.

Beginning at the wide end, roll up dough. Place with point down on a greased baking sheet. Brush with egg; sprinkle with sesame and/or poppy seeds. Bake at 375° for 11-13 minutes or until golden brown. Serve warm. **Yield:** 2 servings.

Peachy Banana Splits

Diane Hixon, Niceville, Florida

This is a simple yet perfect ending to a meal for two on a summer's evening. Whenever I make this dessert, I'm reminded of my childhood, when my favorite treat at the soda fountain was a huge banana split.

- 1/4 cup flaked coconut
- 1/4 cup butter *or* margarine
- 1 can (8-1/2 ounces) sliced peaches, drained
- 1/4 cup packed brown sugar
- 1/2 teaspoon ground cinnamon
- 2 small firm bananas, halved lengthwise
- 2 scoops *each* vanilla, chocolate and strawberry ice cream
- 4 maraschino cherries with stems

In a skillet over medium-high heat, brown coconut in butter. Remove coconut with a slotted spoon and set aside. Add peaches, brown sugar and cinnamon to skillet; cook and stir over low heat for 8-10 minutes or until heated through. Meanwhile, place bananas in two shallow bowls. Top with ice cream. Spoon peach sauce over ice cream; sprinkle with toasted coconut. Garnish with cherries. **Yield:** 2 servings.

Mushroom Olive Salad

Mary Johnston, Palestine, Texas

(Not pictured)

We like fresh mushrooms and have them often. This salad "happened" one night when there was nothing but a carton of mushrooms in the refrigerator. The simple addition of chopped stuffed olives was such a hit that this salad has been one of our favorites ever since.

- 1/4 pound fresh mushrooms, chopped
- 2 tablespoons chopped stuffed olives
- 2 tablespoons olive *or* vegetable oil
- 1 garlic clove, minced
- 1/8 teaspoon dried basil

Salt and pepper to taste

In a bowl, combine all ingredients. Cover and refrigerate for at least 1-1/2 hours before serving. **Yield:** 2 servings.

APPLE SWISS CHICKEN

Lynne Glashoerster, Edmonton, Alberta

My mother and I both like to experiment with recipes and created this one almost 45 years ago. It has come to the rescue for many impromptu occasions when I've had to adjust the serving sizes to unexpected numbers. My family really enjoys chicken, so I'm always looking for new ways to prepare it.

- 2 boneless skinless chicken breast halves
- 1/2 teaspoon dried rosemary, crushed
- 2 thin slices fully cooked ham
- 1 medium tart apple, peeled and thinly sliced, *divided*
- 1 tablespoon vegetable oil
- 2 thin slices Swiss cheese
- 1 tablespoon apple juice *or* chicken broth

Paprika

Flatten chicken breasts to 1/4-in. thickness; rub with rosemary. Top each with a ham slice and a few apple slices; roll up tightly. Secure with toothpicks. Place in a greased 1-qt. baking dish. Drizzle with oil. Bake, uncovered, at 350° for 20 minutes. Top with cheese and remaining apple slices; drizzle with apple juice. Sprinkle with paprika. Bake 10-15 minutes longer or until chicken juices run clear and cheese is melted. Discard toothpicks. **Yield:** 2 servings.

HONEYED CARROT COINS

Annie Hicks, Zephyrhills, Florida

It seems fresh carrots are frequently on my menu. They're so easy to work with and are usually on hand in my refrigerator. This is one of my favorite recipes. I got it from a neighbor. We like to share recipes at our potluck suppers while we're eating all those delicious home-cooked dishes.

☑ **Uses less fat, sugar or salt. Includes Nutritional Analysis and Diabetic Exchanges.**

- 1-1/2 cups sliced carrots
- 1/2 cup apple juice
- 1 tablespoon honey
- 1 teaspoon grated orange peel
- 1 teaspoon grated lemon peel
- 1 teaspoon butter *or* margarine
- 1/4 teaspoon salt, optional

In a small saucepan, combine the carrots and apple juice. Cover and cook over medium heat for 10 minutes or until tender. Stir in the honey, orange and lemon peels, butter and salt if desired. Serve with a slotted spoon. **Yield:** 2 servings. **Nu-**tritional Analysis: One 3/4-cup serving (prepared with margarine and without salt) equals 119 calories, 57 mg sodium, 0 cholesterol, 26 gm carbohydrate, 1 gm protein, 2 gm fat. **Diabetic Exchanges:** 2 vegetable, 1 fruit.

GARLIC POTATO BALLS

Alpha Wilson, Roswell, New Mexico

I've used this recipe since I was married, almost 50 years ago. Both my husband and I worked, and we liked to have hearty, hot meals when we came home in the evening. This was easy and quick to make on busy days. With the amount of potatoes used, there were never any leftovers.

- 1 tablespoon butter *or* margarine
- 1 can (15 ounces) small whole potatoes, drained
- 1/4 teaspoon garlic salt
- 1/2 teaspoon minced fresh parsley

In a skillet, melt butter over medium heat. Add potatoes; sprinkle with garlic salt. Cook and stir for 15-18 minutes or until golden brown. Sprinkle with parsley. **Yield:** 2 servings.

BREAD PUDDING FOR TWO

Jean Loomer, South Windsor, Connecticut

The two best things about this comforting dessert are it's easy to make and uses convenient ingredients I usually have in my kitchen. Besides making it often for my husband and me, I have made it several times for unexpected company. Everyone agrees it satisfies a sweet tooth without being too rich.

- 1 cup soft bread cubes
- 1 egg
- 2/3 cup milk
- 3 tablespoons brown sugar
- 1 tablespoon butter *or* margarine, melted
- 1/2 teaspoon ground cinnamon
- 1/4 teaspoon ground nutmeg

Dash salt

- 1/3 cup raisins

Vanilla ice cream

Place bread in a greased 1-qt. baking dish. In a bowl, whisk egg and milk. Stir in the brown sugar, butter, cinnamon, nutmeg and salt. Pour over bread; sprinkle with raisins. Bake, uncovered, at 350° for 30-35 minutes or until a knife inserted near the center comes out clean. Serve warm with ice cream. **Yield:** 2 servings.

General Recipe Index

✓*Recipe includes Nutritional Analysis and Diabetic Exchanges*

✓*Recipe includes **Nutritional Analysis**
and **Diabetic Exchanges***

General Recipe Index

✓*Recipe includes Nutritional Analysis
and Diabetic Exchanges*

Alphabetical Recipe Index

✓*Recipe includes Nutritional Analysis and Diabetic Exchanges*

✓*Recipe includes Nutritional Analysis
and Diabetic Exchanges*